the South.
Reconstruction

ASC
19303

The American South

The American South

SEVEN BOOKS SUGGESTED
FOR REPRINTING BY
C. VANN WOODWARD

THE

SOUTHERN STATES

SINCE THE WAR

1870–1

BY

ROBERT SOMERS

ARNO PRESS

1930 3

A NEW YORK TIMES COMPANY

New York ☆ 1973

Reprint Edition 1973 by Arno Press Inc.

Reprinted from a copy in
  The University of Illinois Library

The American South
ISBN for complete set: 0-405-05058-5

Manufactured in the United States of America

———◆———

Library of Congress Cataloging in Publication Data

Somers, Robert, 1822-1891.
  The Southern States since the war, 1870-1.

  (The American South)
  Reprint of the 1871 ed. published by Macmillan,
London, New York.
  1. Southern States--Social conditions. 2. Southern
States--Economic conditions. I. Title. II. Series.
[HN79.A13S57 1973b]   309.1'75'04   72-11347
ISBN 0-405-05063-1

THE

SOUTHERN STATES SINCE THE WAR.

THE

SOUTHERN STATES

SINCE THE WAR.

1870–1.

BY

ROBERT SOMERS.

WITH MAP.

London and New York:
MACMILLAN AND CO.
1871.

LONDON :
R. CLAY, SONS, AND TAYLOR, PRINTERS,
BREAD STREET HILL.

PREFACE.

THERE is little to say by way of preface to this book. To explain how it came to be written would lead only to personal details of no interest to the reader. Its defects cannot be extenuated nor its merits enhanced by any statement in this form; and a Preface might as well be wholly dispensed with but for a tribute of thanks which it is alike incumbent and pleasing to pay.

To John Pender, of Manchester, who warmly encouraged my design from first to last, and gave me letters of introduction that proved most valuable—to Robert Dalglish, M.P. for Glasgow, who readily obtained from the Foreign Office a letter commending Her Majesty's Consuls to render me such assistance as they could properly afford—and to all in the United States, too numerous to name, from whom through these and other relationships much information was received—I owe the most cordial acknowledgments. Nor can I omit to express my admiration of the general civility of the American people, from whom, during a sojourn of months among them with all the curiosity of an inquirer, not a word escaped in my hearing unwelcome to a stranger or a British subject to hear.

This Inquiry has been accomplished without connection with any Association, mercantile or political. The Author alone is responsible for the manner in which it has been performed, and the conclusions to which it comes.

Among the many writers who visit the United States with somewhat similar purposes of observation, one so seldom directs his steps to the South that I am fain to hope there may be found in this circumstance alone an ample warrant of publication.

CONTENTS.

THE

SOUTHERN STATES SINCE THE WAR.

CHAPTER I.

Introduction : General Subjects of Inquiry.

[WASHINGTON—*October* 23.]

I PURPOSE, in a not too hurried tour of the Southern States, to give some account of their condition under the new social and political system introduced by the civil war. I shall endeavour to collect such notes of the progress of their cotton plantations, of the state of their labouring population and of their industrial enterprises, as may help the reader to a safe opinion of their means and prospects of development. It will no doubt also fall to me to give such information of their natural resources, railways, and other public works, as may tend to show to what extent they are fitted to become a profitable field of enlarged immigration, settlement, and foreign trade. It is a prevailing idea on both sides of the Atlantic that the Southern States are likely to make vast progress in the next ten or twenty years, and it must be matter of common interest to see, by a near though brief view, how far this idea is supported by their actual circumstances.

The production of cotton is the chief material interest in the Southern States. It is the supply of cotton wool they have yielded, and may be made to yield, which gives them so powerful a hold on the attention of the manufacturing interests of the world. But while I shall make close observation of the state and prospects of cotton culture in the South, I must guard this inquiry against all supposed intention of trying to affect the current price of cotton, or of making guesses at the crop of the coming year or the next. Such questions are discussed in a thousand quarters, and from every possible point of view, with a keenness and intelligence that no single individual could hope to rival. My inquiry will be one of a more general, though at the same time, perhaps, of a somewhat deeper and more permanent character. The desirable end is that the Southern

B

States, in due course, should produce two, five, or tenfold the
quantity of cotton they have yielded any year since the war.
It is probable that only through a reduction of price can any
such expansion take place. A few cents per lb. may decide
whether the looms of Lancashire are to be half idle, to work full
time, or to be increased in power and number with a rapidity
that would speedily overtake the largest crops which America
and other cotton regions of the world might produce. But
whatever the possible demand for cotton-cloth may be were it
only cheap enough, and whatever the manufacturing resources of
Great Britain, it is clear that the growers of cotton will not produce increased crops save on terms which, in the whole circumstances of their agriculture, will yield them a satisfactory profit,
and that the two interests thus involved can only move forward
in harmony and in step with each other. The question of a
larger supply and lower price of cotton resolves itself practically
into a question of greater skill of culture, greater efficiency and
economy of labour, better handling in all respects of the whole
agricultural resources of farms and plantations, whereby the
necessary profit may accrue from the larger quantity of cotton
produced at the same cost. This is a problem which has been
solved satisfactorily in nearly every department of industry. It
is a problem which the Southern planters have to solve, not only
in competition with one another, but in competition with other
cotton-growing countries which now occupy a much higher position in cotton supply than before the American civil war, and
which, though not so capable in some respects as the Southern
States, have peculiar advantages of their own—such as cheap
labour and notions of profit quite un-American—that have kept
them steadily for years, and may keep them permanently, as
effective competitors in this branch of production.

It may be well, while on this point, to give the relative
proportions of cotton supply in Great Britain during the three
years following the close of the American War:—

COTTON IMPORTED INTO THE UNITED KINGDOM IN BALES.[1]

	1866.	1867.	1868.
American	1,162,740	1,225,690	1,262,060
Brazil	407,650	437,210	636,807
Egypt	167,450	181,170	188,689
Turkey, &c.	32,770	16,990	12,758
West India, &c.	111,830	129,020	100,651
Surat	1,206,660	1,095,440	1,038,925
Madras	294,370	163,400	243,949
Bengal	346,730	249,910	169,198
China and Japan	18,840	1,940	—
	3,749,040	3,500,770	3,660,127
Exports from U.S. to all countries	1,548,000	1,553,000	1,656,000

[1] John Pender and Co.'s "Statistics of Trade."

So that the total exports of cotton to all countries from the United States have for these years been less than half the cotton of all countries imported into the United Kingdom; while of the British imports of cotton the United States have contributed less than India alone, after making allowance for their somewhat heavier bales.

It is important to note in connection with these facts that Great Britain retains for her own factories but a moiety of the cotton she imports from her possessions in India: while she now re-exports a smaller proportion of her shipments from the United States than in former times. Thus, of the total Indian exports in 1868 the Continent took 720,000 bales, or 46·73 per cent., and Great Britain retained 821,000 bales, or 53·27 per cent. In the same year Great Britain exported only 197,000 bales of American cotton. Whether the cotton of India be worked up in France and Germany and other Continental countries, or in Great Britain, it enters equally into competition with the cotton of the Southern States. But the fact that Great Britain parts so largely with the cotton of India in favour of American proves the identity of interest which subsists betwixt her manufacturers and the growers of the United States. If cotton is to be the chief staple of the South, and if by its extended production she is not only to restore her prosperity but to develop her vast resources to an extent hitherto unknown, it is only through the instrumentality of the cotton manufactures of England and Scotland that the process can be carried out. The cotton trade of the United Kingdom leans to American cotton. It is the United Kingdom which has its hand on the fabrics, the markets, and all the mechanical, artistic, and commercial resources by which the produce of the Southern plantations can find a profitable outlet. The British merchants and manufacturers say they can take an indefinitely increasing quantity of American cotton, but it must be produced at softening rather than hardening prices, since every substantial advance in value at once checks in all the markets of the world the profitable consumption of cotton goods. If the South cannot meet these conditions, the progress of British manufacturing industry will be so far retarded. If the British manufacturers cannot extend their operations at the price necessary to produce the raw material, the progress of the South, so far as it depends on the growth of cotton, will be retarded also. Such is the equal disability which the question of cotton supply imposes on both sides, and there does not appear to be the slightest room for any misunderstanding.

There are questions at issue in the Southern States worthy of investigation, which, however closely bound up in the com-

mercial problem, have also a moral significance of the highest
human interest. The emancipation of four millions of negro
slaves is in itself a revolution of which the world has seldom
seen the like, either in magnitude, in suddenness and completeness, in the desolation of war amidst which it was
accomplished, or in the influence of its ulterior results on the
future of mankind. In contemplating such an event one is
raised above commercial interests to the borders of the divine
and the religious in human destiny.   To observe the effect
of such a total change of personal standing and social relations on the character, the industry, the sense of responsibility,
and general habits of the negroes—how well or ill they adapt
themselves to their new conditions of life, and whether they are
likely, as free people, to rise in dignity and prosperity, or to
stumble downward into deeper physical and social degradation
—must be acknowledged to be matter of more than merely commercial interest. Yet, in such a line of inquiry there is obviously
the key to the immediate future industrial condition of the
Southern States.   In its economic bearings, it is the question of
the relative value and efficiency of slave and free labour in the
South, with negroes as the labourers, so often contested in theory,
but now put to the test of practical experiment. The five years
that have elapsed since the war cannot be expected to have solved
this question, worth so many years of valiant trial and endeavour. But it may be discovered whether, so far, there be signs
of that success of free negro labour so much to be desired, or of
that failure so often feared. | Nor can it be much less interesting
to see how the white population of the South, more especially
the owners of slave property, are bearing themselves under the
new system. They were doubly crushed—crushed by a war in
which they engaged with reckless bravery, and crushed under
the fall of a system of servile labour with which their wealth
and fortune, the cultivation and existence of their estates, were
so closely intertwined that to destroy it seemed to be utter ruin.
The mettle of the Southern people is thus put to a severe trial.
If the well-doing and well-being of the emancipated negroes
would be gratifying to every benevolent feeling of the human
heart, a course of fresh energy and enterprise on the part of the
white population of the South would be honourable to the
courage and resource of the superior race. Are they throwing
off all lethargy and despondency, and exerting themselves with
hearty resolve and enlightened effort to build up the prosperity
of the country on a new and more stable basis? What improvements have been made in the system of cultivation, and in the
means of economising labour and fertilising the soil, to compensate the lost profits of slavery?   And to what extent does
Federal legislation aid and encourage, or hinder and discourage,

the freed labourers and the owners and occupiers of land in the South to accomplish the great work which they are called upon to do? If taxation be necessarily heavy, is it levied with equity and justice? Does the tariff give fair play to the agricultural industry of the South and West, or, in being made more consistent with the just interests of these great sections of the Union, may it become more consistent with the interests of the whole American people? I am indicating the questions which must occupy any investigation of the condition of the Southern States, and do not know that I have nearly exhausted them. It would be vain to think that a definite and conclusive reply could be given to so many queries; but as they have all been more or less keenly canvassed by an extremely intelligent and energetic population, and are amenable to facts, it may be possible to throw some light on a subject so deeply interesting. It is manifest that great caution will have to be observed against too hasty conclusions. I shall have, in the first instance, to describe simply, and to collect facts and corroborations, and allow evidence to accumulate, before attempting to arrive at results.

It must be said that, so far as the production of cotton goes, the South is giving proof of gradual recovery from the exhaustion and disorganization of the war. It may be wrong to rest on cotton as the sole test of Southern prosperity. Yet, as cotton is the chief product of the South, it is a good index, and it may be well, as evidence of the progress made under free labour and of what had been done under the slave system, to put on record here the crops in the following years:—

UNDER SLAVE LABOUR.[1]

	Bales.
1858-9	4,019,000
1859-60	4,861,000
1860-1	3,850,000

UNDER FREE LABOUR.[2]

1866	1,900,000
1867	2,340,000
1868	2,380,000

The crop of 1869 shows a further increase, and has been stated unofficially to have been fully 3,000,000 bales; while the crop of this season promises a much larger annual increase than any year since the war. On the other hand, there are some unfavourable symptoms in the Southern States. There is not only much political agitation, which may be sound and unavoidable enough, but there are signs of disaffection to Federal rule, and occasional outbreaks of violence, engendered apparently by fierce party

[1] Report of B. F. Nourse, United States Commissioner to Paris Exposition of 1867.   [2] Department of Agriculture, Report, 1868.

hatred, that may be of small moment in presence of returning
prosperity, but, if spreading or long-continued, cannot fail to
react unfavourably on the material interests of the country, and
require to be taken into account.

It may be added in these introductory remarks that I did not
leave home without recommendations and facilities of access to the
best information in the principal Southern States ; and that I
have also cordially to acknowledge the courtesy of the heads of
various departments of the Administration at Washington.
With respect to the census returns, I must own a certain degree
of disappointment. A census of the whole United States is
taken, by Act of Congress, at the close of every decennial period.
Many of the States also take a decennial census within their
respective bounds, and so order it in point of time as to make it
fall in the middle term of the decennial period of the Union
census.   Had this outline been filled up, there would have been
a return of the population of the United States in 1860, when
the war was just beginning ; again in 1865, when the war had
just closed ; and now in 1870, when five years of peace have
followed five years of sanguinary intestine strife.   But a census
is not taken, probably cannot be taken, in the United States,
even in time of peace, with the swiftness and accuracy of the
smaller though more densely peopled areas of European countries.
There are consequently both blanks and delays in the census
returns of the United States, and I may not derive so much
advantage from this source as I anticipated.

Still, incidental advantages and disadvantages apart, the
period at least is not ill-chosen for the purpose I have set before me ; and, considering the magnitude of the subject and its
numerous ramifications, the utmost any writer can well hope or
promise to do, is, while keeping a steady eye on the more important practical questions at issue, to convey such knowledge
of the country and such means of judgment as may be gathered
only by personal travel and observation.

CHAPTER II.

Mount Vernon.—Washington's life as a Planter.—The Woods of Virginia.—
Aspect of the Country from Acquia Creek to Richmond.—Agricultural
Divisions of Virginia.—Their general Characteristics.

[RICHMOND, VA.—*Oct.* 26 to *Nov.* 3.]

BEFORE proceeding from the American capital southward into
Virginia, I could not deny myself the pleasure of a visit to the
ancient homestead of Washington, whose historic figure and
noble character are ever present to the mind at the quiet city
in which the Republic has not unwisely established its seat
of government. The pilgrimage to Mount Vernon is easily
accomplished. A sail down the Potomac is almost as delightful
as a sail on one of the Highland lochs of the Clyde. The
scenery, indeed, is neither bold nor picturesque, but is well defined, and in many of its features beautiful. The shore on either
side is traced by a line of yellowish sandy bluffs, not very high,
but wavy in their outline, and clothed to the water edge with
young forest wood, arrayed at this season in all the colours of the
rainbow; with a background of rolling upland, on which there
is the same crown of forest timber, sombre in the distance, and
stretches of córn and pasture visible in the middle space, over
which a brown and moorish aspect rests. I had noticed a similar
air as of wilderness on more level tracts, all the way from New
York to Philadelphia. The stalks of Indian corn in autumn are
either gathered up in large sheaves, or left standing gaunt-like
where they grew, shorn only of their richly-laden ears, with no
white stubble, but only the red-brown till beneath. On pasture
land the wild grasses have sprung far up in autumn, and over-
shadowed the more tender blade, which, after the scorching heat,
has begun to grow green again under the rains and temperate
sun of a second summer. With Maryland on one shore of the
Potomac and Virginia on the other, both of which States have
passed in a few years from slave culture to war and devastation,
and not infrequent desertion of lands, the darkening effect of
such natural causes can only be increased. But as the great
white-coated steamboat, drawing only two or three feet of water,
glides rapidly on, there is no want of objects made memor-

able by the war, if nothing else, to arrest attention. Without
even looking back on the city of Washington, with the dome of
its Capitol always prominent, but always less enchanting as
distance brings it into more critical view, there is the long
bridge, slanting many miles over the shallows of the estuary
from Washington towards Alexandria, across which the Federal
troops defiled to meet the hosts of the Confederacy; overlooking
it is Arlington House, the residence in ante-war times of General
Lee, now the property of the Federal Government on an arrear-
of-taxes title, and converted into a military cemetery; on the
other side is Navy Yard, and away down on the Virginia shore
is Alexandria, with the steeple visible of Christchurch, to which,
though ten miles from Mount Vernon, General Washington was
accustomed to go with his household for Divine worship, and
where a pew Bible of his is still preserved as a sacred relic. The
remains of earthworks are seen on some of the higher ground on
both banks, and Fort Foote, an extempore construction, armed
with heavy guns, is still a power on the Maryland shore. On
the same side is Fort Washington, an old defence of solid mason-
work, which was destroyed in the war of 1812, and afterwards
rebuilt. Such is the approach from the city of Washington to
the country-seat of the Commander-in-Chief of the War of
Independence.

Mount Vernon is situated on a somewhat higher bluff, and its
woods are richer than most others on the Potomac. Its little
cupola and grey roof, when first seen, are not striking. It is
only on ascending to the colonnade of the mansion, formed of
eight stately pillars, and looking round, that one perceives the
beauty of the site, the good taste, the simple dignity, the fine
order and arrangement of the whole place. The Potomac, as
seen from the piazza, and in reality the rear of the building, is
more like an inland lake than an estuary or a river. It is land-
locked towards the capital by the ridge on which Fort Washington is erected, and by the sinuous shores towards the sea; there
is a grassy plot down to the edge of the shelving bank of
forest; and as one looks through the openings among the trees
upon the smooth and glistening waters of the Potomac, and a
coasting schooner or oyster wherry with her white sails passes
by, the effect in the pure bright atmosphere of this part of the
world is extremely lovely. The landward front of Mount
Vernon is not less interesting in its way. On one side is the
kitchen and on the other the domestic servants' apartments. A
covered way of light open arches connects these houses with the
main building. The lawn, though not extensive, is neatly laid
out. First, a circular plot, then a long rectangle of grass, flanked
on both sides by old trees and avenues. At the end of the lawn
is a gateway which appears to have been the main entrance;

beyond is a grass park, with orchards sloping downward on either hand; behind all, woods and woods. One could hardly imagine a more exact reproduction of an old English country seat. Parallel to the lawn there is a vegetable garden on the same side as the kitchen, and on the other side a flower garden, with the remains of a row of negro houses, the windows of which seem to have had the full benefit of the fragrant flowers and plants of which Washington was evidently an ardent admirer and cultivator. There are still shown in this garden two "sweet-scented shrubs" (Calycanthus Floridus), presented to him by his compatriot and successor in the Presidential chair —Jefferson. The leaves of this plant shed a delightful odour, and when in full flower its sweetness fills the whole air. The offices are situated in a hollow part of the ground, to which a paved way descends from the front of the mansion. Considering that Mount Vernon is a frame building, it seems in a quite wonderful state of preservation. The frames are raised above the ground-level over cellars extending under the whole building, and entered by a flight of steps and wide door at each end of the colonnade. These doors, when left open, allow a current of fresh air to pass through all this under-story, in which Washington kept his wine and other household stores. It is hardly necessary to speak of the interior, which has been so often described. There are the quaint rooms and quaint stair-cases one expects to find in old country houses, and various relics which have hardly a place in these notes. There is a noble dining-room, that appears, with the apartments above it, to have been an addition to the original building, and from which a door opens on the colonnade, and on the cool and refreshing breeze and charming scene of the Potomac. One can fancy Lafayette retiring here from the table to smoke his pipe or cigar of pure Virginian, and, in presence of his sincere and noble-minded host, indulging in delightful dreams of the coming age of "liberty, equality, and fraternity." All the details of Mount Vernon, apart from political associations, convey a vivid impression of a planter's life and surroundings in America a hundred years ago. Washington is said to have possessed ten miles of river shore and six miles inland. There was accommodation at Mount Vernon for all the service required in the household, the gardens and orchards, the stables and dairy, and such work of cultivation and forestry as belonged to the establishment of a country gentleman. But Washington had his extensive territory to reclaim by degrees, and he would have his cleared ground and labour settlements among the woods, and the work of the axe and the plough would go on from year to year under his wise guidance, with occasional military operations against the Indians, in which his heroic spirit would find vent

through all the kindly tendencies of his nature. Still, with all
this activity, the passion of money-making, so rampant in the
present day, could scarcely have been felt by Washington.
Mount Vernon is not in the tobacco region of Virginia. It was
the Westmoreland, even by name, of this second England. It
had soil, and sun, and variety of product, in comparison with
which, indeed, the northern moorland of England was but a
desert. There would be abundance of Indian corn, some wheat,
every variety of fruit and fowl, traffickings in timber, and all the
rude plenty of a wild but teeming land. But no money-bags,
no accumulation of speculative stocks, or of solid capital in the
Funds. The only plan of life which can be conceived as followed
by Washington is that of working out, by great personal sacrifice and heroism, in Virginian wilds, the highest form of life then
known in England. A great change seems to have passed over
the world since those days. To be master of thousands, tens of
thousands, and millions of dollars in "cash down" is now the
ruling passion. There are multitudes of rich men and their sons
in New York, and other great American towns, who, if animated
by only a little of the spirit of Washington, could plant many
a Mount Vernon, and cause many a wilderness in the United
States to blossom like the rose. But the spirit which founded
America and American Independence is not remarkably prevalent in the world to-day. The fortunes made by trade and
commerce in the old country are often turned with happy and
beautifying effect on the waste places of England and Scotland ;
yet this seldom occurs in the United States, where the heroic
work of subduing the untamed land is left for the most part to
the poor tempest-tossed emigrants of Europe.

The Virginian shore of the Potomac down to Acquia Creek
is of the same type as at Mount Vernon. The sand bluff is
more or less naked to the eye, the foliage more or less varied
and brilliant in its hues. A few miles past Mount Vernon
there is a long range of building, not in very good repair, but
which yet might be supposed to be the residence of a landholder
struggling under difficulties of labour and want of capital. It
is occupied as a fishing-station, at a rent of 1,000 dollars per
annum. There are shad and herring fishings on the Potomac.
The herring shoals begin to come in the spring, and there is
probably a busy scene at that period of the year. But there is
little mark of extensive fishery operations on the Potomac, and
the herring probably have a good time of it in these and other
American waters. I should scarcely have noticed this fishing
station but for the bright and exquisitely blended colour of the
trees amid which it is set. The composition of the Virginian
woods affords scope for a much deeper study than I can give
to it. The very brushwood develops elements of commercial

value. But besides the hickory, the cedars, and maples, one is struck by the various oaks, the ashes, the chestnuts, and beeches, so familiar in the "Old Country," and some of the species may not be indigenous. Six or seven generations of British planters have passed over this memorable land of Virginia.

The leaves were falling fast towards the end of October, but the bare branches, seen from a little distance, only added a new variety of colour to the beauty of the woods. The Richmond and Potomac Railroad soon passes literally from the bosom of the water to a table-land of considerable elevation, which drops down again into the valley of the Rappahannock, where Fredericksburg, the scene of a heavy Federal defeat in the war, comes·in view. The old town does not seem to have suffered much from the furious cannonade which the hostile forces poured over the tops of its highest steeples from the opposite banks of the river, and there was a stir of people about the station, including not a few thriving-like country folk, that was cheering to see. The heights behind Fredericksburg, on which the Confederates were posted, are neither so steep nor so lofty as the accounts of the battle might have led one to imagine. The character of the country, indeed, all the way from the Potomac to near Richmond, is the same. There are no mountains or hills, and no rock, but a rolling alluvial country, broken only by ravines where the streams in the course of ages have washed a deep bed out of the unresisting soil. The deepest cuttings of the railroad track reveal only the same bottomless deposit of clayey sand, with but a light top-dressing of vegetable mould, as is seen on the exposed bank of the Potomac. The land is well cleared, the woods in many places having been cut down to mere belts, the boundaries betwixt one property and another, and not more than are necessary for shelter. The soil has also at one time been nearly all cultivated. The marks of the plough are everywhere seen. But thousands of acres are rapidly returning to a state of nature, and little forests of young pines are springing where Indian corn and even wheat may have recently grown. There is a curious fact mentioned in connection with the Virginian woods. When the oaks are cut down, they are followed by a crop of pines, and when the pines fall under the axe the oaks come again. When the soil has been exhausted by bad cultivation, and is left to take its own way, it is prolific of pines. Of this peculiarity I had ocular proof in many fields, over which the furrows were still traceable, covered with little pine-shoots, thick as if planted in a nursery. The soil in this district of Virginia is certainly not so rich as to dispense with the aid of skilful and liberal culture; but the tracts on which crops had·been grown this year showed, in the standing stalks of corn, fair powers of vegetation; and the alluvial character of the soil must render it duly responsive to subsoil ploughing and manure. Along the Orange and Alexandria Railroad, which passes from Washington to Richmond farther to the west, there are richer and more peopled districts, and yet much land ready for new owners, the highest price expected for which is twenty dollars, or 4*l.* to 5*l.* per acre; but from five to ten dollars per acre would probably purchase farms of any size along the railway route from Acquia Creek.

The district to which I have been referring is the last which the people of Virginia wish a stranger to see. It is held to be the poorest part of the State, and is "the Wilderness" of the war times, where most of the great battles were providently fought. Yet from Fredericksburg to Ashland, some fifteen miles from Richmond—a pretty little place, with several fine houses, and a Methodist College, attended by a large number of hearty young men—there must be tens of thousands of acres, in the immediate vicinity of a great line of railway communication, capable of successful settlement, and of developing all the conditions of fruitful, prosperous, and happy country life. In thus attempting to estimate the worst part of Virginia there is at least the advantage of arriving *à fortiori* at a conception of what the better parts must be.

At Richmond the scene changes, and it is only in the capital of the State that one finds a key to all the various districts and agricultural resources of Virginia. The tide flows up the deep channel of the James River to Richmond, bearing large sea-going vessels to the bridges; but it flows no farther, a series of falls immediately above Richmond stopping thus abruptly the tidal flow. This has led to a division, not infrequent on the American continent, into "Tide-water Virginia," applied to the territory along both banks of the James River betwixt Richmond and the Atlantic, and "Granite or Piedmont Virginia," the region round the upper course of the James, terminated by the famous Blue Ridge Mountain chain, where the sulphur springs are found, and whither the Americans, from New York to New Orleans, repair every summer season for health, pleasure, and invigoration. There are many large and productive farms along the tidal course of the James, and in the peninsular countries formed by the James and York Rivers. Two sons of General Lee, whose death has called forth profound marks of respect in Richmond as well as all parts of the South, cultivate large estates in tide-water Virginia; and new families, both from the Northern States and from England, have purchased land and settled in this part of the State. But the heat in summer is severe to all but the acclimatised. The land is low, and in some places swampy; and near Norfolk, the great shipping port of Virginia, with probably the best and most capacious harbourage on the American shores, there is the " Dismal Swamp," which is neither agreeable in aspect nor salubrious in effects. The Virginians themselves are of opinion that the " Piedmont" of the State, from its European temperature and upland character, the variety and homeliness of its agricultural productions, its water power, and its facilities for manufacturing industry, is the best adapted for British settlers. Betwixt the Blue Ridge and the Alleghany range is the great valley of Virginia, that, with the exception probably of the Shenandoah Valley, its northern part, has been less disturbed and impaired by the war than any other section of the State. Then there are the midland counties, where tobacco is the principal crop, and where "planting," as it may be distinguished from simple farming, is carried on with no inconsiderable prosperity. The southern counties along the border of North Carolina have many cotton-fields. All the way from Petersburg to Weldon the white woolly bolls are seen at this season gleaming deep down among the green leaves of the cotton shrub. In all these various divisions of Virginia, though in some more than in others, properties which in any other part of the world would be deemed valuable are offered for sale greatly in excess of the demand.

CHAPTER III.

City of Richmond.—Some features of its Trade and Industry.—Tone of
Politics.—The General Assembly.—Testimony borne of the Freedmen by
Employers.—Rate of Wages.—Dearness of Articles of Consumption, and
its Causes.—Population of the State and City.—Schools for the Negro
Children.

[RICHMOND, VA.—*Oct.* 26 to *Nov.* 3.]

THE capital of Virginia, and erewhile of the Southern Confederation, is a busy and spirited town, and has a very engaging
population. But all its importance does not strike one at the
first glance, and many a traveller on the through route to the
South may pass away from it with an inadequate opinion of a
place rendered historical by recent events. The city is situated
on a series of hills and vales, and only a small part of it is seen
on entering or passing through the streets, until some elevation
is reached where the eye takes an extended view. It is pleasing
and animating to look down a busy and stately street from the
top of one of the heights, and see it, after traversing the valley
below, rising in a straight line up the side of the hill beyond;
and of such *coups-d'œil* there are many in Richmond. Like
most of the American towns, its streets are laid off in straight
lines, and crossed by others equally straight. It may be called,
as well as Washington, a "city of magnificent distances," for the
outlines traced for the future expansion of the capital of Virginia
much exceed its actual development. It has its Broad Street, like
Philadelphia, intended to be the main artery of a great city, and
yet occupying but a subordinate, and certainly not a central,
place in the existing organization of the town. The lower
ground along the bank of the James River is busy and dusty,
the seat of tobacco and other produce warehouses, ironworks and
foundries, factories and workshops, and rattles all day long with
the noise of lorries drawn by four mules, with a negro mounted
postilion-wise, who loves dearly to crack his whip, and cries to
his animals more than enough. Sambo is a natural-born Cockney.
Whether one meets him in the hotels, or driving his lorry in the
streets, or roaring at the railway stations for the honour of carrying one's luggage, he gives assurance of a man who imbibes aptly

the *genius loci,* and contributes his full share to all the smartness and animation, polite or noisy, of the scene.

It is not within my purpose to describe the trade, the mechanical industries, or the various phases of civic life in Richmond. But some leading features may be mentioned in a few sentences. The Tredegar Ironworks, reconstituted since the war, if not the largest of the kind in the United States, execute an almost unequalled variety of work, not only making iron, but every kind of iron castings—from railway spikes to field artillery—with equal resource and success, and are carried on with vigour and activity, employing a thousand hands. The Company use annually a certain portion of Scotch pig, notwithstanding the high tariff duty of seven dollars per ton, as a sort of luxury on account of its greater fluidity and adaptation for foundry purposes. Various smaller foundries and machine shops in Richmond display much spirit and ingenuity in the manufacture of engines and other implements for agricultural purposes. I have also remarked the great number of warehouses for the sale of phosphates and artificial manures, as well as guano, ground bones, and other natural fertilisers, showing how much the attention of the agricultural community is directed to the means of enriching the soil. Virginia has within herself an active propaganda, both chemical and manufacturing, of this new philosophy; but manufacturers of soluble phosphates from Baltimore and other northern seaports visit Richmond regularly, and pass down south through all the leading centres and seaports as far as Montgomery and Selma in Alabama, doing a satisfactory trade. The discovery of marl deposits in the tidal region of Virginia, as well as of the Carolinas, has given an impulse to this question of fertilisation that is daily extending. Though the use of artificial manures may not be so widely spread among the farming population, yet there is no part probably of England or Scotland where more genuine interest is taken in the question, and as the movement is not confined to this State, where it is not least important, it is well worthy of being noted as a sign of reviving agricultural improvement and enterprise in the Southern States.

The war, heavily as it pressed by fire and sword and siege upon Richmond, has left but few traces in the external aspect of the city. A few blocks of building still stand in all the ruin in which they were left by the fires lighted on the night of the evacuation. The tobacco warehouses burned down on that wild occasion have been replaced by temporary erections. But the "Libby Prison" and "Castle Thunder," and other great houses of business, which were devoted to the reception of Federal prisoners and Confederate wounded, are now restored to trade. A sober sadness may be described as the prevailing mood of the

people, which the death of General Lee has probably at the
present moment deepened. There is no dejection, no loss of
honourable pride, and little repining at the bitter consequences
of the war, but a resolve, more deeply felt than strongly expressed, not only to accept the situation, but to turn it to
account of improvement, and to build up anew the prosperity
of the old Commonwealth, which the Virginians love with an
ardour and a faith in the future hardly credible in a community
so greatly shattered, and so bereft for the time of the prestige it
long maintained in the Union.

The tone of politics in Virginia, after some experience of New
York, seems to me very temperate. The old party in the State,
called in electioneering parlance Democrats, as distinguished
from the Republicans and Radicals, or the new party introduced
by the issue of the war and upheld by the authority of the
Federal Government, has regained in the recent elections a
moderate ascendency. An incident, which has just occurred in
the Courts, appears also to be regarded with no little quiet grati-
fication by the native Virginians. One Chahoon, a lawyer, who
was made Mayor of Richmond by the Federal Executive at the
close of the war, and who failed to be elected in regular course
under the Act of Reconstruction, has been tried and sentenced
to four years in the Penitentiary for attempting to defraud the
State of 7,000 dollars by forgery. It was the case of an estate
left without heirs, of which Chahoon attempted to secure possession by forging documents in the name of fictitious claimants.
The Federal Government could hardly avoid making what are
called "military appointments" to civil offices in the state of
affairs which arose on the dissolution of the Confederate Government ; and where these appointments were in favour of officers of
repute and discretion in the Federal army, there was a guarantee
not only of honour and integrity, but of the temporary character
of such infraction of the regular course of election. But Chahoon
appears to have been an adventurer—a specimen, pure and simple,
of the "carpet-bagger"—and his conviction and punishment have
given undisguised joy to the native party of the State, who see
in them a sign that things are coming right again, and that law
and justice will have free course in Virginia.

The General Assembly of Virginia has been holding for a
week or two an adjourned session, and transacting without
excitement a good deal of important State business. As I had
strolled up to look at the Capitol, which—as well as a very pleasant West End, equal in beauty and retirement to the best parts
of Brooklyn or New York, with much more notable in Richmond
—is only discovered as one mounts one eminence after another,
I stepped in to see the Virginian Parliament. The Speaker
of the House of Delegates was a reflective and intellectual-

looking gentleman, himself a Delegate, and perfectly versed in the duties of his place. The Clerk, owing to some pain or weakness in his eyes, had a white bandage round his temples, but was equally master of his position. I counted among the delegates three or four coloured men, one of whom was a pure negro, very well attired, and displaying not more jewellery than a gentleman might wear; while another, who seemed to have some white blood in his veins, was a quite masculine-looking person, both physically and mentally. The Senate was presided over by the Lieutenant-Governor of the State, who was altogether like a young member of the British House of Lords, as the Senate itself had a country-gentleman sort of air not perceptible in the Lower House, which more resembled a Town Council or Parochial Board than the House of Commons. There were two coloured Senators among the number, quite black, but senatorial enough, and like men who in Africa would probably have been chiefs. In the Lower House the coloured delegates mingled freely with the other members, but in the Senate these two sat in a corner by themselves. Yet they seemed to take a cordial interest in the proceedings, and manifested all sympathy with the Senators who addressed the House. As I have never been able to understand the official monotone of our own courts, I cannot profess to have been able to follow every word with all the differences of intonation here; but the procedure was quite intelligible, and I was pleased and amused to see how truly the form and pressure of the "Mother of Parliaments," after a century of separation, were reproduced in her Virginian child. The presence of coloured men in the British Parliament is impossible, simply because the negro element is not among us; but the Virginian feature I have ventured to notice is only a practical reflection of the great deliverance of Lord Mansfield —that slavery is incompatible with the law, air, and soil of England. As long as the political equality of the negro is not pushed to any greater extreme than it is like to be in Virginia, or made the factious instrument of bad and trading politicians, it can hardly be the cause of much trouble or discord in any part of the United States.

The testimony generally borne of the negroes is that they work readily when regularly paid. Wherever I have consulted an effective employer, whether in the manufacturing works of Richmond or on the farms and plantations, such is the opinion, with little variation, that has been given. In the country, negroes get from eight to ten dollars a month, with house and provisions. In Richmond, for common and ordinary labour, they are paid fifteen dollars a month with provisions, or thirty dollars and find themselves in the necessaries of life. In various branches of more or less skilled labour of which negroes are capable the wages are much higher, and approach the standard of remuneration to white men in the same occupations. A dollar a day for common labour will appear high to the best labourers in England or Scotland, but there is a necessary qualification to be made in any comparison of the relative rates of wages in the two countries. The dollar does not go so far as its exchange-worth in British money would imply. The price of nearly everything bought in the shops is very high; the labourer cannot command the same comfort as the labourer of other countries, save at a much higher monetary rate of wages, which necessarily augments the cost of American products, and impairs the commercial and competitive power of American industry. This state of things, arising from artificial causes operating over the whole United States, and inflating the monetary rate, not of wages alone, but of every form of profit, without making the working or any other class richer (what is gained nominally in wages and profits passing away in expenditure), has already all but destroyed various branches of American trade, and enhances materially the productive cost even of such staples as wheat, tobacco, and cotton, in which the United States have a natural pre-eminence. This will probably be more apparent now every year, until it forces itself on the public mind, and brings about a wholesome rectification.

Richmond has several fine streets of shops and warehouses, that are not so well or fully stocked as similar places of business in towns of inferior importance in England, and yet where every article needful in any rank of life may usually be purchased. But one is astonished at the prices demanded and paid, and when the shopkeeper is asked he says it is the result of the high tariff on foreign goods, which is no doubt largely true. The difference, however, betwixt his price and the real value of the goods is three or four times the amount of the Customs duty, suggesting other evils, starting probably from the tariff, but in active independent operation. The duties, being high, are more conveniently paid in New York than they could be in the South, where capital is scarce. This leads to indirect trade as well as transit, and the piling of one large profit on the top of another before the goods reach the consumer. Prices, moreover, received an inflation from the enormous expenditure and paper currency of the war, which the approximation now of the paper dollar to gold value and the pressure of taxation do not appear in many cases to have materially reduced. People speak, in giving an estimate of values, of " ante-bellum " and "post-bellum " prices. Things are thus floating along on an artificial level produced by all these derangements, rendering the cost of living and the cost of production in every department expressed in money very high as compared with other countries. It is evident what a heavy incubus such a state of things must be on a State like Virginia, impoverished and crippled by years of devastating war, and needing supremely every natural facility in the cultivation of her soil and the increase of her wealth and produce.

The census returns of the City or State have not yet been published, but I have been politely informed by Colonel Parker, the United States Marshal here, that the population of Virginia may be taken as 1,245,000, showing a decrease of the population of the State since 1860 of from 20,000 to 30,000. The population of the city of Richmond is 51,093. In 1860 Richmond had not more than 35,000 inhabitants, but the apparent increase is mainly the result of an extension of the municipal boundaries. The Marshal, however, claims for Richmond, as it was before the enlargement of the bounds, an increase of 5,000. This result is questioned by citizens of much information, who are disposed to think the population both of State and of city lower than in the return. It is quite usual to find the census questioned in the United States, and the mode of taking it—not all in one day as in Great Britain, but by piecemeal and irregularly—is certainly not compatible with strict accuracy. The President has ordered a new census in New York, and will probably do so also in Philadelphia and other places where the returns have excited dissatisfaction. The decrease in Virginia is believed to be chiefly in negroes, who were accustomed under the slave system to be sent South in considerable numbers, and who have migrated in the same direction voluntarily since their emancipation. Contractors, themselves coloured men, also come down from the hotels in Boston and other Northern towns, and engage negroes to go to them as servants. But the tendency of the black man is to go South, and the probability is that Virginia will continue to supply the Southern plantations with less or more labour.

The Radical party in the State take credit for having opened schools in Richmond immediately after the war for the education of negro children. They say that from 5,000 to 6,000 were thus brought under instruction, and that the consequence now is that black children can read and write, while many of the white children are untaught. There has been no school assessment hitherto in Virginia, but the Constitution under the Act of Reconstruction requires free schools to be established by assessment over the whole State, and this provision is being carried out with the assent of all parties. The city of Richmond has already appropriated 100,000 dollars for education. The practice is to have separate schools for the negroes. I have been shown a large building in what was not long ago the fashionable quarter of the town, and then used as a grand hotel, which has been purchased for conversion into a free school for the negroes, and in magnitude will vie with the splendid free schools of New York or Philadelphia. Seeing that buildings have to be provided, and that there are no reserved lands, as in the Western States, for the aid of common school education, the school-rate in Virginia will be pretty high for some time ; but it will be a source of much profit in the end, and will make her labour more valuable, and her wide domains more attractive and more pleasant to settlers of every class.

CHAPTER IV.

The Land Question in Virginia.—Estates and Farms for Sale without Purchasers.—Effects of War and Revolution.—The Annual State Fair.—Abundant natural Fertilisers. — New Industries. — Regularity of the Markets for Tobacco and other Agricultural Produce.—Railways.—Desirableness of Virginia to Middle-class Settlers.

[RICHMOND, VA.—*Oct.* 26 *to Nov.* 23.]

THE land question is the absorbing question in Virginia. How to get the estates formerly productive again brought into cultivation—how to attract settlers of a superior class from England and Scotland, who would take their place in Virginian society as landowners and give a fresh impulse to the work of improvement going on—how to fertilise the soil and increase and improve the farm stock—how to turn the woods, the mines, the beds of marl, the streams and waterfalls, the fruits and game, and all the abundance of nature to productive account, and so fill with new blood the wasted frame of the old Commonwealth, occupies the minds of all classes with an intensity of interest to which no other public concern can be compared. The first question asked of a stranger is whether he has come to look at land. I was not three minutes in Richmond till a pushing Irishman offered to sell me a very fine milch cow and calf on the spot, or tell me where I could get a nice bit of land on very economical terms. But the stranger who is landward-bound is not left to such chance means of information. There are dozens of respectable estate-agents, every one of whom has lists of farms and estates for sale which he advertises in the newspapers, and offers in fee-simple at a rate per acre that in England or Scotland, or even Ireland, would be deemed but a moderate annual rent, and payment of which he is willing to take in cash just enough to pay the expenses of suit, with the balance in instalments spread over three or four years. Every one of them states in private that he has even more lands on his list for sale than he advertises. Nor is this all. The State of Virginia has appointed a Board of Emigration, composed of gentlemen of the highest standing and reputation, with General Richardson, the Adjutant-General of the State, as secretary, whose sole object is to guide and assist, by every kindly office, persons from abroad wishing to invest a little capital and settle on the soil of Virginia. I might fill pages with a description of farms and plantations, and lots, large and small, of land that are thus in the market. But I shall only mention a few particulars from a list presented to me by General Richardson. To show the great variety of choice, as regards situation for example, some of these farms and estates are in the immediate neighbourhood of Richmond, some are in Roxbridge county, some in Orange county, others in Culpeper county, Chesterfield county, King William county, Louisa county, James City county, New Kent county, and so on. One is a tobacco plantation in Fluvanna, one of the most famous tobacco counties in Virginia. In the county of Orange there is an estate of 6,000 acres of improved land, with several dwelling-houses on it, the purchaser of which could make a large home-farm for himself, and have besides half a dozen or even a dozen farm tenants. The lands are " very fertile, and suited to grass." The purchase-money of this estate would be taken in instalments, spread over ten years if necessary. There are also many small farms, and lots of 20 to 50 acres. The highest price asked for any of these lands, which are improved, is 4l. per acre. One estate of 800 acres, "land good, with abundance of greensand marl only four feet below the surface," could be bought for fifteen dollars an acre. Among the number there are " 2,000 acres of undeveloped coal lands." Land rights are carefully registered and guarded in Virginia, and there is seldom any difficulty in tracing a clear title back through a long period of years.

To understand the avalanche of land bargains at present in Virginia, one has to remember that before the war the soil was owned chiefly by slaveholders, who had large estates which they never fully cultivated, but on which they shifted their crops about from one place to another, and who, finding themselves with plenty of money and little trouble under this system, allowed their overseers and the slave-dealers to settle all the hard matters between them. At the close of the war, when the slaves became free, it is easy to perceive that with no means left to cultivate such large tracts of land under the new conditions, it became a necessity, as well as the best thing the owners could do, to sell large portions of their estates, and to retain just as much as they had capital and labour to cultivate; and this they have done and are doing to some extent. In many other cases, proprietors, not rich save in land before the war, have since become embarrassed, and, falling into debt and arrears of taxes, have had decrees passed against them in the courts, under which sales are ordered to proceed. There have been instances also of gentlemen "slain in battle," or driven from the country, or flying from it in despair, and of every form of vicissitude and ruin that follows in the train of war and social revolution. The consequence is that a

large proportion of the landed property of a great and long
settled State is literally going a-begging for people to come and
take it. The like has seldom been seen before. The deluge of
encumbered estates in Ireland was nothing compared to it, for
the land in Ireland, when brought to sale under a Parliamentary
title, readily commanded purchasers at good prices. Yet there
are no agrarian murders in Virginia. Nor is it a new and undeveloped country, where every element of civilization has to be
introduced, but an old land of renown, where law and order prevail and every social comfort may be enjoyed. There is hardly
any part of Virginia where a settler on the soil would not only
find towns and markets, and roads and railways, but have as his
neighbours gentlemen who are no mean agriculturists, who are
versed in all the science of husbandry, many of them breeders
of the rarest and finest stock, and deeply imbued with the spirit
of agricultural progress and improvement.

The annual State Fair at Richmond has been held this week.
This is an institution which is spreading rapidly in the Southern
States. I had early note of agricultural fairs at Augusta and
Atlanta, in Georgia, but found it impossible to be present. The
Georgia fairs from all accounts have been most spirited gatherings. Charleston has also its first fair since the war this week,
which I may be just in time to get a glimpse of. There have
already been fairs in Lynchburg and Petersburg, in this State,
and these now culminate in Richmond. The fairs are competitive exhibitions of stock, produce, implements, and manufactures,
where planters, farmers, and engineers meet to compare notes,
and where the young country people of far distant counties come
to enjoy town-life for a few days, to assist at races and other
field amusements in the afternoons, to fill the great hotels with
balls and routs at night, and let all the gay spirit out, as most
young country people everywhere love to do. The fair at Richmond was held on a large open space that was the *Champ de
Mars* of the South in the war times. I was struck by the completeness and permanence of the erections for this annual
gathering. The Royal Societies of England and Scotland themselves cannot vie, in the temporary fabrics of their great peri-
patetic shows, with the pavilions, committee-rooms, grand stands,
restaurants, ware-rooms, and stalls for stock, made to last, on the
fair-ground at Richmond. A circular racecourse, formed within
the square outer enclosure, is exactly one mile round. The
exhibition of stock was not very extensive, but it contained
some superb specimens of Hereford and Durham shorthorns,
Ayrshire and Devon cows, and immense fat bullocks, all native-
bred. There were many notable fine-wool sheep—South-downs,
Cotswold lambs, one Cotswold ram (a very fine animal, imported from Gloucestershire), and Spanish merinoes, which are

a favourite stock in Virginia. The merinoes were from Culpeper county. The British races of sheep and cattle seem to thrive, and to be capable of the same high development as at home. The large breeds of swine probably exceed in size anything seen in the old country—Chesters, Bedfords, and Woburns being prominent. There was as fine a show of light thoroughbred horses as could be seen anywhere, but very few draught animals. I saw a grey Norman stallion, that had been imported, as large as a Clydesdale, but with a longer and smaller body than the barrel-like trunk that gives the characteristic aspect of concentrated strength and power to that famous breed. There were some fine mules, and a few donkeys which seemed as large as horses, and brayed with corresponding volume. The implements and machines formed, perhaps, the most extensive display in the agricultural department of the Fair, and several steam-engines were at work on the ground, including a road-engine, with broad wheels, but of the ordinary type, and wanting in the properties of the india-rubber tire and other adaptations for draught and ploughing invented by Mr. Thomson of Leith. A show-room contained specimens of the varied manufactures of Virginia, and a large open shed was devoted to the raw materials and produce of the State. In this latter department I saw marls from various counties in the tidal region, and from Hanover county, north from Richmond; puddling clay and fine moulding sands; and manganese from the Cabell mine in Nelson county. On the day of opening, Mr. Jefferson Davis, who was on his return home from Europe to Mississippi, appeared on the platform with the President and office bearers, accompanied by General Early and other associates in the war, and delivered a short speech, in which he congratulated the Virginians on the reviving prosperity of the State, and made passing allusion to former days and circumstances. Mr. Davis is an accomplished speaker, and expresses himself with a nervous force that thrills and rouses his audience. No politics were spoken, but it was obvious that the people retain a deep respect for their former leaders in the Senate and the field. The trotting races were a source of great attraction, and the Virginian horses certainly display amazing powers in this line. The light buggies in which they were harnessed flew round the course like chariots of the sun. There is an amusement on these occasions which must be regarded, I suppose, as an outcome of the "chivalry" of the South. It is a tournament, wherein young men mounted on fine bloods, and dressed in fancy costumes of the olden time, endeavour at full gallop to run their lances through iron rings about two inches and a half in diameter, suspended from cross-trees placed in a line at some distance from each other on the field. The gallant knight who excels in this achievement has the honour of naming among the fair ladies "the Queen of the Tournament," whom he crowns with roses amidst the cheers of the spectators.

Whatever inroads may be made on tender hearts at these Southern fairs, there can be no doubt that they have many useful results, and are a manifestation of public spirit of the most commendable kind. The agricultural characteristics and resources of the various districts are arrayed before the eye till they become familiar to all; and every new invention, discovery, or means of improvement receives a degree of publicity and discussion which could not be so effectually attained in any other way. The Fair at Richmond this year is deemed scarcely up to the mark of former seasons; but it was anticipated that a great flood which, three weeks ago, swept the banks of the James and North Rivers, destroying life and property, and washing away soil to an extent of which there has been no precedent for a hundred years, would interfere most materially with the exhibition. "The hand of God," a pious old statesman said to me, "has lain heavily on Virginia for some years, and this flood is our most recent visitation." It must be regarded as a signal proof of the buoyant spirit and substantial resources of Virginia that "twenty thousand people," as the local papers reckon, should have flocked into Richmond on this occasion, and that so varied and excellent an exhibition of agricultural stock, and of the materials and products of industry, should have been made.

Since the discovery of the great marl deposits in South Carolina keen interest has been excited and eager search made for similar treasures in the neighbouring Atlantic States. Virginia has shared this excitement, and every year seems to add to her discoveries of these native means of fertilisation. There can be no doubt that from Acquia Creek in the north-west of the State to south of Richmond, and from Richmond towards the sea, beds of marl are to be found not far from the surface, more or less rich in phosphates and ammonia. The marl is of various kinds. There are blue marls, white marls, greensand marls, and other sorts, the composition of which differs; but they are all beds of shells and fossil remains, and by proper treatment and manufacture yield phosphates of the highest utility in fertilising the soil. Along the eastern shore numerous banks of half-decomposed oyster shells have been found, which, without any manufacture, have since the war enabled the agriculturists to dispense with lime. The Piedmont or Granite region, from the less exhausting nature of its husbandry, stands in less need of chemical manures than the tobacco, cotton, and wheat lands; but in the Great Valley limestone everywhere abounds, and there can be no question of the ample and convenient means which Virginia possesses for the renovation and enrichment of her soil. Necessity is the

mother of invention, and not only. is this manure-question giving
rise to promising developments, but new uses are being found for
materials with which the woods and wildest parts of Virginia
abound. The bark of the oak-trees is made in Richmond to
yield tannin capable of profitable exportation to the most distant
markets. Shumac, worth 70 to 90 dollars per ton, is now produced
in increasing quantities from a till lately neglected shrub; and
the bark of the black oak of Virginia is ground into quercitron,
used in Glasgow and elsewhere for dyeing purposes, and fetching
35 dollars per ton. The reeds of the Dismal and other swamps,
by a machine which I can only liken to a big gun, are torn into
rags, and the rind completely separated from the inner pulp,
which makes excellent paper,—a manufacture of unlimited demand in the United States. For the great products of Virginia
there are the best of markets. Every pound of tobacco-leaf is
bought in the Tobacco Exchanges of Richmond and the other
towns for cash by firms of the most ample resources, and by
agents of the French, Austrian, and other Continental Governments, as soon as sent in. The Corn Exchanges of the various
towns are conducted with similar regularity, and there is an
advantage to the wheat of Virginia in being so near the seaboard
that it gains in cheapness of transit what it loses in yield as
compared with new and more productive soils. The farmer in
the virgin lands of the Far West has to produce two bushels of
wheat to carry one to the consumer. The minor farm products
of Virginia find ready sale in all the principal towns, at prices
which the inhabitants of even a European city would consider
high. Thus, in Petersburg, I find eggs 18 to 20 cents a dozen;
butter, 35 to 40 cents per lb.; chickens, 25 to 35 cents each,
wholesale prices. Fruit of every kind in Virginia is produced
in larger quantities than can be consumed on the spot, but is
preserved in various forms and sent abroad, and, raw, is daily
bought and sold in the domestic markets. It seems only a
nightmare, or some hideous misunderstanding, or unaccountable
caprice of evil fortune, that can retard the progress of Virginia to
prosperity and wealth greater and more substantial than she has
known at any former period.

The following figures show the crops of tobacco in the four
years before and four years after the war :—

	Hhds.		Hhds.
1856-7	52,909	1866-7	43,717
1857-8	72,720	1867-8	47,211
1858-9	68,593	1868-9	47,400
1859-60	76,950	1869,70	33,721

The average value of this produce would be about 150 dollars
currency per hhd. Last year's crop was exceptionally small, but
will be made up this year, which has been very favourable to the

plant, as regards both quantity and quality. It is estimated on the Tobacco Exchanges that from 50,000 to 60,000 hhds. of superior Virginian will be sent into market before next year's crop. Virginia devotes about 120,000 acres to tobacco. Her crop of cotton before the war was only from 10,000 to 12,000 bales of 400 lbs., though a large quantity passes through her port of Norfolk from other States. It is in her wheat crop that the effect of so many uncultivated farms, and the diminution of her agricultural production, is most plainly seen. In 1860 she produced 13,130,977 bushels of wheat. In 1868 her crop of wheat only amounted to 6,914,000 bushels. In Indian corn and other cereals the lost ground is equally conspicuous.

The State is well intersected by the great through lines of railway, both south and west, and the formation of cheap branches in the interior will now doubtless be a main object. But attention is chiefly directed in the meantime to the completion of the connections betwixt the spacious harbour of Norfolk, on the Atlantic seaboard, and the Western and Pacific routes, so as to place Virginia direct on the highway of future commerce.

People who desire to change the Old World for the New, and to acquire either small or large farms without great change of circumstance, may do so more easily in Virginia than probably in any other part of the United States. For emigrants of a superior class, with a moderate capital to invest in land, Virginia has peculiar attractions. Englishmen and Scotchmen will find here Episcopalian, Presbyterian, and Independent Churches, and a well-organized and agreeable society. They will find a population scarcely distinguishable from their own countrymen in anything—a population proud, indeed, of their State and of themselves, but still prouder of their mother-land, and equally proud to welcome and hold out the hand to all worthy of the mother-land who may come to settle among them.

CHAPTER V.

[GOLDSBORO'—*Nov.* 5-6. WILMINGTON—*Nov.* 7-9.]

THE sun was just rising as the railway train, on my way southward from Petersburg, plunged into the depths of the great pine forests of North Carolina. The scene by this time was not quite new to me. The Atlantic slope southward from New Jersey through Pennsylvania and Virginia to this point, so far, has all much the same natural features, but Pennsylvania is more cleared of wood, though (what I saw of it) not much better cultivated than Virginia, and the woods of Virginia have more variety than the forests of almost pure pine which flourish in North Carolina. The rising sun, as seen through these dense thickets, suffuses a vast golden radiance from a burnished centre, on which the eye can look steadily, and trace from background to foreground, and on this side and that, the lines of light with which it pierces the glades, brightens the leaves, and plays round the dark trunks of the forest. It is as if all the distant outer edge of the wood were on fire, without smoke, or noise, or flame—aglow, simply, with irresistible, advancing, and spreading fire. But as the cars sweep on, the tall pines begin to whirl round in an endless dance, and the golden radiance seems to move through the wood with the speed of lightning, till the eye grows weary, and the brain, overtasked, and itself ablaze with the fire of imagination, becomes dizzy. One is glad to fall back on the seats for relief, but again and again leans forward to gaze anew on the glorious scene. The pines, which, as far as I can estimate, grow to a height of 70 to 80 feet, are bare and straight as the masts of a ship, with only a small cupola of branches and leaves at the top. It seems as if the very thickness with which they spring up precludes any other development. They crowd and jostle one another into nakedness. In the fierce contest to go ahead, the lower branches, "cabined and confined," and choked to death, fall off till nothing but the bare stem with its hood of foliage remains. The very brushwood cannot live amidst the affluence and mastery of the pine in the Carolinian forests. Long as the woods of North Carolina have yielded enormous quantities of turpentine and naval stores to the world, it proves the inexhaustibility of the sources of these valuable products, that I must have travelled fifty or sixty miles through forest scenery without seeing a single tree that had been tapped for oil. It is only in the interior, and as one approaches nearer the port of Wilmington, that the manufacture of "naval stores" becomes visible in incised trees and turpentine distilleries.

Yet the hand of man has long been busy over all these north-eastern tracts of North Carolina. There are numerous clearings in the woods under cultivation, and farms and plantations, which yield Indian corn in abundance, and always cotton more or less successfully. Many of the cotton-fields, indeed, show but an inferior growth, but others in their immediate vicinity are flourishing, even luxuriant. In some instances the heads only of the negro pickers were seen above the tops of the plant, while in others, no doubt the majority, the plant was not more than a foot and a half or two feet high, with considerable portions of the fields here and there showing either a total failure or a partial extinction of the culture by overgrowth of grass and weeds. The best crops are usually found in the neighbourhood of the dwelling-houses of the larger plantations and of the villages, and are the result obviously of manuring and more careful handling. The negroes and other small cultivators have settled on many of the clearings in the forest, and have not yet the art or the means either of growing or picking their cotton well. Yet one could not but observe the abundance of bolls on fields where the plants were smallest. An English pasture, covered with white daisies, is the closest simile which can be given of the aspect of many of these cotton patches. The picking was not more up to the mark than the preliminary culture, and, generally speaking, was most advanced where the cotton plant was largest and most carefully cultivated. I must remark, at the same time, that several negro lots have come under my observation which are little models of industry and improvement, from the cottage outward. The dwellings in this part of North Carolina are for the most part very poor—mere wooden shanties, without paint, or any other mark of comfort or substance. But this is by no means the universal character of the country. The railways pass through the poorest districts lying between important points of traffic, and it is only by getting away from the tracks of the cars and behind the woods that one discovers all the rural development. There are many large planters in this region, who grow spacious breadths of cotton, and send as well-pressed iron-tied bales to market as are to be seen anywhere. The extent of cotton culture in North Carolina, and the fervour and energy with which it is prosecuted, are much greater, indeed, than one expects to find so near the northern limit of the Cotton Belt. The area within which cotton is grown in North Carolina may be defined by lines drawn from Northampton county on the northern frontier, eastward through Halifax and Martin counties to Pamlico Sound, south-westward through Halifax, Nash, and Johnston counties, and thence direct westward as far as Mecklenburg county, which is said to be one of the best cotton districts in the State.

An extension of the area of cotton culture is not at the moment a question of supreme importance as regards either the Southern States or an ample supply of the staple to the factories of Europe. The area may be extended without materially increasing the aggregate produce, and the question of the time appears to be how, by skilful culture and the application of manures, the same area may be made to yield a larger crop. It is to this object that the attention of growers in the South appears to be mainly addressed. Yet it is the opinion of persons of experience here that in North Carolina there is probably 20 per cent. greater breadth of cotton this year than last, though doubts are expressed whether the increase of produce will be in proportion. The weather, however, is favourable beyond expectation for the utmost yield of the cotton plant. The difficulty so far north is the shortness of the season, but up to this date there has not been a nip of frost; the days are as warm as in July in England, the nights clear and pleasant, and there has been neither rain nor storm to retard the labour or destroy the hopes of the planter. With such weather, there is no reason why cotton should not turn out as well for the grower, even in North Carolina, as any crop that could be cultivated. Since long before the war this State has suffered from emigration to the richer cotton lands of the South, and this is one of the social difficulties arising from the very superabundance of natural resources in America which it is hard to overcome. Some say that for every native in the State there are two strangers, and ask how any proper consolidation of society or stable industrial progress is possible in such circumstances? But an extended cultivation of cotton is at least not a bad symptom in the meantime. The testimony borne of the negroes by candid and substantial people is that, while they do not afford the supply of steady labour necessary, and there is room for more of them, or of more efficient labourers, they are doing much better than was expected before emancipation. They are paid on the cotton farms in some instances by wages, and in others by a share of the produce, the relative merits of which modes of remuneration are likely to become an important practical question in the Southern States. The acknowledged disadvantage of the latter mode is the uncertainty and inequality of the return for labour. The negroes on the share system, for example, had a larger remuneration last year, when the price of cotton was high, than they will have this year, when it has suffered a heavy decline. Can the negro be expected to understand or be satisfied with this fluctuating scale of remuneration for his toil? Is it desirable that he should be dragged, at his present stage of progress, into all the ups and downs of cotton speculation? Is he likely to comprehend that, while doing his best probably in both years, he should have less this year than last, because France and Prussia have gone to war? And if he cannot comprehend this, is there not a danger that he may be discontented, and think himself the victim of some fraud or injustice nearer home?

Railways generally are—or, if not, ought to be—made at very little cost in this part of the world. On my way to Wilmington, I have remarked about forty miles over which the rails pass in as straight a line as could be drawn mathematically, on ground almost as level as a bowling-green, and with only the fine, light, marlly soil of the Atlantic slope to cut through. Not a rock, scarce a creek or stream, or marsh, in all this long distance. The American engineers have usually carried their lines along the ridge of the country to be traversed, and hence the few bridges, and the forest land with which the traveller in America becomes so familiar. On looking down on the track—for which, by the way, the construction of the cars, allowing free passage at all times from one end of the train to the other, affords peculiar facility—one sees for the most part a simple narrow clearing through the forest, a certain amount of spade and barrow work, with embankments here and there only a few feet deep; ribs of timber, or "railway sleepers," laid across; and then, longitudinally, the iron rails, bound together by bolts, without the "chairs" and jointings which the heavy traffic on British railways renders necessary. Two light trains a day, with probably one freight train in the same period, form the general average of traffic, and can be conducted safely without the elaborate expenditure on "way" and "maintenance of way" in other circumstances indispensable. The railways hereabouts have numerous stations, which are simply landing-places, without buildings of any kind, for letting down passengers to farms and little centres of population in the neighbourhood; and they have also " depôts" where there may be a little town or not, but where there are great amounts of produce to be "shipped," and where the companies erect sheds and provide every structural convenience necessary to the traffic. The main outlay of American railways, however, away from the great cities, is the iron rail. The timber is got on either hand in abundance at every step of the road, and the proprietors of the lands are so eager to have railway communication that they not only open their woods, but give tens of thousands of acres along the track for ever to the companies. The earthworks, and all into which labour on the spot enters, have to bear, indeed, the great inflation of prices which dates from the war, and which renders the monetary cost nearly double what it was before. But the iron rails are the most formidable difficulty.

Wilmington is the only shipping port of any magnitude in North Carolina. The railway system of the State, converging at Goldsboro', has been extended to Beaufort, about 100 miles north of Wilmington, where there is said to be deeper water, and other advantages, and which is expected to compete with Wilmington for the export and import trade. But the results hitherto have not been equal to the most sober expectations. It is always a difficult and tardy process to divert trade from an established channel. Wilmington, like all the old Atlantic ports, has great depth of water up to its warehouses. It was the chief port for blockade-runners during the war, and the success with which that trade was conducted in the face of the Federal cruisers is adduced as a proof of the safety and convenience of the harbourage and its outlets. The stormy dangers of Cape Hatteras, which increase the rate of insurance at New York, may be a drawback in the coasting trade betwixt Wilmington and seaports to the north, but not betwixt Wilmington and any port south of North Carolina, while they can hardly affect, in any degree, the direct trade of Wilmington with Europe. The cotton steam-press here was destroyed in the war, and has not yet been replaced. There is a great number of intelligent, energetic, and honourable men of business in Wilmington, including a few prominent Northern men, who have made money in North Carolina, are imbued with an earnest desire to develop the prosperity of the State, and will not readily allow the trade of the port to dwindle.

The exports of North Carolina, of which the great bulk passes through Wilmington, have been steadily on the increase since the close of the war. With the exception of 1866, the first year of peace, when a considerable quantity of produce stored up during the blockade found outlet, and when the export of cotton amounted to 64,000 bales, the cotton exported annually has been 38,000 bales till the past season, in which it has increased to 57,855 bales. The production of cotton in a State can seldom be inferred from the exports of its own harbours, owing to the divers lines of transit by which cotton finds its way to market, and North Carolina itself is not an exception to the general rule in this respect, since some of its cotton, with much more from farther South, goes to Norfolk in Virginia, and some to Charleston in South Carolina. But North Carolina exports hardly any cotton which is not the produce of its own soil, and the rapid increase of export during the past year shows a largely extended internal production. The average price of cotton realized in North and South Carolina in the four years after the war was 28¾ cents per lb., while in 1869-70 it was but 22½ cents per lb., and has since been still further reduced. But it is worthy of observation, that while the average value of the dollar, in the four years succeeding the war, was 6·49 to the pound sterling, during 1869-70 it has been as high as 5·70 to the pound sterling. This difference may not be immediately felt by the grower under the roundabout style of business and the elaborate frustration of economic principles prevailing in the United States, but it shows that a fall of the currency price of cotton is not exactly equivalent to a fall of value, and that, under any moderate approach to free trade, and a fair rating of goods and materials of every kind, the possibilities of American production of cotton and other staples, with a handsome profit to the producer, would be immensely increased. The exports of spirit of turpentine from North Carolina in 1866 were 57,000 casks, in 1867 they rose to 89,000 casks, in 1868 to 96,000, and last year to 120,000 casks. In 1870 the same ratio of increase will not be shown. The production has not been so great as in 1869. The benzoin spirit distilled from petroleum is interfering with the demand for spirit of turpentine, and the increased labour and energy thrown into the production of cotton naturally marks a diminished attention to the industry of the forests. The price of the spirit of turpentine has fallen since the war from 25 dollars to 15 dollars per cask, and crude has declined in equal proportion. Yet, what with the increased quantity produced, and the higher value of American currency, North Carolina has been receiving annually an almost uniform sum in pounds sterling for her turpentine and other naval stores. The export of rosin has increased from 343,451 barrels in 1866 to 544,498 barrels in 1869. The price has dropped in the same period from 5 to 2½ dollars per barrel, but the dollar is worth in British money from 15 to 18 per cent. more than in 1866. The export of lumber of all kinds has been well maintained year after year since the close of the war, and though at slightly reduced rates, has of late been increased; so that, with the extended cultivation of cotton and other marks of reviving agriculture, the gradual recuperation of North Carolina seems beyond question.

Wilmington is striving in various ways to develop the resources

of the State and to improve its own position as the port of shipment. Chief among the objects anxiously promoted by its
leading men is the completion of the Wilmington, Charlotte, and
Rutherford Railroad. There are 170 miles of this line in operation, but a considerable extension is still necessary to render the
projected communication complete. Along the southern border
of North Carolina there are several well-settled and productive
counties which have no railway communication with the coast,
and the object of the promoters of the railway is to open up
these counties and to form a connection with the Tennessee line
and the great thoroughfares to the South and West. The leading
ports on the Atlantic seaboard have all a lively ambition to get
into direct railway communication with the Western States and
the route to the Pacific. This appears to them to be the great
highway of future commerce, while at the same time the extension of their lines westward meanwhile serves most important
local objects. There is little reason to doubt that, by means of
direct railway communication with Tennessee, Kentucky, Ohio,
and Illinois, Wilmington as well as other Southern seaports
would command a share of the Western traffic with Europe, at
present carried by a longer route to New York, Philadelphia,
and Baltimore. New York more especially, by its great concentration of capital and means of communication, and the keenness, not to say unscrupulousness, with which the latter are
worked in its favour, overshadows and overlays as with an incubus the natural and regular development of the Southern seaports, and introduces some very uneconomic elements into the
trade of the South and West with Europe. Whether this want
of balance can be corrected remains to be seen, but, at all events,
there is every propriety in North Carolina seeking to have the
means of carrying her own produce quickly and cheaply to the
seaboard. The counties yet to be penetrated by the Wilmington
and Rutherford line are rich in agricultural and mineral resources.
Mecklenburg, one of the number, has long been among the foremost cotton-growing counties in the State. The whole district
is largely peopled by thrifty and industrious Scotch settlers
of long standing. On being shown the book of a cotton factor
here, I found, with some surprise, that fully one-half of his con-
signers were " Macs." Many of the planters of North Carolina
send down their cotton to Wilmington, bale by bale as they
gather it, under heavy charges of transit, which, in a state of
declining prices, may one day turn the scale against production.
As it is, there is much grumbling this season. The growers say
that 15 cents per lb. at the gin is the lowest price at which
they can produce cotton, as 15 cents go at present in the United
States. The cheapest access to market is thus of the most vital
importance. Yet the promoters of the Wilmington and Ruther-

ford Railroad, notwithstanding all the outlay and substantial progress they have made, are met by great difficulty. Three years ago they were authorized by their charter to borrow 2,500,000 dollars on first mortgage bonds, than which there is no better security; but there would seem to be little hope of getting the money on this Continent unless the company sell its bonds at 50 for 100 at 8 per cent. interest, or, in other words, borrow at 16 per cent. and pay at last in principal 100 for every 50 borrowed! New York, which is the chief centre of these financial operations, has probably no great disposition to promote railways which threaten in some degree its own imperial monopoly, or it may not have funds enough for all the projects of this kind urged on its attention; but such things might surely somehow be better and more easily accomplished.

The want of confidence betwixt the white people of North Carolina and the State Government that followed upon the war continues to prevail, though in a limited and subsiding degree. Notwithstanding the test oath, by which persons who took part in the war are excluded from office, the negro mass vote, and the high-handed measures of the party in power, the white population of the State are gradually acquiring influence, and have made considerable gains in the elections this autumn. The Governor, Holden, has weakened rather than strengthened his influence by a cry which he raised, in a case of supposed murder, against Ku-Klux conspiracy and outrage in the State, and the military and other measures he adopted on the occasion. The fact that a murder had been committed might be clear enough, but that a secret confederacy existed among the white people for purposes of violence was denounced as an invention of the Governor to agitate the negroes, and to keep them banded on his side in the elections. The case at all events broke completely down on inquiry, and the parties arraigned right and left on a charge of complicity were discharged by the Radical judges. Governor Holden is not a "carpet-bagger." He is what is called here a "scallowag," or what in the amenities of electioneering parlance in England would be termed "turncoat." He is said to have been more fiercely Confederate than the Confederates themselves during the war, but upon the surrender to have turned round, and, placing himself at the head of the negroes, secured his pre-eminence.[1] The fierce passions excited betwixt North and South by the war are kept alive by the system of rule which has almost inevitably followed, but there are symptoms that bitter feelings and inane resentments will gradually give way. A Northern man of business readily

---

[1] Governor Holden, since the above was written, has been impeached, found guilty of high crimes and misdemeanours against the State and the liberties of the citizens, and expelled from office.

attains the position due to him among his fellow-citizens in the South. Mr. Silas Martin, the present Mayor of Wilmington, though a Northerner, was freely elected to his office, and is held in deserved respect by all classes of the population for his business qualities and standing, and the zeal and probity with which he promotes the interests of the port and of the State.

The white and coloured population of North Carolina are nearly equal in number. Here in Wilmington the negroes are in a large majority, the census of this year having brought out the following results :—

White males	2,697	
White females	2,832	
Total whites		—— 5,529
Coloured males	3,446	
Coloured females	4,455	
Total coloured . . .		—— 7,901
Foreign males	348	
Foreign females	200	
Total foreign . . .		—— 548
Total population of Wilmington . .		13,978

This is an increase of fully 4,000 since the previous census, which is remarkable, considering the vicissitudes through which the town has passed in these ten years, and is indicative, not only from the large majority of negroes, but the large excess of coloured females over coloured males, of the tendency of the negro, since emancipation, to desert the country for the town, and to do so in a loose and vagrant fashion. Society cannot be in the most healthy condition where the coloured females are four to three coloured males. But there is abundance of employment most part of the year in Wilmington for all the able-bodied negroes willing to work. The rate of wages paid them for common labour is from 1 to 1·25 dollars a day, and for whitewashing, bricklaying, and labour more or less skilled to which negroes have been trained, as high as from 2·50 to 3 dollars a day.

CHAPTER VI.

City of Charleston—Its Ruin in the War—Marks of gradual Restoration.—
The Battery.—Great Fire of 1862.—Charleston account of the Losses of
the Southern States.— Loud Complaints of Misgovernment and Financial
Jobbery.—Majority of Negroes in the Legislature.—Atmosphere of Political Suspicion.—Efforts of the Whites to regain a share of Representation.—The Reform Union.

[CHARLESTON, S.C.—*Nov.* 10 to *Nov.* 14.]

CHARLESTON—" old Charleston," fondly so called by its citizens
—that has braved " the battle and the breeze," if not a
thousand, a good hundred years—the centre of Carolinian trade
and commerce, the centre always of strong political emotion,
and the centre also where the negro element was densest and
negro slavery was intrenched as in a stronghold alike by fear
and interest—is getting, slowly but surely, on its legs again
from the downfall inflicted by the war. Never had a completer
ruin fallen upon any city than fell upon Charleston in the years
from 1860 to 1865. Her planters, who, with noble country
seats on the banks of pleasant streams, amid groves of live oaks
affording deep shade from the summer sun, could afford to have
their winter residences here in town, were reduced, as by the
grinding of a nether millstone, from affluence to poverty—her
merchants were scattered to the four winds of heaven—her
shopkeepers closed their doors, or contrived to support a pre-
carious existence on contraband of war—her young men went
to die on the battlefield or in the military prisons of the North
—her women and children, who could, fled to the country. The
Federal Government, mindful of Fort Sumter and the first
indignity to the Union flag, kept Charleston under close blockade, and added to its miseries by occasional bombardments.
When this process in five years had reached the last stage of
exhaustion, and the military surrender gave practical effect to
emancipation, the negroes in the country parts, following up the
child-like instinct of former days that Charleston was the El
Dorado of the world, flocked into the ruined town, and made its
aspect of misery and desolation more complete. The streets
were empty of all but themselves; the houses had not only

lost all their bright paint without, but were mostly tenantless within; many fine mansions, long deserted, were fast mouldering into decay and ruin; and the demand for labour and the supply of provisions were at the lowest point. Seldom, with a deeper ruin of the old, has there been a more hopeless chaos out of which to construct a new order of things than Charleston presented in those days. Yet the process of amelioration has year by year been going steadily forward. Many of the old merchants of the city, and many active agents of exchange, both new and old, have come to put the wheels of trade once more in motion. Some of the old planters have also survived, and are seen, though in diminished numbers and with saddened countenances, yet with the steady fire of Anglo-Saxon courage in their eyes, attending to affairs like men determined to conquer fortune even in the depths of ruin and on the brink of the grave; while others, not so much to be respected, unwilling to work and ashamed to beg, seek to maintain some remnant of the ancient dignity no one knows how. The quays and wharves are busy; new ones, to meet new branches of trade, have been built with files of counting-rooms to suit; the cotton presses are again at work; lorries laden with the staple products of the interior pour the livelong day along the streets towards the river; revival is extending from the business parts of the town to the quiet quarters of private residence; and the hotels, always of the first consideration in America, are already, with their stately colonnades of white pillars, their freshly painted fronts, and their troops of polished waiters of various hues of ebony, magnificent in Charleston. I went down one evening to the Battery, an esplanade at the seaward end of the peninsula, formed by the Cooper and Ashley Rivers, on which Charleston is built—not of great compass, seeing that the embouchure of the two rivers here draws the land to a narrow point, but beautiful and refreshing, looking out on the spacious bay direct to Fort Sumter and the far Atlantic, and calling up associations of the Spanish Main and the West Indies, the distant British Islands, and of naval and historic glory, at the crowding thoughts of which the heart of every English-speaking man leaps to his mouth. Though Charleston, like other cities, has its West-End —as I have seen from the tower of the Orphan Asylum, a noble institution which the war has left in full vigour—where goodly houses along stretching avenues of trees, and ample garden grounds, afford a happy and elegant retreat to prosperous men of business, yet there is reason enough why the Battery should be a point of peculiar eminence and fashion in Charleston. The residences round the esplanade—palaces in their way—after long neglect, are undergoing rapid renovation. I am told that, apart from the "nabobs" who live in these charming marine villas, the

Battery in ante-war times was the resort every evening of a long array of carriages, in which fair ladies reclined, and happy gentlemen cooled themselves after the heat and toil of the day. The only equipage I saw was the handsome buggy of a dry-goods man from the North, who is rather liked for the spirit he displays. But the ladies of Charleston meantime take a constitutional walk on the Battery with their babies and nurses, and the gentlemen say the carriages will come again in due time.

Such is the hopeful uprising of commercial progress in Charleston just now. But the old town has much to recover. In the winter of 1862 a calamity more destructive and terrible than all the Federal bombardments befell the devoted city. A fire broke out in some negro shanty on the Cooper River, and, favoured by the wind, spread and swept down all before it in a curious zigzag but generally straight line through the centre of the town, till stopped by the Ashley River on the other side. This appalling conflagration, the desolation and misery cuased and the hospitality evoked by which, amidst all the troubles of the war, cannot be described, still leaves its mark, like the course of a caterpillar that has eaten its way over a cotton leaf, upon the city of Charleston. Fires, once sprung, must propagate here with fearful rapidity. A large proportion of the side streets of Charleston are built of wood. The houses are simply frame erections. They are all dry as tinder, and airy as they can be made. An accidental spark or flame which in our British towns would be instantly smothered by the damp atmosphere, the stone walls, the dense fogs, and the absence of sun and ventilation, is here fraught sometimes with alarming consequences. Not the slightest suspicion of incendiarism rested upon the great Charleston fire of 1862. The negro is not given to the folly of setting his house on fire to roast an egg for somebody else to eat; and such is the power of discipline and habit over him, that he continues, save on election nights or other periods of great excitement, to turn into bed at the early hour in the evening prescribed to him by a sort of curfew law in the days of slavery. The question asked when one surveys the vast ruin caused by this fire is, What became of the insurance companies? The insurance companies of the South? The war soon rendered their position untenable. The number of persons caring to insure rapidly diminished, and as the destruction of fire and sword spread wider and wider, the companies went down by the board, till the whole insurance capital of the Southern States, and all the interests centred round it, shrivelled up like a scroll and disappeared. One must go to Charleston in order to hear all the ruin of the war summed up in good round emphatic English. Any old merchant citizen will reckon on his fingers what the war lost of property, capital, and substance of every kind to the South.

First, the property in negroes, which, whether property in right
reason and natural equity or not, was introduced under the sway
of England, was recognised by the Constitution of the Republic,
was protected by the laws of the United States, and was to all
material intents and purposes as essentially property in the South
as anything elsewhere which makes profit and can be bought and
sold;—this property was abolished, and was four hundred millions
sterling. The whole banking capital of the South, which cannot be estimated at less than two hundred millions more, was
swamped in the extinction of all profitable banking business,
and, finally, in a residuary flood of worthless Confederate money.
The whole insurance capital of the South—probably a hundred
millions more—also perished. The well-organized cotton, sugar,
and tobacco plantations, mills, factories, coal and iron mines, and
commercial and industrial establishments, built up by private
capital, the value of which in millions of pounds sterling cannot
be computed—all sank and were engulfed in the same wave.
Every form of mortgage claim, with the exception of two or
three proud State stocks, shared for the time being the fate of
the principal, and only now crops up amidst the subsiding
deluge like the stumps of a submerged forest. And so on the
account goes as long as the fingers hold out, till the demonstration made is that the South by the war was peeled to the bone,
and left not only without a cent in its pocket, but without anything by which a cent could be made, save the rude but productive land and the bright sun, powerful indeed as natural germs
of wealth and prosperity, but needing, to give them vitality,
more capital and labour, more invention and ingenuity, more of
everything which it seemed most difficult to supply.[1] Terrible
though the picture of ruin and impoverishment be, as thus

---

[1] The census returns of the total value of the taxable property of many of
the States have been published since my visit. The basis may not be a very
accurate one, but is doubtless an approximation to accuracy. Referring to
the figures, the total valuation of Florida has *declined* from $68,929,685 in
1860 to $31,167,464 in 1870; Georgia, from $618,232,387 in 1860 to
$202,563,557 in 1870; Louisiana, from $435,787,265 in 1860 to $250,588,510
in 1870; while in Mississippi the decrease has been from $509,427,912 in
1860 to $154,635,527 last year. South Carolina has not suffered as great
a depreciation as some other States, the returns placing her present valuation
at $174,409,491 against $489,319,128 in 1860. The valuation of Virginia
and West Virginia in 1870 was $480,800,267 against $657,021,336 ten years
ago. Kentucky appears to be recuperating, her valuation in 1870 being
$423,776,099 against $528,212,693. The impoverishment of the South has
told materially on the total taxable property of the Union. This value
increased betwixt 1850 and 1860 from £1,200,000,000 to £2,100,000,000, or
75 per cent. The increase in the last ten years has been only 25 per cent.,
or about £500,000,000. The country, on the other hand, now owes a National
Debt, without reckoning State and City debts, of an amount nearly equal to
what appears to be the whole increase of taxable property in ten years.

drawn here in Charleston, I suspect it is in the main true of the whole South, and the marvel must be that affairs should already be so lively, so hopeful and elastic, as they everywhere appear. It was to be expected that the young men would enter upon business with fresh life and energy; but more remarkable than they are the men of advanced life who, still on the top of the wave, are guiding and controlling by their experience the new order of things.

Charleston, like Boston—for a good comparison there is nothing like the antipodes—has an English look about it. The old city has not fallen so mathematically into the parallelogram formation as the cities of the United States in general. The inhabitants still cast many a fond look towards the old country, and contrast the present misrule with the time when the laws of England were the laws of South Carolina. Such is the deep sense of change and revolution produced by the downfall of State Rights and the inroad of Federal power and innovation, that they profess not to know what the laws of South Carolina now are, or whether she has any laws at all. Ask what the system of rule is, and the reply will uniformly be that it is "nigger rule," which is in one sense true. The negroes are more numerous than the whites in South Carolina. Being all citizens of the United States, they have all the right of voting, while many of the whites are not naturalized; and the War Radicals who came in to take the lead in political affairs, and to hold offices for which the prominent men of the State were disqualified by the test oath, have succeeded in controlling the negro vote, and casting it almost *en masse* in their favour at the polls. There not being "carpet-baggers" or "scallowags" enough in the State to fill all the seats in the Legislature, the negroes have largely returned men of their own race to watch over "laws and learning," and "ships, colonies, and commerce," at the Capitol. The House of Representatives consists of 80 coloured men and 44 whites, and the Senate of 11 coloured men and 20 whites—there being one seat vacant just now. The white people of South Carolina are thus practically disfranchised, and a proletariat Parliament has been constituted, the like of which could not be produced under the widest suffrage in any part of the world save in some of these Southern States. The outcry of misgovernment, extravagant expenditure, jobbery, and corruption is both loud and general. The negroes are declared to be the dupes of designing men, comparative strangers to the State, whose object is simply to fill their pockets out of the public spoil. Political charges are not minced in South Carolina. There is room, indeed, to hope for a good deal of exaggeration. The exclusion of the superior part of the population from all influence in public affairs must of itself tend to magnify the

enormity of everything enormous, and to distort everything not
quite square that is done. The members and dependants of the
State Administration are said, after having depreciated the South
Carolina bonds to 40 and 35 cents, and bought in largely at such
prices, to have then offered gold interest at New York, which at
once advanced the price to 95 cents, and enabled them to pocket
millions. Possible and condemnatory enough, but it was a good
thing in itself to restore the financial credit of the State; and in
North Carolina, for example, the business men and the proprietors have since the war urged upon the Legislature to place
the public credit of the State on the best footing, and will not
desist till they succeed, under the conviction that honesty to the
public creditor is the best policy, and the corner-stone of all
progress and improvement. State Commissions are said to be
issued on roads, lands, and other departments, the members of
which do little but job and make profit to themselves and their
friends. The State Government buys lands on which to settle
and give homes to negroes. This is commissioned, and land
is said to undergo sale and resale before it becomes the property
of the State. It is not believed that the negroes will in any
considerable number make homes on these properties, and the
only advantage I have incidentally discovered from such settlements is in one instance where the negroes, not having crops
enough of their own to occupy their labour, formed a reserve
force from which a neighbouring planter has drawn extra hands
to gather in his cotton. Railway contracts and railway bonds,
in which the State has its finger, are also suspected of offering
opportunities not exactly consistent with the public good. The
phosphate deposits in the bay and rivers have been leased at a
royalty of a dollar per ton to a single company, not, I am to
believe, without heavy sums distributed in the House of Representatives; but the principle of this transaction is discussed
freely by all parties, and it is thought by some that the law of
the United States will not sanction a commercial monopoly of
what is public estate. A State census was taken last year,
which is thought to have been a superfluous labour, seeing that
the decennial census ordered by Congress fell to be taken this
year, and the Governor is supposed to have sought in this way
to give employment to partisans, and to secure votes. Everything thus moves in an atmosphere of political suspicion. One
of the most favourable signs, indeed, is the keenness with which
the acts of the State Government and Legislature are scrutinized,
and the activity with which the native white population endeavour to recover influence and authority both in the State and in
Congress. Prior to the recent elections, they organised a Reform
Union on the basis of the political and civil equality of the
negroes, turned out in large numbers to the ballot-boxes, pro-

tected the negroes who were voting on their side, and in
Charleston succeeded. But, throughout the State, the movement so far has failed to divide the negro vote with the Radical
party, who remain in a large majority. The principles of the
Reform Union seem to be consistently maintained in practice.
Many of the white electors in the city voted for Delarge, a negro
tailor, as representative of their district in Congress, because
they believed him to be more trustworthy than his white
opponents.

I allude at this length to political affairs in South Carolina,
because it is very obvious that a system of government resting
almost wholly on the votes of the negroes is not a desirable state
of affairs as regards either the State itself or the general interests
of the Union. It destroys confidence in the integrity and
stability of the Administration, prevents the investment of
money, and renders impossible that hearty co-operation of the
public authorities with the substantial people of the State which
is so essential to the interests of all classes of the community.

CHAPTER VII.

Exports of Cotton from Charleston before and since the War.—Opening
made for New York Speculators.—Decrease of Banking Capital in South
Carolina.—A Fortunate Development.—The Phosphate Deposits—Their
Extent and Characteristics—Manufacture into Manures.—Great activity
of the New Trade.—Rice Cultivation likely to diminish.—The Environs of
Charleston.

[CHARLESTON, S.C.—*Nov.* 10 to *Nov.* 14.]

IMMEDIATELY before the war the port of Charleston passed out
to sea as many as half a million of bales of cotton in a year.
This large supply was drawn from many wide districts beyond
the borders of South Carolina, the total production of ginned
cotton in which was 300,900 bales in 1850, and 354,412 bales in
1860, this latter being the largest crop which the State had ever
produced. The extended commercial relations of Charleston,
and its convenience as a place of shipment for the cotton of
parts of North Carolina, Middle Georgia, the Sea Islands, and
regions still more distant, were thus well established before the
war. Charleston is resuming all her old connections, but has to
contend with new conditions of railway communication in the
interior, as well as with the fresh flow of capital and commercial
energy into ports formerly occupying a subordinate position
which has characterised the last few years of reviving industry
and enterprise in the South. But all the old sections of the
country from which cotton came to Charleston continue to send
her more or less still; and with some further development of her
railway system, and an increase of banking and commercial
capital, Charleston is certain to maintain a leading position both
as a market and a port of shipment for cotton. She exported
in the year ended August 31 last, 238,000 bales of Upland cotton
and 13,000 bales of Sea Island, which, though much short of
ante-war times, show a large increase on preceding years since
the war, and from the high prices realized present a volume of
trade in money value which compares favourably with the most
prosperous times in Charleston. The cotton exported here in the
past year is estimated at 25,750,000 dollars, and, with a new
crop still larger coming forward rapidly to market, has produced

a very satisfactory feeling, both retrospectively and prospectively. There is probably, in the meantime, a larger proportion of the cotton exported from Charleston sent forward here simply for shipment, and giving little return to the town itself, than in former times. The cotton speculators at New York push over the heads of the local merchants and factors, and, by cutting before the point, do little good probably to themselves, while impoverishing the trade of the Southern seaports and muddling and confusing the market. Instances have occurred in which they have bought cotton in the interior, cash on the spot, upon which advances had already been made by Southern merchants; but this, of course, is a practice which cannot extend, and immediately checks itself. Yet the excessive activity of speculation in buying and moving cotton is very apparent, and is of doubtful benefit either to the planter or to the consumer. The poverty to which the cotton dealers of Charleston were reduced by the war, and the ruin which fell upon all her financial resources, made an opening for the capital of speculators of which they have availed themselves, and which only closes up as the profits of trade once more accumulate and the town becomes richer. Before the war Charleston had a banking capital of 13,000,000 dollars, whereas to-day she has a banking capital of only 1,892,000 dollars. The State of South Carolina, outside of Charleston, had a banking capital before the war of 3,000,000 dollars, but now of only 300,000 dollars. The crippled capacity of planters and merchants to raise and move such large crops of exportable produce as those of South Carolina may be inferred from these facts. The charges for the use of money are enormous. The banks turn over money at the rate of 18 to 24 per cent., on a class of business which presents little or no risk. In the country districts the rates are still more exorbitant, so that it is with money as with everything else that enters into the production and transport of cotton—it is loaded with a costliness in dollars of now all but par value with gold, which to an Englishman or Scotchman appears simply unbearable. Hence the cry for a high price; hence the difficulty and discontent into which every fall seems to plunge the producer; and hence the struggling condition of the Southern States despite their natural advantages and hold on the commercial world. Until capital be more largely established on the spot for the trading purposes of the country, and substantial reductions of the tariff permit a more direct trade between the South and Europe, and bills on England become saleable in the great depots of Southern produce, the cotton trade can hardly be in a sound condition, while it is impossible that such cities as Charleston can be enriched by the vast inland countries behind them, or be to them in return the strength, support, and ornament they might well be.

Meanwhile, the most fortunate thing that could have occurred in the present circumstances of Charleston has occurred, and is in full progress of commercial development. It has been found within the last two or three years that all round Charleston, and at a few feet from the surface, there are immense marl deposits, so full of phosphates that they cannot be anything else than incalculable heaps of animal remains thrown or washed together, such as science has hitherto not been able to explain, and as commerce, with its clear eye for means of wealth and profit, has not hitherto discovered in any part of the world. The deposits are in the form of little lime-like nodules, light in weight and easily crushed and pulverized. Mixed with these are all but completely petrified ribs, vertebræ, tusks, and other bones of both land and sea monsters of the early tertiary period. So perfect in form are these petrified bones, that, with a collection ample enough, an Owen might have little difficulty in constructing skeletons of the original animals. From some specimens as much as 85 per cent. of pure bone phosphate has been obtained by chemical analysis. But the petrifaction in most cases is too complete for easy treatment, and the great matter commercially at present are the little chalky and irregularly rounded nodules, which yield from 45 to 65 per cent. of bone phosphate. They are found lying in layers under a thin top-dressing of sandy soil, embedded in a bluish clay and earth, and are dug out by pick and shovel much in the same fashion as potatoes. The scientific record is that these layers extend over an area of 70 miles by 60, but, as known to commerce here, there is given an area of 60 miles by 20, including the river beds. The deposit is found in the beds of all the shore rivers, and on the land lying between. The layers vary from six inches to several feet deep. The digging, being done by hand, is not pursued beyond four feet, but a new trench is opened, and the digging carried on in the easiest form. An acre has been known to yield 1,300 tons of nodules. The river and marine deposit differs from the land deposit in being of a blackish colour, harder, and with not so large a percentage of phosphate. The average richness in phosphate of these deposits is usually given at 45 for river and 57 for land. The nodules, when dug up, are washed in long troughs with paddles worked by a strong stream of water from a force-pump, and, thus freed from clay and sand, are sold on the wharves or conveyed into the factories constructed at Charleston for their conversion into soluble phosphate manures. These establishments first put them through kilns to dry them thoroughly, then crush them into pebbles, and afterwards grind them into fine powder by the ordinary circular millstones. In this state the material is taken to a loft, where it is washed with sulphuric acid, and subjected to such varied chemical treatment and composition as may be desired in the final product. When wheeled off from the chemical apparatus into a heap, it cakes, and has to be ground again, after which it is put into bags, and is ready to be transported and applied to the soil. An immense business has already been done both in the raw and manufactured article. The nodules were first extracted for manufacture into manure in the North, but the whole business has been taken up briskly in Charleston, and to import artificial manures into South Carolina is now like carrying coals to Newcastle. An export of the nodules to the most distant parts is growing into magnitude. Vessels are loading just now with this phosphate deposit for England and Scotland; and such is the energy with which the Charleston men have thrown themselves into the utilisation of this mine of wealth round their shores, that the export of the raw material is likely to increase with rapid stride, freight being probably the greatest difficulty in the case. As for the manufacture of superphosphate manures here for local purposes of fertilisation, the result is placed beyond all doubt. The Wando Company, which was the first to enter fully into the trade, divided 30 per cent. of profit, and created by its success a little *furore* for phosphate digging and manufacture. There are now twelve companies operating or about to operate in this new industry, and local works for the manufacture of sulphuric acid have also been set agoing. The planters are taking the manure freely. On the day I arrived in Charleston, bills for a million dollars of this home-made manure fell due and were satisfactorily discharged. One effect has been to benefit the railways in giving them more inland freight, of which they have hitherto felt the scarcity. Some of the planters I have met with say that the manure is as good as Peruvian guano, while others do not give quite so favourable a report. The price is 30 per cent. less than guano; and with an expenditure of three to five dollars to the acre there is the most abundant practical testimony of its productive and profitable results. The scientific men have hitherto not thrown much light on this remarkable natural phenomenon. I believe Dr. Shephard, of the Medical College here, has had more to do in bringing this extraordinary deposit into notice than any other. Agassiz came and looked at it, and was deeply interested, but declined to enter into any elaborate scientific diagnosis or investigation. It seems that the people had been long carting the nodules off the soil as an obstruction to the plough, and were laying the streets with them, ignorant or heedless of their valuable properties. They are, no doubt, a superficial deposit, and cannot be dug out to much depth. There is usually a rapid end to such concentrated animal remains. The nodules overlie an immensely deep bed of white limestone marl, in which Dr. Shephard has found from 2 to 9 per cent. of phosphate of lime. There is an artesian well in Charleston, that has been bored down 1,200 feet for water, passing through eight or nine hundred feet of this white limestone marl, which has been recognized as underlying all the country round. Over this dense bed of marl the phosphate nodules are found, sprinkled as in a layer in some places of a few inches deep, and cropping out in stray pieces on the surface of the soil; but from the varying thickness of the layers, and the frequency with which the diggers have not exhausted them at the depth of three or four feet, the probability is that they will be found in pockets of occasionally great richness. The deposit has already, at all events, been found uniformly over an immense area, and science has begun to forecast its discovery at other points of the coast from Acquia Creek to the shores of Florida. The remarkable thing commercially is that these phosphate deposits of South Carolina have been brought into daylight and practical use at the moment when they are most needed to fertilise the sandy and exhausted soils of the Atlantic States, and to bring them up to a better competitive level with the richer lands of the Gulf and the Mississippi. To South Carolina they are indeed twice blessed, for while increasing the productiveness of the inland soil, they will gather immediately at Charleston a large amount of capital, which is here one of the things most wanted.

The phosphate " diggings " may be expected to make serious inroads on the rice lands round Charleston. But this is probably no great loss. Nothing could be easier than to extend the cultivation of rice all about Charleston, which on various sides has broad, shallow, sedgy swamps, through which the tide flows from the rivers. I went out a few miles to a cotton plantation, and a part of the road—made by a heavy deposit of shells—passed through a section of this swampy ground. The part of the swamp thus separated was rapidly forming into good agricultural soil. The tidal water must be banked off from rice land, and a free command of fresh obtained for irrigation. It would not be difficult, by a few embankments, to make much new rice ground about Charleston; but the wet culture of rice is admitted, even in these parts, to be more fatal to human life than almost anything else, and to extend it up to the very streets of a large town would be bad policy. Rice was a diminishing product of the United States for ten years before the war. Yet South Carolina sold of her crop of the year just ended 40,000 tierces, which were not only an increase on the previous year, but were two-fifths of the total production of rice in the American Union. Almost the whole went to home consumption. South Carolina rice has all but ceased to be an article of export to foreign countries. The cotton plantation

which I went to see did not present a paradise to be put in
contrast with a rice-field.   It had been the pet place of the
owner and cultivator of several plantations.   There was a
splendid mansion closed up, and flower and vegetable gardens
over which the pigs of the negroes had free "ish and entry,"
and a noble verandah from which there was a delightful view
of the Cooper River and of fine avenues of trees by which the
plantation was approached and bounded on all sides.   There
were also superior fields of cotton, sown with Dickson's seed
and amply phosphated, and so full of young bolls that it was
doubtful whether so late they could ever come to maturity.   Yet
it was confessed to me that all would not pay.   This is probably
not the way in which cotton can be profitably cultivated in these
days, and my city friend, who pays a rent of 700 dollars for the
place, seemed quite conscious of the fact, and not to care much
about it one way or other.   Yet I could not but admire the
environs of Charleston—good roads which one expects to see on
approaching any place of importance, whether it be the chief
city of a State or the residence of a duke or a millionaire—
noble trees, too deeply draped perhaps with the mossy veils
peculiar to miasmatic regions—summer gardens which adverse
circumstances have closed, and many other places of public
and private resort, now silent and neglected, but capable of
being repaired and reanimated with a richer and brighter life
than that of former days.

E

CHAPTER VIII.

The Negro's "best Friends."—Sinister complexion of Politics.—Kindly Social Influences at work.— State of Education.—System of Medical Relief in Charleston.—The Health Statistics.—Proportionate Mortality of Whites and Blacks.—Salubrity of the Climate.—Freedmen's Savings Banks.

[CHARLESTON, S.C.—*Nov.* 10 to *Nov.* 14.]

APART from the passing excitement of the elections just over, and the disappointment of the white population at the voting of the negroes *en masse* for the Republican or Radical party, the general tone of social life in Charleston is kindly and temperate, and all classes of society are working together with considerable harmony for mutual good. The negro is beset at present by two parties who claim to be his "best friends." The Republicans, who came in with the close of the war, appeal to him as his best if not only friends; and, looking at the political issues of the war, and the decree of emancipation, with its elaborate guarantees of reconstruction, the negroes could not but regard the Republican party politically as their friends. Nor can it be denied that the organs of the Federal Government have laboured to introduce institutions for the moral and social benefit of the negroes, and, as far as their limited means would allow, have befriended that large portion of the population. I have not found any one on the other side who is prepared to blame the negroes for voting almost universally as they did in the elections which raised General Grant to the Presidentship, or who appears to have expected that they would or should have been other than fast adherents of their emancipators. But the political agitators and hungry spoil-and-office hunters of the party are accused of appealing to the ignorance and passions of the negro population —of telling them that the white people of the State are eagerly seeking an opportunity of restoring slavery, which they have certainly no wish to do, and which they could not do even if they would; and now, after five years of this, it is considered hard that the negroes—when there are great public objects of economy, protection from jobbery and corruption, and a sound and healthy administration of the affairs of the State to promote,

in which the blacks are as closely interested as others—should
cast their votes in a body against the great majority of the white
population, and terrorise such of their own colour as are disposed
to act differently.   This feeling breaks out violently just now
in bar-rooms and at street corners, and is often expressed more
quietly and reasonably, yet firmly, in private circles.   Many
seem ready to despair of the negro as a politician, while others
talk of a " war of races " and other disorders sure to arise.   The
feeling is no doubt all the stronger since the evils of "carpet-
bagging " and negro demagoguery are apparent to respectable
men of both parties, and, while violently denounced on one side,
are not denied, but sometimes admitted and deplored, on the
other.   Though politics in South Carolina thus wear a somewhat sinister complexion, yet there is a healthy action and a
sober practical opinion underneath the surface that promise
beneficial results.   The issues left by the war are being rapidly
closed; the *Reform Union*, which has figured prominently in
the late elections as the organ of the native white people of the
State, recognizes fully the civil and political equality of the
negroes not only as an election platform, but as the fundamental
law of the United States; this position is likely to be maintained, and may be expected soon to bring about in this, as in
other Southern States, a better balance of parties.   Meanwhile
social bonds are being knit together, and many ameliorative
influences are quietly at work.   The ladies, who had a long
apprenticeship of self-devotion during the war, are exerting
themselves to give work, and to sell the work of poor needle-
women of both races.   Nearly all the old charities of Charleston
remain in operation, and schools and missions are doing much
to improve the population.

By a law passed five years before the war a public school
system was introduced into South Carolina, which became well
developed in Charleston; and now the State has passed under
the new free-school principle, embodied in the Constitutions of
the Southern States under the Acts of Reconstruction.   It is
only by degrees that this system can get into general operation,
and, indeed, it is doubtful whether the ground lost in education
during the war has yet been recovered.   The official statistics
for 1860 give 20,716 pupils in 757 public schools, whereas they
show for 1869 only 381 public schools and 16,418 pupils.   The
new law is now, however, being put into operation; the State
has appropriated 50,000 dollars to this object, and, aided by the
Peabody Fund and other voluntary contributions, South Carolina
may be expected soon to be tolerably well furnished with the
means of education for the whole population.   Charleston is
probably more advanced in this respect than any other part of
the State, and the education of negro children is already quite a

prominent feature, one building devoted to the coloured people being capable of receiving 1,000 scholars.

There is in Charleston a well-organized system of medical relief, and much attention is paid to sanitary conditions and arrangements. The city is divided into five health districts, over each of which there is appointed a physician in charge, with an office and dispensary, where attendance is given an hour every morning and an hour every afternoon. The physicians are also required, when called upon, to visit certain public institutions—such as the Alms House, the Old Folks' Home, the Small-pox Hospital—situated in their districts. From the annual report for last year of Dr. Lebby, the City Registrar, which is very full, it appears that the total mortality of whites was 220 males and 233 females—453 ; and of blacks, 421 males and 497 females —918. The greatest mortality of whites occurred in the months of June, July, and August, and of blacks in July, August, September, and October. Of the 453 whites who died, 181 were children of five years and under ; and of the 918 blacks who died, 461 were children of five years and under—the mortality of infants among the coloured people being proportionately much greater than among the whites. Both races seem equally long-lived, though the coloured people would seem to have the advantage. Among the deaths are recorded 33 whites from 70 to 80 years, 9 from 80 to 90 years, and 6 from 90 to 100 years ; and 44 blacks from 70 to 80 years, 29 from 80 to 90 years, and 10 from 90 to 100 years. But the remarkable fact is the greatly larger mortality of the negroes, in proportion to their total number, as compared with the white people. The census taken last year by order of the Governor, and generally accepted as substantially correct for Charleston, gave the population of the city as 20,354 whites, and 24,570 blacks and coloured. On this basis, the mortality of 1869 shows one death in 44·93 whites, and one death in 26·77 coloured people. In other words, very nearly twice as many coloured people died as white people in proportion to their respective numbers. Before the war this disparity in the mortality of the two races was not so marked. The returned population of Charleston in 1860 was 26,969 whites, and 21,440 coloured. The mortality of whites in that year was 719, or one in 37·5, and the mortality of coloured people 753, or one in 28·47. The health of the whites has greatly improved since the war, while the health of the negroes has declined, till the mortality of the coloured population, greater than the mortality of the whites before the war, has now become so markedly greater, that nearly two coloured die for every one white person out of equal numbers of each. To those accustomed to think of slavery only as prolific of every form of evil, this increased mortality of the negroes under emancipation may appear surprising. But when one considers the strict, almost domestic control under which the slaves were kept in Charleston, how they were cared for when young and provided for when old, and how their number in the city was kept down to the actual demand for their services, one finds natural reasons enough for an increased liability to death in the severe ordeal they have passed through since their emancipation. In 1860 there were 5,529 more white than coloured people in Charleston. There are now 4,217 more black and coloured than whites. The absolute increase of the negro population of Charleston since 1860 is 3,130. They flocked in from the country at the close of the war, deserting the Sea Islands in large bodies, and produced all the evils of overcrowding at a time when the white population, who could alone employ and maintain them, were not only thinned in numbers, but reduced to poverty, and the trade and wealth of the town were destroyed. Such a state of things could only have a disastrous effect on health and life, the traces of which still remain. The physicians in charge of the health districts also complain of the extreme carelessness of the negroes in following their advice, and administering the medicines prescribed. A negro woman will come with her sick child to the dispensary at the morning hour, but does not return in the afternoon or next day as she ought, but makes her appearance a few days after to announce that she administered some charm of her own, and that the little patient is dead. New classes of disease are also notable in the returns of negro mortality—such as consumption, from which they used to be peculiarly exempt, and diseases which spring from immoral causes. Yet with all this access of negro mortality in Charleston, the whole deaths in 1869 were not more than 1 in 32·77, which it would be quite possible to match, and even exceed, in the mortality returns of various large cities of the United Kingdom. But if the negro population and mortality of Charleston be excluded, and the white population only considered, there is a degree of healthfulness which is almost unequalled in large towns of the old country. The mortality of whites in 1869 in Charleston was only 1 in 44·93. The mortality of all England in the same year I find to have been 1 in 44·17, and of all Scotland 1 in 42·52.

I imagine there is much nonsense thought and spoken about the unhealthiness of these Southern countries and Southern seaports. Any passing impressions of mine, indeed, would be a very unsafe guide; for I have been travelling in an atmosphere so bright and clear, and yet so temperate and agreeable, and so pleasant by night and day, as to form a rather fascinating contrast to the climate of the United Kingdom at the same season of the year. This is the famous "Indian summer" of the South, and Charleston has its earlier and fiercer summer, when there is a considerable amount of sickness, and when febrile affections prevail. But this city has been singularly free from all epidemic disease for some years past. On the hottest day in 1869 the mean temperature at 2 P.M. was 86·77, and the thermometer is never known to rise above 97 degrees; while in eight months of the year the temperature has an equable range from 50 to 65 degrees, with fair weather, and rainfall only heavy at very rare intervals, as the prevailing characteristics of the climate. No doubt the health of the town owes much to the well-organized staff of medical officers and the efficient arrangements made for the treatment of disease among the poorer classes. I was politely shown through the City Hospital by Dr. Lebby—an establishment of great extent, marked by scrupulous cleanliness and order, and devoted equally to white and coloured subjects. The white female ward is probably as lightsome, airy, and fine a sick-room as is to be seen in a public hospital anywhere. There is a lunatic ward, the inmates of which are chiefly blacks of a very low order. There were only two white women in the number—one of whom, a lady of Italian origin, had been driven to distraction in her matrimonial relations. Surgical cases, some of them very difficult, are also treated with marked success, the proportion of negroes operated upon being about 6 to 1 of whites. There is no general registry of births and marriages in Charleston, which detracts from the light thrown by its otherwise ample vital statistics on the physical and social condition of the population.

That the negroes are improving, and many of them rising under freedom into a very comfortable and civilized condition, is not only admitted in all the upper circles of society, but would strike even a transient wayfarer like myself in the great number of decent coloured men of the labouring class and of happy coloured families that one meets. There is an institution in Charleston which early attracted my attention. In Broad Street one sees the office of the National Freedmen's Savings and Trust Company. I believe this form of National Savings Bank for the negroes was founded by the Freedmen's Bureau in the first years after the war. It has spread over all the chief towns of the South, and has already in deposit upwards of two millions of dollars, almost entirely the savings of the negro population. The deposits in the Charleston branch were 165,000 dollars at the end of October, and are monthly on the increase. Go in any forenoon, and the office is found full of negroes depositing little sums of money, drawing little sums, or remitting to distant parts of the country where they have relatives to support or debts to discharge. The Freedmen's Savings Bank transacts a general exchange business betwixt the various points at which it has branches. Perhaps "branches" is not the exactly proper designation, for each bank is an independent corporation in itself, has a subscribed capital, is governed by its stockholders, and is altogether probably too like an ordinary commercial bank for the humble functions it has to discharge.   Yet there is a certain degree of national concentration and control. The banks are under the patronage and protection of the Federal Government, and from the centre at Washington a monthly Circular is published, which reports the progress of all the various offices, and contains an amount of general matter very suitable to the negroes, and very desirable for them to read. The funds are for the most part invested in the Federal Debt, the high interest of which enables from 5 to 6 per cent. to be paid to the depositors.   But the Federal Government does not appear to be bound to make good to the depositors any loss accruing from the failure of a bank through embezzlement or any other cause.   The responsibility in such a case would fall on the subscribed capital of the stockholders so far as it was sufficient to make good the deficiency.   There is an opening in this state of affairs for partial and local disasters, which is happily closed in the National Security Savings Banks of the United Kingdom.   But practically the Freedmen's Savings and Trust Companies do for the negroes what our National Savings Banks do for the working classes of England, Scotland, and Ireland; and it is gratifying to find that the negroes have in five years accumulated nearly half a million sterling of deposits. This result is the more significant since it is confined almost wholly to what were formerly the Slave States, and is but very feebly developed in New York and other Northern towns where it has been tried.   The number of depositors in Charleston is 2,790, of whom nine-tenths are negroes.   The average amount at the credit of individual depositors is about 60 dollars.   The negro begins to deposit usually with some special object in view. He wishes to buy a mule and cart, or a house, or a piece of land, or a shop, or simply to provide a fund against death, sickness, or accident, and pursues his object frequently until it has been accomplished.

While some portion of the former slaves are probably sinking into an even worse condition than the first, there are others who are clearly rising, both morally and socially.   The system of free labour, as was to be expected, will thus, in its own rough but salutary way, sift the chaff from the wheat; and but for the electoral antagonism of the moment, and the parading more than enough of negroes as senators, as policemen, as militia, as the armed force and the dominant power of the State, the relations of the two races on both sides would here be more kindly and cordial, and the prospects of the negroes themselves more hopeful than could well have been anticipated.

CHAPTER IX.

The Capital of South Carolina.—The State Fair a failure.—Usury.—Governor Scott on the Position of Affairs. The Blue Ridge Railway project.—Mr. Treasurer Parker on Taxation and Negro Free Labour.—Political Opinions of the Farmers.—Arguments for and against Payment of Negro Farmlabourers by Wages or Share of the Crops.—Railway Freight.—Cotton bagging and the Price of Cotton.

[Columbia, S.C.—*Nov.* 15–16.]

It was on the morning of the first frost this season in the South that I was landed on the railway platform here from Charleston. Day had just broke, and nothing could be more inspiriting than the clear sky and sharp air, the paling moon and stars being just visible and no more, as the glorious effulgence along the eastern horizon shot its golden light up to the zenith. The country all round cultivated and interesting. The hills, or rather mounds, lower and rounder, the hollows less deep and abrupt, and the whole landscape presenting a more swelling outline than at Richmond in Virginia, with woods no more than enough for ornament. The hotels in these parts are very obliging. They send carriages to the railway depôts for guests, whether they can entertain them or not, while an express company's van picks up the baggage, for both of which services a handsome fee has to be paid. Columbia is a city of such "magnificent distances" that a stranger is never quite sure when he is in it or out of it. I am conscious of having arrived at the depôt, and of being there in the country; of having by-and-by seen a stately building on an eminence which was clearly the Capitol, and two or three church spires about as widely apart as such objects may be seen in any English country landscape; of having been set down at a hotel full from floor to roof with country-people who had come in to the State Fair; and finally, of having sauntered forth to look for another inn and found myself in the country again. Columbia, it will be remembered, was completely burned down by Sherman in the war, the State House being almost the only building that was spared or, fireproof, proved impervious to the flames. The town is being built up anew by degrees, and many fine brick houses have been erected since the close of the war. But what magnificent outlines of streets sweeping spaciously for miles over the heights and hollows of that rich landscape, having rows of fine old trees on either side, and, intersected by other wooded avenues equally broad and long, opening up in all directions the most delightful vistas! These vacant streets have solitary residences here and there, and since it must have cost a good deal to lay them out, and perhaps something considerable to keep them up, the suburban residents of the capital of South Carolina enjoy for nothing an amenity which money could hardly command in any part of Western Europe.

The State Fair, though attended by a multitude of happy-looking people, was a failure as regards agricultural interest or display. There was little or no stock, which surprised me more in Columbia than in Charleston, where the same deficiency was very observable. The South Carolinians cannot vie in this respect with the Virginians. There is either no superior stock in this State, or the stockowners have not sufficient interest in its extension to be at the trouble to show it. The present disjointed state of political relations has also probably something to do with it. But the truth is that the Atlantic Cotton States have, till very recently, neglected stock-raising, for which they have some excuse, not only in the absorbing attention which the cotton-plant requires, but in the nature of the soil, which is un-favourable to the development of good pasture land or winter forage. The difficulty may, no doubt, be overcome with care and perseverance, and it is only now that agriculturists in these parts are awakening to the importance of combining general elements of agricultural wealth with the growth of cotton.

The cotton-growers are not in the most satisfied mood this season. The heavy fall in the price of cotton—partly in consequence of the Franco-Prussian war, and partly owing to the large crop of last year, now reckoned to have been 3,300,000 bales, and the still larger being gathered—has occurred when they had placed themselves under heavy accounts for manures, and disappoints their expectations of profit. The phosphates are generally allowed, however, to have had a marked and favourable effect on the crop, and increased quantity will probably in many cases retrieve the fall in value. Complaints of the usurious rates charged for money are general among the farming community. Twenty-five and even thirty per cent. is taken by banks and people who have money to lend as a quite ordinary rate; and it is doubtful whether the planters are as thriving as the commercial interests around them.

Governor Scott, whose administration I had heard severely blamed, courteously favoured me with an interview, and entered freely into conversation on the condition and prospects of the

State. He said that some official protection of the negroes was necessary, and, indeed, found to be unavoidable by persons in authority. Alluding to the dictum of Chief-Justice Tanpey on the Dred Scott case, that "a negro had no rights which a white man was bound to respect," he remarked that there were still some who seemed to be actuated by that view of the question. He had had to give safe-conducts to negroes leaving the State; and subordinate magistrates were not unfrequently called upon, and felt bound, in the discharge of their duty, to throw the protection of the law over the coloured race. Governor Scott expressed a very hopeful view of the progress of South Carolina, and explained to me on the map the merits of the Blue Ridge Railway, the formation of which he is most anxious to promote. This project, which was prepared two years ago, and for which a company has been organized, and the necessary powers obtained to subscribe capital and borrow on mortgage bonds endorsed by the State, is designed to connect the existing railway communications of South Carolina from Anderson county with Knoxville in Tennessee and with the lines to Kentucky and the Western States. To get into direct and continuous communication by rail with the great West is a common object of ambition to all the Atlantic Cotton States and their seaports, and may be said to have become an absolute necessity of South Carolina if she is to keep pace with the progress made in this direction by her sister States. The Blue Ridge Railroad would not only be of essential importance to Charleston and Port Royal, but would develop a large traffic betwixt the interior of South Carolina and the rich and productive States both to the west and the south. The produce of Kentucky is sent round eleven or twelve hundred miles, and brought back to points in South Carolina within a hundred miles or two of the place from which it started. The line is being extended at both ends, and some grading or earthwork is being done, but the borrowing powers of the company have not yet been exercised. Upon my observing that American railroad companies sometimes provided that their rails should be home-made, the Governor said that this was not the case in South Carolina, and that, on the contrary, it was a condition of the Blue Ridge Company that the road should be laid with the best English rails. Mr. Parker, the State Treasurer, with whom I conversed for some time, stated that, before the war, the assessment for State purposes was levied, among other means and substance, on the slaves; that this source of revenue was now, of course, abolished; and that a larger rate had to be laid on land and other substance proper, all of which had been greatly reduced by the war, and was only being gradually, though rapidly, restored. Mr. Parker is of opinion that the labour of the negro as a free man is more efficient than when he was a slave ; and in proof of this conclusion adduces that many of the negroes perished during the war and immediately after it, that the negro women are now almost wholly withdrawn from field labour, that the children who were made available under slavery for industrial purposes are being more and more absorbed by the schools, and yet that, with all these diminutions of the labour power, the production of South Carolina and other Cotton States is rapidly rising to a magnitude equal to that of any former time.

The "fairs" in the South afford a good opportunity for obtaining information on country affairs. The hotels are filled with intelligent men, who all seem to know one another, and who are ready enough to enter into conversation with strangers ; while the railway cars form a sort of free assembly, in which affairs are discussed with all openness. In my travels from Columbia towards Georgia I gathered much opinion, as it were, in the mass. The dissatisfaction of these country folks of South Carolina with the present state of government in the United States is palpable enough. They exclaim bitterly against the corruption which prevails in public life ; they are utterly opposed to the high tariff on European goods, looking upon it simply as a means of plundering the cultivators of the soil in the South and West for the benefit of Northern manufacturers, overgrown, they say, in wealth, and adepts in bribery and lobby-rolling ; they point to the enormous prices of goods sold in the Southern towns, and long for the growth of manufactures among themselves, and the direct importation of foreign goods into their own' seaports ; they express disappointment that more direct trade has not sprung up with the South since the close of the war, the high tariff notwithstanding ; they declare American statesmen of the present day to be dwarfs and nobodies compared with those of former times ; and when the whole gamut of political discontent has been sounded, one often hears the remark, so startling to any European admirer of American Independence, that Washington made a capital mistake, and that it would have been better for the country to have remained under the rule of England. To such an appeal to British patriotism I could only reply that England could scarcely, in any circumstances, have continued to govern so great a country as the United States, and would certainly not be inclined to undertake the responsibility now. On political subjects the people are very emphatic, if not a little excited, and the party newspapers are more emphatic and excited still. But on agricultural and business matters they at once become cool, practical, and reasonable, and talk with acute apprehension of the point in hand, whatever it may be. It is felt that the old system of cultivation, or rather want of cultivation, is no longer suitable or possible, and that there must be deeper ploughing, more attention paid to stock and to the formation of good farm-yards, with plenty of manure and vegetable compost from the forest and the ditches, so as to give heart, vigour, and greater variety of elements to the soil. There is little or no disparagement of the negro as a labourer among respectable countrymen, who need his services and employ him. On the contrary, there is much appreciation of his good qualities, a good deal of kindly patience towards his bad qualities, and much greater satisfaction with what he has done, and may yet be trained to do, as a free labourer, than one might be prepared to find. How to shape his relations as a farm labourer is thoroughly well canvassed. The alternative presented is that of paying him by a share of the crop or by wages, both of which plans have obtained a footing, and each of which is acknowledged by the practical mind of the planter to have its advantages. A summary of the arguments I have heard *pro* and *con* on this question would occupy a considerable space. But on the whole, so far, the preponderance of reason, as well as weight of testimony, inclines to the side of wages. One objection to the share system, which goes much deeper in my opinion than at first appears, is that it renders the negro indifferent to and reluctant to perform any kind of work on a plantation which does not bear immediately on the corn and cotton crops in which he has a share. A planter who cultivates on the share system must see his fences falling out of order, his manure heaps a diminishing quantity, and his hogs and cattle strayed, stolen, or starved ; or, resorting to the wages system after all, must employ special hands to do these and other kinds of farm work. As the system of agriculture improves, the necessary labour on plantations will become more and more varied, with the direct result of increasing the corn and cotton crops per acre ; and to pay wages to one class of men, probably whites, to do various kinds of work, in order that another class, certainly blacks, may share an increased abundance to which they have contributed nothing, will prove too unjust to be practicable. The rapid and regular picking of the cotton crop, which is the greatest difficulty of the planter, has kept the share system more in countenance than probably anything else, but in practical experience it seems to fail at this point as at others. The share system implies rations to the negro from the beginning of the year to the end, and if the rations for a week are consumed in half that time, an additional supply must be given, which places the negro so heavily in debt to his employer by the time the picking season has come, that he is apt, more especially under declining prices as this year, to be regardless of the financial results of the partnership with his employer into which he entered in January. The picking of cotton, as far as I know, does not involve any greater natural difficulty than harvest season in all countries, when extra labour, stimulated by higher pay, flows freely into the fields, and crowns the labours of the husbandman with a success in which all feel they have a personal interest. But in the thinly populated Cotton States of America, with labour on every plantation too inadequate for its ordinary routine of work, and vast spaces of mere wood, without town or village, betwixt one plantation and another, the social conditions are, of course, different. Yet some planters in South Carolina succeed in employing extra hands in the picking season, giving rations and 50 cents per 100 lbs. of cotton picked. The production of cotton per acre is no doubt very varied, but one hand and a mule in general cultivate 20 acres of cotton and 10 of corn, producing 10 bales of cotton and 100 bushels of corn.[1] One bale of cotton on good land per acre, with the help of phosphates and good picking, may be attained in some instances ; but half a bale of cotton per acre is deemed a very favourable result in these parts.

The railways in South Carolina conduct the cotton freight on a rough-and-ready rate of a dollar per bale to Charleston, without being particular as to the weight of the bales, or a handful of miles of transport. One result is that the bales are becoming always heavier. Another curious instance of turning the penny to advantage is that the late high price of cotton has created a demand for heavy bagging, sold with the bale at the cotton price, which only the coarsest hempen looms of Kentucky can supply. As the price of cotton falls this temptation is reduced, and the point is just about reached when the protected hempen stuff of Kentucky is dearer than the unprotected cotton wool of the Southern States.

[1] A negro usually works two mules, but he cannot cultivate or gather the crop which his mules plough and "lay by, that is, finish for the season." He requires several hands, a little staff of labour, to make and gather the crop.

CHAPTER X.

[AUGUSTA, GA.—*Nov.* 17–19.]

MY first acquaintance with the State of Georgia has been made at the thriving and busy town of Augusta, situated on the border line of South Carolina, and connected with Columbia by an excellent railroad. The town at once establishes in the mind of a stranger a favourable prepossession of the State. It is lively, well built, well organized, and as amply furnished with merchandise as any small inland town of the most flourishing province could be expected to be. Augusta escaped direct devastation by the Federal armies during the war, and no doubt owes much of its compact condition and steady march to that happy immunity. But it was finally cut off from all its communications, and its inhabitants shared the general impoverishment which blighted every portion of the Southern States. It is surprising, therefore, to see already so much spirit and abundance as prevail in Augusta. The town has a "Broadway," before which the imperial street of New York must, all circumstances considered, hide its diminished head; for the Augusta Broadway is three times as broad as that of New York, and has a neatly-constructed market-place at either end, with as much space for expansion as in future may be necessary. But the Broadway of Augusta is really no make-believe. Nearly the whole ground-space is occupied with well-stocked stores, in which everything, from a needle to an anchor, from the humble fabrics woven on the spot to the finest cloths of Europe, from the commonest earthenware to the choicest crystal, and all the products of the soil from cranberries to cotton, may be bought. And how substantial the houses are, and how many fine buildings meet the eye! The Freemasons have a pillared edifice as chaste and pure as the White House at Washington, with their insignia brightly gilt on a ground as of alabaster. The dry and brilliant atmosphere encourages everywhere a cheerful style of ornamentation. It is remarkable how widely the ancient Order of Freemasonry is spread throughout the Southern States. I find traces of it everywhere, and traces which sometimes reflect no little honour on the brotherhood. For example, a tract of land laid out in lots, with cottages and cultivation, where the widows and orphans of deceased Freemasons find quiet and comfortable homes ; or a school-house in some solitary district where it is difficult to discover a population, built by the Freemasons, who, content with the second story for their lodge-room, have devoted the lower to the educational purposes of the community.

Augusta is an extensive cotton market. Since the lifting of this year's crop began, the receipts have been about 1,500 bales a day. The railroads place Augusta in rapid communication with the adjoining counties of South Carolina, and with all parts of Middle Georgia, and the cotton collected from these wide districts is poured down by rail to Savannah for shipment. The telegraph works all day betwixt Augusta and Savannah, and betwixt Augusta and towns farther inland, telling what cotton can be bought or is selling for; while prices at New York and Liverpool are eagerly scanned, and form the basis of the day's transactions. The local factors and merchants deal freely in cotton, though the former operate chiefly on order from Savannah, Charleston, and New York. Seldom has cotton been brought more rapidly to market than this season, which is to be ascribed not only to the favourable weather, but to the activity of buyers and speculators, and the necessity, rather than the interest, of the planters ; for under the heavy fall of prices, generally attributed here to the war in Europe, and scarce at all to the yearly expansion of the crop, the planter might be tempted, with the stock of American at Liverpool still low, and the return of peace probably not distant, to hold back in expectation of better prices. But the growers of cotton, though restoring rapidly their plantations and their stock of implements, are, for the most part, still poor in purse, and have to draw heavy advances on the growing crop. Paying from 2 to 2½ per cent. for money per month, with storage and insurance charges to boot, the planter finds that to hold is a costly business, and that it is better to sell at once than to extend his borrowings and charges in the expectation of an advance of two or three cents per lb. The crop, save in so far as it may be interrupted by the action of middlemen and speculators, is therefore rolled from the field, over hundreds of miles of railway and thousands of miles of ocean, to the great markets with marvellous despatch. Though insurance in the South was swept away during the war, yet it is growing up again with great rapidity ; and statesmen and generals, whose names were famous in the war, preside over local companies or act as agents of New York or British corporations.

A great revolution in agriculture is going forward in this district, and indeed throughout the whole of Georgia. The most lively discussion is kept up on such points as the preparation of land for crops, the selection of cotton seed, the use of fertilisers, the improvement and increase of live stock, and a more careful and varied cultivation than has hitherto been followed. There appears to be a strong feeling of the necessity of bringing intelligence and an active spirit of improvement to bear on the management of plantations, which, in ante-war times, were allowed to drag along with slave labour and overseers, as they had done for generations. Agricultural Societies have been formed in all parts of the State, and have been consolidated into a general institution, which holds two conventions every year for the discussion of agricultural questions, and for making arrangements for the holding of annual fairs or exhibitions of industry. Numerous periodicals are published here, and throughout the State, which are chiefly devoted to the land interest, and discuss practical farming in all its branches with much vigour and intelligence. Farmers and landholders constantly interchange their views and experience in these organs, and the actual results obtained from the use of phosphate and other manures, or from Dickson's and other classes of cotton seed, and the advantages of various kinds of implements, or the payment of labour by wages or shares in the crops, are chronicled with business-like detail. The consequence is that the production of cotton per acre has been sensibly increased on the middle quality of land in Georgia, the soil of which in general has hitherto borne but an inferior reputation. Half a bale per acre is becoming more of an average than it once was; two bales to the three acres is deemed a super-excellent result on the best land with guano or phosphates, and a bale to the acre is said to be attainable when land, seed, manure, season, and mode of cultivation are all favourable, though I rather think there are very few instances of such a rate of production in Georgia.

Of the vital importance of good selected seed there can be no doubt, and much of the inferior crop seen throughout the Atlantic States is probably to be ascribed to carelessness in this particular. Mr. Dickson's seed and its offspring are now extensively propagated throughout this and neighbouring States. But the best seed will rapidly deteriorate without careful and annual selection, and probably the greatest service rendered by Mr. Dickson and other agitators of this cardinal point is seen in the increased care which planters bestow on the quality of the seed annually set apart from their own crops. One could purchase here two thousand bushels of a seed that appears to be peculiar in species, and is certainly remarkable in its fruitfulness. The branches of the plant grow up more straight from the stem, and thus cover less room in the drill than most other cotton, while the number of bolls produced is much above the average. On one branch I have counted ninety bolls, the great majority not only mature but picked of cotton. The grower began by purchasing as much seed as planted ten acres, the product of which gave him seed next year for the whole plantation. But, in order to keep up the quality, he carefully selects his seed each year by setting two trusty negroes to pick only from the stems bearing the greatest number of full, sound, and ripe bolls.

In Middle Georgia, as well as in South Carolina, much cotton is now grown by white labour. This occurs chiefly on small farms, the proprietors of which were formerly unable to compete with the large combinations of slave labour, but are now raising a considerable amount of cotton. There are now also many small patches of cotton in the neighbourhood of towns and villages, where fruits and vegetables cannot be so well preserved from depredation by vagrant or destitute negroes as in former times. It is the outcome of cotton from these and other unusual quarters that has probably caused the estimates of crops since the war so habitually to fall short of actual results. Speculators, looking only at the diminution of negro labour, and at the state of the large plantations, the disorganization and diminished productiveness of which are very apparent, have formed erroneous conclusions. The large planters, who cannot command labour or capital to cultivate more than a section of their former cotton area, endeavour to sell or to farm out portions of their plantations; but this process can only be developed slowly in a country where there is so much land in this state and so few people. Yet some land is farmed out at a crop-rent of one-fourth the produce; while a good many strangers come into this part of the State, buy land, and settle down to its cultivation. Estates bring from five to fifty dollars per acre, according to the quality of the land and the degree of improvement. The average purchase-money of an improved farm is from fifteen to twenty dollars per acre. The field negroes command from eight to twelve and a half dollars a month, with rations, houses, and fire; women, from five to eight dollars. But the share system of paying labour prevails more than that of wages, at the rate of one-third of the crop with rations, or one-half without rations. "The negroes," says a very competent authority to me, "are working better and stealing less every year, and would be well enough if the political agitators would only let them alone." The agitators complained of are "the carpet-baggers," who come into the South with very light equipment, for the sole purpose of getting themselves elected Representatives by the negro vote, and of working themselves into some office in which they may

F

make rich, by not the most honest means, at the public expense.
The tactics of these trading politicians are declared to be sometimes of the most wild and desperate description. It is said the
negroes have been told from the stump that their former masters
owe them wages from the date of Mr. Lincoln's proclamation,
and that anything stolen from them now is but in fair liquida-
tion of the account !

There is a prosperous cotton factory in Augusta, of no mean
extent, which produces sheetings and shirtings, and other plain
domestic fabrics. The hands are all white people, male and
female, and differ little from factory operatives in the smaller
towns of England or Scotland. The capital of the company is
600,000 dollars, on which a profit of 5 per cent. a quarter, or
20 per cent. per annum, has for some time been regularly
realized and paid. The factory has both steam and water
power, and has established a basis of skilled labour that is
not likely in a town of such considerable population to fail in
the future. But the large profit made by this manufacturing
concern of late years probably requires that the facts should be
stated, that in its early history it was unfortunate to the share-
holders, that it was sold to a new company at much less than it
had cost, that it remained in undisturbed operation during the
war, when the simplest domestic manufactures were in the
highest request, and that the factory thus obtained a vantage
ground which it has hitherto held with happy success. In such
considerable towns as Augusta a large amount of labour, otherwise idle and unprofitable, may be utilised without impairing in
any degree the main interest of agriculture, and this cotton
factory proves with what advantage various manufactures may
be prosecuted in the Southern States.

The Legislature of Georgia has passed an Act to carry out the
system of free public schools, which has become, with certain
local modifications, a fundamental law of the United States.
Much attention is paid to the Act, and to the steps necessary
to bring it into operation.

Augusta passes on the Sabbath Day into as profound a tranquillity as any town in England, or even in Scotland. The
Georgian newspapers have adopted a plan of publication which
can only have been suggested by a determination to observe
with Hebrew precision a rest from labour during the day of
twenty-four hours as defined throughout all the European and
Western worlds. They are issued on Sunday mornings as on
other days of the week, because the labour essential to their
production, though not to their distribution, can be completed
by twelve o'clock on Saturday night. It has not occurred to the
Georgian newspaper people, that while the Western day begins
and ends at twelve at midnight, the Hebrew and Eastern day

begins and ends at six p.m.   The consequence is that they give
to the people their mass of secular ·print on Sabbath morning
when they would rather not have it, and withhold it from them
on Monday morning when it would be acceptable to all.   I
walked out on Sunday afternoon towards the country.   Not a
beer saloon or even a candy shop was open, scarcely a person
walking about, and only a street car at long intervals passing
along.   At length I met a grave-looking man with a lively little
girl in his hand, whom I congratulated on the delightful weather,
to which he cheerfully responded.· Was Augusta advancing
rapidly? He did not think it was.   I then ventured to ask him
whether the churches in Augusta had an evening service, to
which he replied that he really did not know; that the only
thing he knew was there was no Universalist Church, morning
or evening, in Augusta.   It was easy to perceive that my friend
was himself a Universalist; and that in a community of Presbyterians, Episcopalians, Baptists, and Methodists, he did not
think it worth his while to know whether there were any evening diets of worship in Augusta, because there was not a
Universalist Church!   Religious sects may be more numerous in
the United States than in any other part of the Christian world,
but there·is nothing essentially distinctive in this little incident,
the like of which might befall anywhere.

CHAPTER XI.

The country from Augusta to Savannah.—Alleged poorness of the Soil.—
Population of the State.—Competition betwixt the Cotton Lands of Georgia
and the Mississippi "Bottom."—Probable effects of Good Farming.—
Want of Stock and Grass.—The Central Railroad Company.

[SAVANNAH, GA.—*Nov.* 20-23.]

THE distance from Augusta to Savannah, the great seaport of
Georgia, is 132 miles by rail, and is travelled, with frequent
stoppages for freight, in eight to nine hours. The aspect of the
country gives an impression of a rather poor soil. There is the
same white sandy surface as strikes one all the way down the
Atlantic States. The crops of corn and cotton are not heavy,
though often wonderfully fruity; and the woods, which abound,
are of lighter timber than in many other parts of the South.
Pine prevails almost without a rival, and an extensive lumber
trade is done in all the counties east and west of this line of
railway. Burke County, on one side, is a large and comparatively rich county, with its agriculture well developed; and
Emmanuel County, on the other, produces large quantities of
good timber, and has a social life more rude than is probably
characteristic of the vast rural spaces of Georgia. The name
attracted my attention to this county, which I thought must
necessarily be the home of piety, virtue, and every Christian
felicity. But these are fruits not the first to bloom in the
American wilds. Yet Emmanuel County has an ideal in its
name which in due time, with the spread of culture and population, it may approach. The old pine of the primeval forest
serves so many purposes that it must be pronounced a most
useful tree. But it is also, when prepared and polished, a very
beautiful wood. Some of the finest panellings I have seen in
the houses and railway cars are of pine. Though the forests still
occupy an inordinate space in Georgia, yet in the most woody
parts many fine tracts have been opened out, and many garden
spots appear, in the course of a day's travel, where the wilderness really blossoms like the rose. The Georgian woods withal
have often a very old-country aspect that startles one from the
recurring reveries produced by a foreign land. Their light and

varied character, the birds' nests of a departed summer hanging loosely among the rapidly disrobing branches, the wood-pigeons flying swiftly about, and the buzzards poising themselves far above the topmost boughs, under the mild autumnal sky, are very similar to what one may have seen among the copse-woods of England and Scotland; and the squire's mansion, with its park and trees, its dovecot and rookeries, the squire himself with his attendants and goodly villages with their ancient churches and hostelries, are expected every moment to appear, though they never do. I do not think the railway from Augusta to Savannah, while stopping often at depôts and little stations in the woods, touches a single place of such considerable size as to form a small town or village. The landholders and farmers enjoy much sport when so inclined; but they are lost in the woods, and probably do not consider the railway tracks the best ground for game. As for poachers, though the name is hardly known here, the field for them is boundless. One party stepped out from the train, rough and unkempt, with guns and dogs, and blankets rolled in sail-cloth for nightly bivouac, who appeared to me marvellously like persons of this class. I should have been glad to daguerreotype them on the spot, so like were they and yet so unlike what I have seen elsewhere. But amidst all this wildness and solitude, and apparent poorness of soil, it is cheering to see, wherever there are houses and close cultivation, how luxuriant the cotton-fields become, and what varied abundance is revealed. There are fine peach-orchards with rows of cotton-plants betwixt the trees, and vast fields of 60 to 100 acres of cotton and Indian corn, displaying much strength and fertility of soil and sun, and exciting but one regret, that so much cotton should be unpicked, and so little work going on, in these late and precious hours of one of the finest falls ever known even in this propitious clime.

The soil of Georgia, save on the bottoms of the Savannah and other great rivers, is relatively poor; but it has been made poorer by a superficial system of culture, that has left the subsoils untouched, and, after a few years of incessant cropping, has consigned it to waste and barrenness in favour of newer clearings. The Georgian planters and farmers have hopped about from one part of their extensive territory to another, without settling down with a firm grasp upon any; and, while making inroads on the wilderness on one hand, have allowed it to grow up afresh on the other. The ease with which once ploughed land in Georgia becomes a pine barren is commensurate with the difficulty with which it was originally torn from the forest. With this picture constantly before their eyes, and only just beginning to vanish before a larger intelligence and deeper agricultural ideas, people hereabouts wonder that men should wear out their days on such poor soil when there is so much better and richer to be got in other parts of the American continent; and many in Georgia and along the Atlantic slope are nowise loth to act upon this view of life. I have observed trains of bullock waggons carrying farmers and their families from Georgia and South Carolina westward to Texas and Arkansas; and this movement is said to be much more extensive than could be supposed from cursory observation. So that, while the cry of the Atlantic States is for more people, they are losing many of those they have got, and progress is thus made slow and uphill—every step forward being but too likely to be followed by one backward. The population of Georgia, which in 1860 was 1,055,000, is now returned at 1,200,000; but this increase, if real, must be almost wholly confined to the towns. The theory of poor soil, when followed out, raises the question whether the cultivation of cotton in such States as Georgia may not be doomed to disappear before the more productive fields of the Mississippi bottom and the South-West, and it has, no doubt, a severe competition to undergo from that vast region. It is difficult for less than half a bale to the acre to stand against a bale to the acre, or even two bales to the three acres, raised with much less labour and expense. But one can hardly believe that the great Southern districts on the Atlantic seaboard can quickly succumb. They have advantages of health, of proximity to the great cotton markets both of America and Europe, and of greater convenience of settlement to people of capital, which must help to sustain them. Nor can it be admitted that the soil of Georgia is poor in any but a relative sense. A fine sandy-clay soil, of great depth, extremely friable and easily wrought, cannot be called poor. It is soil liberally responsive to the plough and to manure. Any approach, not to "high," but to moderately good farming, would be extremely profitable ; and with deep ploughing, were the application of liquid manure possible, which it cannot well be for a long period, the results would be astonishing. When the Georgian agriculturists learn, as they are fast learning, to spread their labour less about, and to devote themselves on enlightened principles to the steady development of manageable holdings, a meagre cultivation may not be extended over so large a superficies, but a better and more enduring impression will be made upon the land, of which enough has already been cleared for fifty or a hundred years to come.

There is one sad defect that forces itself on attention everywhere. Very little live stock is seen on the plantations or about the farmhouses, while there is also a too apparent difficulty of grass. Only few cattle are visible, save the sturdy animals in yoke pulling patiently their loads of timber and other produce; and the few that do appear are generally in poor condition, with rough coats covering an anatomy of bones. The hogs roaming through the woods are mostly lean, and, from the swiftness with which they run from one feeding-ground to another, seem to have to go through a heavy day's work for their necessary repast of acorns. The Southern States have not yet surmounted the indifference to live stock that prevailed under the system of culture by slave labour. It is also to be remembered that nearly all the live stock on the plantations was consumed by the war, that many of the planters were left without a cow or an ox, with scarce a hog or even a chicken, and that since the war they have had to buy, breed, and recover every useful animal on their lands. It is the forgetfulness of this fact that has led to an exaggerated estimate in Europe of the fortunes made in cotton-planting from the high prices realized since the close of the war. The planters had to resume operations with their farms in ruin, with fences to rebuild, with labour scarce, scattered, and disorganized, with everything to buy at prices three times higher than before the war, and no money to buy with; and it is certain that but for the high price of cotton two-thirds of the plantations could not have continued in cultivation after the first attempt in 1866.

A curious agricultural question might be raised as to whether the deficiency of live stock is the result of the proverbial difficulty of growing grass, or this itself is a natural consequence of that. Of course, a planter who has little or no stock is not apt to trouble himself much about pasture or fodder. Nothing, at all events, is more striking in Georgia and other Atlantic States than the want of herbage. The heights and much of the level land are covered with woods, and at this season withered leaves are strewn over the all but bare earth. On the cultivated spaces the Indian corn-stalks stand in solitary state out of long lines of white sand; while the tracts over which the plough has ceased to go are covered with pine shoots and weedy herbage, or browned like moor and heather by a brittle and "sticky" vegetation, which a forcing sun draws up from weak and frivolous roots into rank and grim luxuriance. Is all this inseparable from the soil and climate?— or is it a mere phase of Nature left to her own wild caprice? Is the green grass, close and tender, always browsed by cattle with avidity, and ever beautiful to human eye, the final polish, the last touch of perennial richness, which cultivation imparts to the soil? In some parts of Georgia what is called "wire-grass" springs up in the woods. The farmers burn it down in winter, and it comes out in spring, sweet and nourishing, and is much liked by cattle; but the heat of summer makes it wiry and unchewable, and fit only for the burning process of the winter. The "impossibility" of grass in

Georgia is somewhat an enigma. One occasionally sees verdant patches of clover, and in many parts the cotton rows, which the planter has much to do to protect from grass all summer, are covered in the fall with a long white fibre, that on being examined is found to be nothing less than the best kind of hay. The influence of soil and climate on any particular growth is not to be disputed; but when live stock on the Georgian farms has had time to increase and improve, and the farmers have begun to experience what an essential element it is of agricultural wealth and prosperity, grass in some form or other will probably be found to grow in Georgia.

The Central Railroad, on which I have passed from Augusta to Savannah, was all but totally destroyed in the war by General Sherman during his famous plunge into the interior of Georgia, so far away from his base of operations as to astonish and alarm his friends. The feat was accomplished by organizing an immense force of cavalry, which, passing Augusta on the left, spread themselves over the centre of the State in such strong and numerous parties as to render effective resistance impossible. In the bewilderment of the Confederates that ensued, the cavalry fell upon the Central Railroad, tore up the rails, and, gathering immense piles of sleepers and timber from the woods, burnt, melted, and twisted them in the flames so as to render them useless. During the war Georgia had been a great source of supply to the Confederate armies, but Sherman's command of the railway from Atlanta to Chattanooga, and this destruction of the Central Road, cut off the State like a dead branch from the Confederation, and contributed materially to the surrender that soon followed. The Central Company had been wise enough to reserve from their earnings a large fund, placed in London, and as soon as the war ended, they relaid their lines with English rails, and resumed a traffic that has been always large and profitable. This company is a banking as well as a railway company, and has just received from the Legislature a renewal of its banking privileges for a term of thirty years. Such conjunction of two very different functions may seem anomalous in countries where abundance of capital has enabled the division of labour to be minutely developed, but no one who has marked on the spot the scarcity of money and exchange, not only in the interior, but in the great seaports of the Southern States, can wonder at the readiness of banking functions to gather round any solid interest or corporation, or doubt that the banking department of the Central Railroad Company of Georgia has done good service to the State. All the older lines of railway in Georgia have been remarkably successful, and have paid larger dividends than most of the leading British and European railways.   Since the war, the railway system in Georgia has been much extended, and new lines and connections are still being devised, and receive the State's endorsement of their bonds with an enterprise which is approaching, if it have not already passed, the limits of discretion.

CHAPTER XII.

The "Forest City."—Abundant demand for Labour.—Great increase of Cotton Exports.—Small proportion of Imports. — Disadvantages to Savannah of indirect Trade.—Rate of Wages. — Relative purchasing power of Money in England and the United States.—Conclusions of the British Consul.—State of Public Health.—Mortality of the Negroes.—Banking in Savannah.—Sylvan features of the City.

[SAVANNAH, GA.—*Nov.* 25.]

THE "Forest City" has made progress since the close of the war, not only in trade and population, but also in healthfulness and general improvement. Buried among trees—that give a novel and striking beauty to the city—and situated on a low delta of the Savannah River, marshy in many places and liable to invasions of yellow fever, Savannah might be expected to be more than usually fatal to human life, and to present more than usual obstacles to the material and social prosperity which depends so essentially on the health, vigour, and increase of the population. But the force and elasticity of rapidly-expanding trade are carrying Savannah successfully over all impediments. The liberation of the negroes, while thinning the number of field hands on the plantations, has thrown an ampler supply of labour into thriving towns and cities in the South than could have been obtained under the slave system. Savannah has had no difficulty, of late years, in absorbing all the labour that has come to it, while stopping up with energy, at the same time, the sources of crime and disease. The Corporation has bought land beyond the municipal boundaries, the cultivation of rice has been pushed back into the interior, and a system of dry culture has been introduced all round the city. Though Savannah was occupied by Union troops after the surrender of the Confederate armies, yet the large number of independent commercial men in the city were resolved not to allow their municipal government to pass into the hands of political adventurers, and the Federal Government was wise enough to let them manage matters in their own way. The consequence is that confidence and contentment prevail in the community. A superior white police has been organized—quiet, intelligent, officer-like men, all of those I have noticed—who not only exercise a wholesome moral influence on the people, but enforce with great care the removal of nuisances and the observance of cleanliness and order.

The business of the port has made a remarkable advance since the close of the war, and the increase of shipments this year has exceeded all former precedent. The receipts of cotton at Savannah in the season of 1869 amounted to 361,285 bales, of which 351,005 were Upland, and 10,280 Sea Island cotton. In the season of 1870 the receipts have been 490,085 bales, of which 473,722 have been Upland, and 16,363 Sea Island—the increase in one year being thus 128,800 bales. Taking the total American crop at 3,150,000 bales, one-seventh of it has passed through the port of Savannah. Of the shipments of cotton the past season at this port—

	Upland.	Sea Island.
Great Britain . . . took	200,284 bales.	4,286 bales.
France . . . . . ,,	41,353 ,,	2,243 ,,
Other Foreign ports . ,,	17,265 ,,	— ,,
The Northern States . ,,	214,188 ,,	9,606 ,,

The money value of exports from Savannah during the past year is estimated at 30,221,576 dollars, of which 17 millions were taken by foreign, chiefly British, vessels. The total imports are valued at not more than 1,115,821 dols. gold. This immense disparity of imports and exports shows how little progress has been made since the war in direct trade betwixt Europe and the Southern States. The tariff operates materially to shut out British goods, and to move such foreign trade as is permitted to New York, whence goods are carried to the South more and more by railway, and less and less by American coasting vessels. This is one cause of that decline of the mercantile marine of the United States to which the citizens of the seaports are becoming so sensitively alive. The restriction of foreign trade by the tariff, and the domination acquired by New York over the whole American trade in imports, are attended with depressing effects on the Southern States. Their chief cities have but half a chance of prosperity. The great power of Savannah in drawing cotton to her wharves would be equally effective in drawing foreign products in exchange, and distributing them over the same wide area as she drains of cotton; but her service in this direction is excluded, while the service she does render is placed under disability. Only few vessels comparatively can come to her port save in ballast. Yet when the cotton season opens, the great demand for tonnage then known to arise brings a forest of masts to the river, and shipmasters crowd the brokers' offices seeking cargo at rates which will pay the expenses of their vessels both ways. The lines of railway traversing the interior from east to west are affected in much the same manner. Trains come to the seaport laden with cotton, but return over their long distances with little or nothing. Were free and direct importation open, the railways would have traffic on both trips, would be more profitable, and could be more successfully extended. At present, of course, their rates are heavier than they would otherwise be, so that much of the cotton crop is carried to market alike by sea and by land under a disability. How many planters in this season of low price for their staple may feel the pinch of this narrow and distorted shoe! All goods, both foreign and domestic, moreover, are much enhanced in price as well as deteriorated in quality to the Southern consumers, who are in this way made to bear a burden to which the whole State and Federal taxation, heavy as it now may be, is light in comparison.

The large increase of receipts of cotton at Savannah during the past season is attributed partly to larger production per acre in Georgia through the use of fertilisers, but still more to the supplies received from other States, and in particular from Alabama, for which latter result the port is indebted to extended railway communications. A large amount of cotton that formerly went to Mobile, and some to New Orleans, now finds its way to Savannah. The prices realized at this port by planters compare favourably with those paid at Mobile and New Orleans. While the Savannah cotton commands about the same rates abroad, the distance of ocean transport is so much shorter that a saving is effected in freight, interest, and insurance.

Though the Sea Islands have reverted in many cases to their former owners, and are still held for cotton culture, yet it is generally thought that the cultivation of the long staple will gradually diminish, owing to the low prices it has commanded of late years relatively to " upland." Egyptian cotton has taken the place of Sea Island to a great extent in Europe. The present season has been unusually propitious for the island crop, and the quality of the staple is better than last year. There have been no caterpillars, and everything has worked well for the plant. But the quantity of land planted has been considerably less, and consequently the crop is estimated to be from 2,000 to 3,000 bales under that of last year. It has so far been sent but slowly to market.

It is generally admitted that the negroes have worked more steadily this year than in any previous year of free labour, and planters have declared to me that they could not do without the "darkies" in the field, so superior are they to any white labour that has yet been tried. Public opinion is well reconciled to free negro labour, and the main cause of dissatisfaction with the coloured population is the too ready ear they lend to political agitators, and the blind persistency with which they are said to enable such persons to acquire predominance in the State Governments against the will of the white citizens. The rate of wages in Savannah for unskilled labour, including such classes as waggoners, is 1½ dollars a day of ten hours; and for skilled labour, such as that of printers, tinsmiths, and carpenters, from two to five dollars a day, according to skill and merit. This nominal high value of labour, however, is largely accounted for by dearness of goods ; or, in other words, the little way a dollar goes in purchasing the necessaries and comforts of life. An impression has been growing on me since my inquiries began that the American currency dollar is little more than equal in purchasing power to the shilling in England. Yet the American currency in all transactions of exchange with foreign countries is only 11 to 13 per cent. less value than gold. This state of things presses with extraordinary severity upon all classes in the United States who produce anything for export, and, if prolonged, must tend to shut American products out of the markets of the world. My impression of the relative purchasing power of money in England and money in the United States was probably based on too narrow a deduction ; but the British Consul here, by entering into a minute analysis as regards such goods and necessaries only as artisans and labourers require, has arrived at the conclusion that the relative purchasing power of money here and in England is in the proportion of 45 to 100. Our Consuls in America, by the way, have had this question brought home rather sharply to themselves. Paid salaries of so many hundred pounds sterling per annum, for each of which they got seven or eight dollars some years ago, they find that their pound sterling does not now bring them more than five dollars, while the dollar has not risen in practical value here in anything like the same proportion. But the hardship this entails on foreign residents falls equally, or rather doubly and trebly, on the producers of the great American staples, who pay for labour, goods, and materials on the inflated scale of prices, and get back their returns on the strict standard of monetary exchange, thus literally buying in the dearest and selling in the cheapest market. It might be some consolation for this anomaly if it could be shown that any class of people is really the better of it. Take, on the Consul's figures, as an example of prices, articles which all would expect to be superlatively cheap in the United States. Thus, beef of the country, lean and leathery, is in Savannah 7*d.* per lb.; Northern beef, prepared for such large cities as New York and Baltimore, and tolerably good, is 1*s.* 3*d.* per lb.; mutton, 7*d.* per lb.; bacon, 1*s.* 1*d.* to 1*s.* 3*d.* per lb.; coffee, 11*d.*; tea, 4*s.* 7*d.*; salt butter, 1*s.* 10*d.*; potatoes, 7*s.* 6*d.* per bushel; and the three-quarter pound loaf, 4*d.*

Among the drawbacks of life and labour in Savannah and

other delta towns in similar latitudes must be placed the effects
of climate, which great sanitary care can only mitigate, and
which are hardly consistent with continuous toil. The average
heat in summer, from 12 to 3 p.m., is about 90 degrees in the
shade, and though the health of the town itself shows great improvement of recent years, yet the suburbs and country are
malarial, and in August, September, and October, malarial fevers
abound, and are often fatal. The health statistics of the city are
undoubtedly reassuring. The population is returned this year
in round numbers at 29,000, of whom 19,000 are white and
10,000 coloured people. The number of deaths among the
whites in 1869 was 423, or 1 in 47·28, which is a low rate of
mortality. The number of deaths among the negroes in the
same year was 429, or 1 in 23·3, being, as in Charleston, fully
double the rate of mortality among the white people. The diseases that cut off the negroes in greatest number were miasmatic, tubercular, nervous, and respiratory: The chief causes
of the white mortality were the three first of these classes of
disorders. The rate of infantile mortality in Savannah, on an
average estimated over a period of sixteen years, is one-fourth of
the total deaths, while in England it is as high as one-third. All
these results, with the exception of the high rate of mortality
among the negroes, are very satisfactory, and are the more remarkable inasmuch as the health of Savannah did not use to stand
so well. In 1854, when the white population was only 12,468,
the number of white deaths was 1,221, or 1 in 10·2, among
which were 625 fatal cases of yellow fever. The blacks escaped
that terrible scourge. Since 1858 there have been few cases of
yellow fever in Savannah. In some subsequent years the mortality was also great, though in most cases the excess was due to
exceptional causes. In 1864 and the following year (the last of the
war), 845 deaths occurred in the military hospitals. But 1866 and
the subsequent years till now have shown a steady progress
towards the excellent health-condition that has been described,
and that is largely to be attributed to the prosperity and good
government of the city, and to the care and vigilance of the
authorities in proscribing and extirpating the more flagrant causes
of disease. Interments are extra-mural, and one of the cemeteries is as beautiful as any institution of the kind can be. The
supply of water is abundant and wholesome, one of the greatest
blessings, since the supply of liquors is of questionable quality.
The negroes in the Southern cities and towns, I fear, are falling
into the habit of drinking inordinate quantities of bad whisky.
The American people generally it must in fairness be observed, are a sober race. But while temperance is ever praise-
worthy, and one of the greatest virtues of a free people, a
little experience of American "drinks" somewhat detracts from

the merit of sobriety in this country. The distillers and liquor merchants, by a short-sighted policy in drugging and poisoning what they produce and sell, have rendered total abstinence almost a necessity of life.

The banking capital of Savannah, which had grown up to eleven or twelve millions, was mostly lost during the war. The Central Railroad Bank alone withstood the melting power of that seven-times heated furnace. The banking capital is now about three millions, quite inadequate to the expanded business of the city, but is being gradually increased. One or two new banks are just being established, one by Northern men who have come down for the purpose, and a very good speculation it seems to be as banking is conducted in the United States, especially in the South. A banking company invests its capital in Federal bonds, deposits these at Washington under receipt of the Treasury, receives 90 per cent. of their value in national currency, and, while paid regularly the full interest on its bonds, proceeds as a thoroughly authorized National Bank to lend its currency on mortgage, bills of lading, and other secure collaterals, at from 15 to 18 per cent. It would be well if all Northern speculations in the South turned out as profitably as National Banks on these terms are sure to do. Several Northern firms commenced business in Savannah after the war as cotton merchants and brokers, but they have all " burst up," as the saying is when a firm either commits a bad bankruptcy and runs away, or honourably withdraws from business when disappointed in its hopes of profit. Cotton-broking is competed so keenly in Savannah as to astonish the older merchants.

The growing commerce and well-being of the " Forest City " are, on the whole, pretty solidly assured. Savannah appears, indeed, destined to become one of the great marts and centres of life and activity in the South. Its common school system has already made satisfactory progress—the negroes and the Roman Catholics being equally furnished with schools of their own, though under the same general superintendence as the schools of the other parts of the population. If the sylvan character of the town be consistent with public health, I can vouch for its charming and picturesque effect. It is very pleasant to saunter along Bull Street from end to end, passing from shops and stores to squares, churches, theatres, and elegant private mansions, the forest shadows deepening as the architecture becomes more choice ; to look on either side down the long wooded streets, two, three, four rows deep in trees, according to their importance in the general intersection ; to dwell for a little in admiration of a fine monument, glistening white as snow amidst the many colours of the autumn forest, erected in honour of Pulaski, who fell for the rights of Georgia in the War of Independence ; to stand with

curiosity before tropical plants that adorn the fronts of the
houses, prominent among them the banana, covering the windows
to the second floor with its great leaves, and suggesting ideas of
some mammoth vegetable world; and again to pass on, with new
sources of attraction at every step, till the avenue debouches on a
small Bois de Boulogne, where an elaborate fountain plays,
pointing the way to shady walks, in which the ladies prome-
nade with their babies and nurses, and lovers meet to exchange
vows of eternal devotion. The spot is cool and sequestered.
One can imagine the delight of it when a hot and scorching sun
drives people in terror from the open sky. The street-ways
betwixt the trees are several inches deep in a blackish sand
that muffles every sound of hoof or wheel. Savannah looks as
if 30,000 people had gone out from town into a bowery forest
glade, and, without disturbing its silence or its beauty, made
summer-houses amidst its flowers and plants, and under the
shade of its spreading trees.

CHAPTER XIII.

The Railway System of Georgia.—Convenience of the Cars.—The " Captains " or Conductors.—Safety of Single-rail Lines.—Greater fertility of the Soil in the Interior.—Want of facilities of Branch Traffic.—Dilatory Cotton-picking.—General characteristics of the various Divisions of Georgia.

[Millen, Ga.—*Nov.* 26.]

The Central Railroad from Savannah to Macon connects at this point with the Augusta and Savannah road, which is also worked by the Central Company.   Various branches and connections have greatly extended the communications of the Central.   The Charleston and Savannah, which has again been opened, runs into its main line; and it has a branch to Milledgeville, the former capital of the State, and Eatonton.   At Macon it gets into connection with all the lines north, east, and west, and by extensions from Columbus, on the western border line of Georgia, is stretching out its communications to Mobile and Montgomery in Alabama.   The business of this old-established company is managed with great ability and prudence; and the same remark may equally be made of the Georgia Railway, from Augusta to Atlanta, and its elongation to West Point, on the Alabama border. Both the Georgia and Central Railroads are now within sight of direct communication across Alabama to Meridian in Mississippi, as well as to Mobile and New Orleans south.   Another great system—the Atlantic and Gulf Railway—is being gradually carried out under the energetic direction of Colonel John Screven, and opening up the southern section of the State, connecting Brunswick, an Atlantic seaport, with Macon north, with Albany and Bainbridge west, and with the Florida Railroad and the Gulf of Mexico south.   The Macon and Brunswick is a separate company, though part of the system.   The South-Western and Muscogar Railways run in a forked form from Macon to Columbus, and from Macon to Eufala in Alabama.   The " Macon and Western " to Atlanta is an essential link in the railway communication of the State north and south; and the Western and Atlantic, or " State Road," as it is called from being the property of the State, carries this trunk system north to Chattanooga in

Eastern Tennessee. These remarks give a skeleton outline of
the principal established lines of railroad in Georgia in active
working condition, but new projects are brought forward in
great number, and receive encouragement from the Legislature
in the cession of State endorsement of their bonds to the extent
of 8,000 to 15,000 dollars per mile.

The railways at this season carry on an extensive traffic. In
my progress hither from Savannah I met four great cotton
trains, twenty trucks at least in each, passing down to the seaport. The passenger trains seldom contain many people, except
when some public gatherings are being held, or when immigrants
and other through passengers happen to be numerous. The
American cars are well adapted to the long distances over which
passengers have usually to travel. The seats are ranged in small
pews on either side, holding two persons each, with a free passage
between, and at both ends there are doors giving communication
with the other cars of the train. The opening and shutting and
slamming of the doors, on a cold or wet day, while the train is
in motion, form probably the only inconvenience of the arrangement ; and though one unaccustomed may feel somewhat dis-
concerted on being set down in the same compartment with so
many passengers, yet the Americans are by no means noisy
when travelling, but for the most part sit as quiet as at church.
There is seldom more than one newspaper editor " on board."
Smoking is prohibited in all but the front car, to which the
smokers go as it suits them. By this subtle arrangement the
railway companies have arrived at a practically dividing line
betwixt first and second class passengers—negroes and others
desiring to travel cheap, and smokers who must smoke all the
time, being required to take their passage in the smoking car,
and not allowed to leave it during the journey. The " ladies'
car " is the choice part of the train, and is strictly guarded from
male intruders at the principal passenger depôts. But the
regulation of the " ladies' car " is somewhat anomalous in practice. The rule being to exclude only such male persons as
happen to be travelling alone, it often occurs that very gentle-
manly people are turned away to an inferior place, while a much
rougher set are freely admitted. Yet, when the train gets in
motion, the free communication from one car to another soon
redresses all inequalities. The railway conductor in America,
or " captain," as he is called (just as the train itself and all
about it are spoken of in nautical phrase), is a high official,
of whom there is no counterpart in the old country. He
collects the fares of the passengers ; in many cases apparently
he keeps no account but the contents of his dollar bill pocket ;
and, having some period of usance in the company's money, he
trades a little betwixt the country and the city, and no doubt

makes a good thing of that. The consequence is that the "captain" is generally an imposing personage, without band or button as a mark of office, but elaborately fixed up in gold jewellery, and not much disposed to give information when asked for it. Many of the stations on the American railways have too small a population, some being merely ends of roads for letting down and taking up country people, to support a ticket office and a station-master; but the habit of paying fares to the conductors has so grown, that even in the larger towns nearly as many pass into the cars without tickets as with them. The passenger traffic is therefore conducted too free from any effective check over the receipts to be quite satisfactory to the boards of directors. The lines in the south are broad-gauge and single-rail lines, and what with the moderate rate of speed, and the necessity of the going train moving into a side track at appointed stations till the coming one has arrived and passed on, collisions seem to be less frequent, and the traffic to be conducted with more security, than on double-rail and more heavily worked lines. One also finds the telegraph in active operation almost everywhere on the American railways.

The country, on the whole, considerably improves in fertility and settlement towards the interior of Georgia. On the road from Millen to Macon farming is carried on with more system; the crops are generally good, sometimes luxuriant; and there are marks of care and vigour in the work of cultivation round the farmhouses and in the fields. Cotton is brought down over twenty and thirty miles of country to some of the railway stations on drays, with four mules to each, and almost as many negroes, a few bales at a time, on tolerable roads. Common roads in Georgia are easily made, and more easily mended than one might suppose—the receptive sandy soil drying and hardening up after moderate rain very soon. The labour required, even with fair roads, in transporting cotton from the plantations to the railways, is enormous, and is often withdrawn from the fields when most needed. Were the railway companies to turn their attention to branch communication, and put on a "road engine" and train of waggons at every principal depôt, great advantage would accrue to themselves as well as to the planters and the cotton trade. The backwardness of picking, while negroes and mules are toiling along the country roads with handfuls of cotton, is everywhere observable. Whole fields along this route, even at this date, are white as snow with cotton wool, which only the extraordinary fineness of the season, liable to break up at any moment, has saved from total loss. The frost, which appeared for the first time ten or twelve days ago, has come more or less at intervals since. Though a "killing frost" probably, in the cotton telegrams, it has con-

sisted hitherto of the slightest bite of cold imaginable, followed
by days of warmth and brightness equal to English summer,
and with neither wind nor rain of any account. The woods
begin to show its effect in diversified change of hue; and the
cotton plant not only shows it in a browner shade, but no doubt
also feels it in a retardation of the latest crop of bolls. But
what signifies the lengthening of the crop, if even the first
and second sheds of fruit have not been gathered? Since the
war picking has seldom been finished till February, and, besides
causing much deterioration of cotton, has cut largely into the
time and labour required to prepare the ensuing crop. Planters
fret and worry under this state of things more, of course, than
anybody else, but it is an evil that injures all. The negroes get
up difficulties of wages, and fall into difficulties of debt and
liens on their share of the crop. The fall of price is even a
difficulty to the negro, for, with the most singular inversion of
reason, he argues that when cotton is cheap it is not worth
while picking it—as if the only way to get the better of the
low price of any crop were not to make the quantity of it as
large as possible. The negroes have some very peculiar traits
of character, and are more like children than grown people.
Served with the stipulated rations for a week, they will sometimes eat them up in three days, and fall into debt to their
employers and their merchants for more than enough. Yet the
prevailing remark is that they are improving. The courts in
Georgia punish them for stealing, and as the resources of theft
and idleness are closed against them, they begin to feel they
must work to live. Such are some of the difficulties of the
negroes on the land; but it must be added that the negroes on
the land are not nearly so many as the land requires. There is
an absolute scarcity of labour for the larger plantations under
culture.

Middle Georgia and the whole Western border from north to
south form the finest and richest agricultural region of the State.
These districts are comparatively well settled, studded with productive farms, and have towns of considerable population and
manufactures. In the south-west there are Albany, Columbus,
Thomaston, where cotton and woollen fabrics are manufactured
with success; in the north-west there are Atlanta, Marietta,
Rome, Dalton, and other towns which are growing in population
and in traffic; while Macon and Augusta may be said to preside
over Middle Georgia, and are at once a result and a source of the
superior agricultural value and higher civilization of that section.
While the cash value of farms in the various counties of Middle
and Western Georgia is estimated by millions, in the other
parts of the State it is more commonly estimated in thousands.
The north-eastern counties of Upper Georgia are. mountainous,

and are impregnated along the river bottoms with gold deposits, which were the cause of a great excitement forty years ago that has broken out at intervals ever since. The deposits, after their first discovery, were deemed so rich that the land was surveyed, and distributed by lottery in forty-acre sections to all who had been three years citizens of the State. There were some prizes, but many blanks. Yet gold-digging continues to be prosecuted among the mountains of Georgia. Copper ore has also been extracted in large quantity. The southern counties of Georgia are the poorest and most thinly peopled. The soil is more sandy, and all but wholly covered with pine forests, on which the lumbermen have hitherto made but small impression. Land in this section of the State is so extremely cheap as to be almost incredible. Purchases have been made at ten cents an acre. Any one ambitious of territorial possession might with little money become lord of a county or two, full of wood, and, in the event of the Baltic forests giving out, might be confessed in some generation or other to have made a splendid investment. At the same time it is very difficult to pronounce in this climate what is poor and worthless land for agricultural purposes. The very different degrees of value of land seem to depend as much on the tract which settlement and population have taken as on the intrinsic qualities of the soil. I have heard it said that the sandy soil of these poor and sparsely-peopled counties, once cleared, would grow long-staple cotton as good as that of the Sea Islands, the season is so much longer than in more northern cotton States. The best crop of cotton I have met with in Georgia is that of a recent settler, who, on what was deemed poor land, has, by close attention and farmyard manuring, raised nine bales from thirteen acres.

The country from Macon to Atlanta, in the north-west of Georgia, is a fine rolling upland, well cleared, with fringes of light forest timber, in which oaks, hickory, and other varieties of tree, as well as the ever-constant pine, are abundant, and where freestone is quarried. The soil assumes a redder colour than at Macon and southward. There is a rich growth of cotton, the picking of which is well up to the mark. Good farming seems well understood in most of this district. The homeliness of the scenery, its gentle hill and dale, its wide sweeps of cultivated land up to the margin of the forest belts, which twine themselves across the heights and skirt the valleys, are peculiarly striking. A more pretty and interesting country than much of it one could hardly desire to see.

CHAPTER XIV.

Central position of Macon.—Command of the Railway System.—Great development of Railway Enterprise.—Success of the Old Lines.—State Endorsement of Railway Bonds.—The system of Railway Financing.—Does State Endorsement add to the Security of a First-Mortgage Bond? —Macon Cotton Manufactures.

[MACON, GA.—*Nov.* 27-28.]

THE position of Macon, in the heart of Middle Georgia, where all the railways—north, south, east, and west—converge as to a common centre, renders it probably the most important and most promising inland town of this lively and enterprising State. It receives from 90,000 to 100,000 bales of cotton annually, and the drafts of planters in the surrounding country are honoured eagerly by merchants and warehousemen to the extent of their resources, with the view of fostering and increasing the importance of the town as a mart for cotton. The railway lines which meet and radiate from Macon would alone be sufficient to give a powerful and permanent impulse to its trade and industry. Extensive railway workshops have been established, and have gathered round them a numerous body of mechanics. A number of the railway directors and capitalists, who are the life and brain of the great system of communication throughout the State, reside in Macon, and act together with much energy and judgment. The various depôts, filled with goods and produce in transit, give an air of business and traffic to the town beyond what one would expect from its general development. Macon is not so compact or so well built as Augusta, but, with a shrewd head on its shoulders, it has also its fingers on a vast network of communication from all parts of the interior and extremities of the State, that will tend every year to increase its means of wealth and employment.

The railway interest, next to the agricultural interest, which is the foundation of all, is at present by much the largest and most prominent interest of Georgia. It is the one interest throughout all the South which, though greatly worn and wrecked by the war, stood erect and vital amidst the general ruin, and that seemed not only able to take care of itself, but to give a

helping-hand to the general recuperation of the various States.
Hence the great development of railway enterprise in the South
since the close of the war. Georgia has probably done more to
restore and extend the connections of its old lines, and to build up
new railways, than any of the other Southern States. The success
which had attended its railways in the ante-war times, and the
strength which they displayed amidst universal weakness when
the war had ended, is no doubt one reason of the almost passionate
activity of the State in this direction during the last four or five
years. The Georgians had come to believe in railways at a crisis
when faith in any other material interest had almost departed.
The Georgia Railroad from Augusta to Atlanta had before the
war repaid in dividends its whole capital and 50 per cent. more,
and remained a clear and going road to its subscribers when the
war had passed away. This company has taken powers to
increase its capital stock to five million dollars, to rebuild depôts
and shops, and replace rolling stock and rails. The Atlanta and
West Point, which was an extension of the Georgia from Atlanta
to the Alabama border, paid 7 per cent. interest from the
day when the money was paid till the line was opened for traffic,
after which it paid 8 per cent.; and in a few years the
reserve had accumulated so much that a bonus of 100 per cent.
was declared to the stockholders in the form of new stock in that
proportion—in other words, every 100 dollars of stock became
200; and yet on the capital, as thus doubled, a dividend of 8
per cent. has been paid from year to year, and no less from all
appearance is ever likely to be paid notwithstanding the competition to which the road has been or may be subjected. The
Central Railroad has regularly paid large dividends to its subscribers—never less, I believe, than 8 to 10 per cent. The State
Road from Atlanta to Chattanooga has also a large, steady, and
prosperous traffic, which was wont to replenish the treasury of the
State, and has only ceased to be profitable under the exoteric and
transitionary rule of recent years. The management of the "State
Road" is a constant topic of attack and defence, and of banter
not always of the pleasant sort, betwixt the local Conservatives
and the party sustained in power by the "Reconstruction" policy
of the North. The Governor and the Legislature, acknowledging
the justice of the complaints made against this department of
the administration, have this year passed an Act to authorize a
lease of the railway to any competent private company for a
term of twenty years. The lessees are required to pay not less
than 25,000 dollars a month into the State treasury, taking over
the road and its appurtenances as they stand, and returning them
in like condition at the end of the period of lease. There would
appear from the terms of this Act to be no decrease of confidence
in the substantial resources of the "State Road," and its pros-

pects of remuneration to the revenue of the State, at the expense
of which it has been built and maintained. This confidence I
hear echoed on all sides. The railway antecedents of Georgia
have thus been peculiarly favourable. Whether under the great
movement of railway extension in progress its future experience
will be equally favourable, depends on many conditions and
considerations not easy at present to resolve. The old Georgian
lines of railroad were urgently needed; they had a traffic ready
for them; they tapped, as it were, the virgin soil of communication in the State; and they were made, step by step, when labour
and commodities were cheap, with cash subscribed, and ready
for every outlay on the neatest ready-money terms. The results
were, economy in the cost of construction, an abounding traffic
as soon as they were constructed, and ample dividends on the
capital of the companies when brought into operation. The new
railway era in this and other States of the South cannot be supposed to present the same advantageous conditions.

Since it was impossible to raise within the State itself the
money necessary to make new railways, the expedient adopted
has been not only to give large borrowing powers by Act
of the Legislature to any projector or company of projectors
who have proposed to make a railroad, but also to give the
State's endorsement of the bonds on which the money is borrowed. The State generally endorses bonds to the amount of
15,000 dollars per mile. The cost of building a railroad in
Georgia, I am informed on competent authority, is from 18,000
to 30,000 dollars a mile, so that on most lines there would
appear to be a considerable margin beyond the amount of State
endorsement, which must be covered by the capital of the stockholders. Still, the money borrowed on the State security bears
an inordinate proportion to the capital invested by the companies, and many do not hesitate to say that in some instances
the roads are made almost wholly from the proceeds of the
mortgage bonds. The Legislature of Georgia has passed an Act
which prohibits the Governor or any other officer of State from
endorsing the bonds of any railroad "until an amount equal to
the amount of bonds for which the guarantee of the State is
applied for has in good faith been first invested, and actually
paid in and expended, by the owners or stockholders of the
road." In the plain meaning of words, the Act imposes a condition that the money borrowed under the State guarantee for
railway purposes shall never exceed the paid-up capital of the
companies; which, if strictly observed, would be alike good for
the State, the bondholders, and the ultimate profit of the railroad projectors and companies themselves. If it should have
the effect of delaying some of the less urgent projects, and
spreading the construction over a longer period of time, nothing

would be lost, and probably much advantage be ultimately gained. The number of railways projected in Georgia is so great as to remind one of periods of railway mania elsewhere of unfortunate memory. The Legislature this year has authorized the endorsement of the bonds of no fewer than thirty-two railroad companies. The endorsement is to be to the amount in some cases of 12,000 dollars and in others of 15,000 dollars a mile. Many of the projects, of course, are only branches or elongations of existing lines from one Georgian town to another; but some are extensive schemes, such as the Atlanta and Blue Ridge, which aims at being a great competing through-line to the North. One wonders where all the money is to come from to carry out so many public works at once, and the expectation that the profits on the plantations will seek investment in railways does not seem to be well founded as an immediate resource, when one considers how much the planters have to do in stocking, fencing, and improving their farms, and getting their affairs into such a train as to enable them to make any profit at all. But there can be no doubt of the immense utility of railways to the agricultural population in the absence of good common roads to market, or of the sacrifices the people are prepared to make in order to attain a railway system reaching and penetrating almost every county in the State. The most ambitious "air-line" through to the great railroads running North and West is always so contrived as to open up new districts within the State itself, and to give an impulse to internal improvement. The State only follows the general bent in helping forward the formation of railways by all legitimate means: and the representatives, as they pass bill after bill, pledging, under conditions, the security of the State, may probably think that to authorize endorsation is one thing and to endorse is another, and that by a natural process of selection a few only of the many projects will be pushed forward for the present.

Southern railway bonds bearing interest of 8 per cent. per annum have already been taken up to a large amount, and, under proper conditions, should be as solid a security as this or any country can offer. But they do not sell very favourably when issued, and they do not sustain well their original price. There is something faulty in the whole system of finance pursued. The guarantee of the State has a large sound; but it is doubtful whether, in present circumstances, it contributes essentially to the value of the bonds. The State debt of Georgia, as well as other Southern States, was inconsiderable at the close of the war, but it has been rapidly increased since, for other purposes as well as railways, and, with its natural result of increased taxation, forms a constant theme of bitter political discussion betwixt the Radical-Negro Governments and the white people of the States. A curious incident has just occurred here, which serves to illustrate the feud that prevails in regard to the State finances. Governor Bullock proceeded to New York some days ago, with the view of negotiating the sale of some amount of State bonds, and was immediately followed by the son of the Treasurer of the State, who reported to the New York banking houses that the bonds which the Governor wished to sell were informal and illegal, that they had not been registered in the terms of the Act, and that no transactions upon them would be binding on the State of Georgia. The Governor has written a note to Atlanta, to the effect that the Treasurer's son has been injuring the credit of the State, and the inference is that his financial mission to the North will be rendered of no avail. Such disclosures as these, commented upon with the utmost asperity by the local press, increase the suspicion of the Southern people as to the integrity with which their affairs are administered, and one of the first steps of the Conservative-Democrat Government, for which the elections are gradually paving the way, will probably be to institute a strict inquiry into the financial proceedings of their predecessors in office. It is undesirable that such a substantial commercial interest as railroads should be embroiled in suspicions and investigations of this description, and the State guarantee, whatever its advantages to the issuers and the holders of the bonds, has obviously its disadvantages also. Its disadvantages, indeed, are more apparent than its advantages. The State engages, in the event of failure on the part of the stockholders, to pay the interest and principal of the bonds. When called upon to fulfil this engagement, the State will proceed to sell, lease, or work the road, and charge itself with the liability to the bondholders. But this is only what the bondholders would have immediate power to do themselves were there no State guarantee or intervention in the matter. The main security of railway bondholders is that the road be one well devised for traffic and for developing traffic, and that it be conducted under the control of the substantial business people of the country through which it operates, who, in virtue of their subscribed capital and commercial interests, have the strongest motive to provide for its economical construction and successful management. Where these conditions are found—and where may they not be found in these great and rising States?—the first mortgage railway bond issued here is as good a security as it can well be made. There are supposable cases in which the superadded State guarantee might save the bondholders trouble; but there are equally supposable cases, on the other hand, in which it might give them a little of that commodity too.

English rails are in favour in Georgia, and, notwithstanding the high tariff duty, are sometimes bought to a large amount on a gold basis, delivered at Savannah. The old lines, I believe, will now re-lay their roads, as required, with the best steel rails.

Macon, like Augusta, has a cotton factory, that has long been a successful element in the industry of the town. The goods manufactured are 36-inch shirtings, one lb. to the three yards, and 30-inch shirtings, four ounces to the yard. The former bring 12½ and the latter 10½ cents per yard. I found the factory working cotton at 12½ to 13 cents per lb. The capital of the company is 128,000 dollars, on which the dividend usually paid is 10 per cent., though sometimes as much as 21 per cent. has been divided; and a surplus fund of 50,000 dollars has been accumulated. This factory has only 5,240 spindles, and works at less advantage than the Augusta factory, which has more extensive and newer machinery. The number of hands employed in the Macon factory is 120. They are all whites. The wages paid to women are 24 to 25 dollars a month, and to boys 13 dollars a month. Another cotton factory is about to be opened in an extensive building that was erected during the war for a Confederate arsenal. It is to have 15,000 spindles, and a 350-horse-power engine. A very general desire is evinced in all parts of the country for the establishment of cotton factories, but the Southern people seem to fall into a series of mistakes on this point. Their ideas of manufacturing run in too narrow a groove. The small factory in Macon has to beat up a good deal for a market for its goods, and the difference in price of cotton here and in New York—two to three cents per lb.—may soon be more than lost in the difficulty and expense of selling the goods when manufactured. There are many branches of manufacture which, both in the towns and country parts of the South, might be prosecuted with probably greater advantage than simple cotton fabrics. Variety of enterprise is eminently desirable. The cotton factories at Columbus are producing cotton blankets, which are a novelty, are well spoken of by those who have used them, and may be capable of introduction into distant markets; but the manufacture of sheetings and shirtings may soon be greatly overdone. It is the North which the South has always in view when it sighs for more and more cotton factories. The people say, Why should we pay Massachusetts a protected and monopoly price for cotton goods, when we grow the raw material and may make them for ourselves? The South, as Mr. Gladstone once allowed himself to say, is thus, after all, a distinct nation in the United States; but the North has to thank, not Mr. Jeff. Davis, but itself, for this distinction, in sacrificing the interests of the great mass of the population in other sections of the Union to a fatly protected

class of Northern manufacturers.   Disaffection is fostered South
and West by this blind and heartless policy.

The best paid class of working people in Macon are mechanics,
who receive from 4½ to 6 dollars a day ; but it is one of the
drawbacks on the supposed high wages of labour in America
that a mechanic, with a wife and family, has to pay as much
as 25 dollars a month for a house or cabin of four rooms.

Macon is finely situated on the side of a sandy hill, broken
into wide and sloping hollows that stretch out in many fine
avenues to be, and are overlooked by eminences that have
already become the sites of spacious and elegant private residences.   The country round is hilly and densely wooded.

CHAPTER XV.

[ATLANTA, GA.—*Nov.* 29-30; CARTERSVILLE—*Dec.* 1.]

I ARRIVED in Atlanta under a shower of rain, the first I had seen in a sojourn of nearly two months in the Southern States. It was really a downfall worth speaking of, enough to make a Mark Tapley feel jolly. "It never rains but it pours" in Atlanta. Sherman poured such a shower of fire upon it as almost swept it from the face of the surrounding wilderness. It is now rising up a grander, fairer, and more ambitious town than before. But an architectural chaos reigns in the meanwhile over all its centre and circumference. The railway from Macon, after gliding through a suburb of cabins and passing a military barracks, begins to toll its bell and perform a sort of funereal procession amidst the *débris* of newly-built houses and the ruins of old ones, pieces of streets to which there is no visible entrance, and deepening files of cars and trucks from which there is no imaginable exit, finally drawing up more apparently from the impossibility of moving backward or forward than from the fact of having arrived anywhere. The various rail- roads which meet at this crowded point do not go to the town; the town is gathering in thick and hot haste about the railways. A general depôt is being built, but, like every- thing else in Atlanta, it is unfinished; and on the arrival of a train under rain the passengers are put down in the mud, to be there screamed at by steam-engines and high-pressure negroes, scared by the tolling of bells, and barricaded on every side by trains of cars, bales of cotton, boxes of merchandise, gable-ends of houses, and all sorts of building materials. "Is there any hotel in this city of Babel?" I cried out, and was immediately told Atlanta had the biggest thing of the kind in creation.

"Where is it?" "There, sare; I take you"— said a darkey, who had already marked me for his own—"there it is," pointing to a really magnificent edifice, which on the side next us seemed to have everything but windows—an edifice forming nearly two streets of Atlanta—so large, indeed, that it seemed impossible to judge where the entrance might be. "The H. I. Kimball House, sir. Have you nary heerd of the H. I.?" said a short, thick man, all beard and no whiskers. I confessed that the Atlanta hieroglyphics were unknown to me, whereupon he put into my hand a printed paper, which, as I was now scaling a heavy intrenchment of brick and mortar, flanked by wet ditches of no mean account, I put into my pocket to cull some particulars from by and by. The inhabited front of the "H. I." was carried without loss of any kind, but not without difficulties that evoked suspicions and objurgations of a serio-comic kind, wherein how much I was deceived will appear from a fact or two. The hall or vestibule of the Kimball House is as big as a church, and prayer-meetings of a certain kind, I believe, are held in it sometimes. This hall is open almost to the roof of the building, with tier upon tier of galleries communicating with the various floors of the hotel, and affording the guests an opportunity of looking down on all that passes below. A gaselier drops from the higher stories over the hall, of such magnitude and brightness as might grace any opera-house in the largest cities of the world. The whole hotel is brilliantly lighted with gas. I was hoisted to my room in a steam-power elevator, surpassing in lubricity of motion the creaky and occasionally foot-crushing machine of the great "Continental" in Philadelphia, so dear to all the "commercials" of the Northern States. The bigger the hotels of America become, the greater nuisance they are generally found to be, but the Kimball House at Atlanta, to whomsoever it may prove a mistake, will be no mistake to any traveller in the upper regions of Georgia who may choose to make it his abode.

The rain having passed away, the first thought that occurred was to walk round what had now for the time become "my hotel;" but this I was never able to do. I found myself, in various attempts, always going away from it and always coming back to it. Parts of it seemed everywhere, and other objects began to distract my attention from its probable lines of circumvallation. Atlanta has several great business houses in the dry goods, hardware, grocery, and confectionery lines, with fine shops on the street for retail business, and upper floors for wholesale trade. One receives at every step a lively impression of the great power residing somewhere in the United States of filling the most distant and unpromising places with wares and traffickers of all kinds. Stores full of "Northern notions,"

New York oyster saloons, and "drummers" of the latest patents out at Washington, are seen on both sides (when they have two sides) of the streets of Atlanta. One man showed me a more perfect kerosene oil or spirit lamp than I had seen or imagined. He lighted three or four of them, and flinging them heedlessly on the floor to burn at leisure in various corners of the store, instantly pulled out a patent washing-machine which is to drive everything else out of the market. He was about to show me a marvellous pot-hook with cradle appendages for weighing babies, when, notwithstanding my deeply awakened interest, I was obliged to come away. The streets of Atlanta are not yet lighted with gas, but the patentee came with me to the door, and sprung an immense spirit torch which threw a blaze of light into the gloom, revealing, in the distance, of course, a wing of the Great Hotel. It is difficult for a guest of the H. I. to lose himself in Atlanta, but it is easy for any one to be abruptly stopped by some impassable barrier, or dangerously inveigled in the network of railway tracks. The railways pass along a narrow defile, and cut Atlanta for the present in two. I found myself standing on one occasion at this Asses' Bridge, beside a grave, elderly man, who was waiting, like myself, for an opening betwixt the long trains that blocked the way. As one moved on, another close behind was sure to give a snort and jolt along too ; and when the down track was a little clear, the tolling bell of a train on the up track gave note of warning to adventurous citizens. I ventured to remark to my patient friend that it was strange the people of Atlanta could bear such an obstruction in the heart of the town. "What would you have them do ?" he asked me. "Petition, of course ; oppose the railway bills, overturn a Governor or two, if necessary ; and insist on right of way." "Friend, you are a stranger—I guess the railways were here before the people of Atlanta," was his reply ; and what he told me I recognized at once to be true. The railways were the beginning and the end of Atlanta in the old times, and the new city rising up around the place where it was erewhile convenient for the railway engine to be fed with wood and water has not yet had time to adjust all its relations. One of the difficulties of the present chaotic stage of Atlanta is that few people in it know anybody else. I had an introduction to a gentleman of some fame, whom I casually met in Macon just as he was going to the train for Atlanta. He had only time to say, " Be sure to *hunt me up* when you come to Atlanta." I did not take up the whole meaning of the phrase at the time, but I learned it afterwards. Yet when all ordinary means of hunting up people in Atlanta fail, there is one resource which, if you are a guest of the H. I., may be reverted to with some confidence. Begin and end your inquiries at the hotel, and ten to one you

find that you have been breakfasting, dining, and supping with
the people you want all the time. The secret of the "big hotels"
in America is that they are designed in a very subordinate
degree for travellers, and that they place their main chance on
town boarders, to whose convenience they conform all their
arrangements. The system of boarding in hotels prevails largely
in the cities of the North, and I am sorry to note its rapid introduction into the Southern States. The ladies, I think, when
the first reluctance has been conquered, rather like the relief
from domestic cares and the mock splendour of living in a grand
hotel. Yet an American wife follows Paterfamilias into the
public dining-room with a subdued sort of air; and more melancholy still, at least to me, are the children who close up the
train with pale faces and precocious eyes, sit down at table
among a crowd of sharp people, and are served by troops of
obsequious waiters. The system may have its origin in Republican ideas carried to an anti-social and burlesque extreme; but
it is not the mould of life in which Republics are made or may
best be preserved, and one cannot but reflect with some misgiving
what a country America may be when a generation has arisen to
whom the sweetest and most potent word in the English language,
"home," has neither present meaning nor past association.

Atlanta is already quite a large place. Its population is given,
in the usual round numbers of the census enumerators, at 28,000
to 29,000. The vague results of the present decennial census in
the United States are somewhat perplexing, but they have more
excuse in a town like Atlanta than in many other places; for if
a census, instead of being taken in a night, be spread over the
greater part of a year, how is it possible to state with precision
the population of a city to which a hundred is added to-day, and
probably half a thousand may be added to-morrow? I am informed, on the best authority, that of the 28,000 to 29,000 souls
in Atlanta, the whites are in the proportion of 15 to 13 coloured.
That the coloured people should be so numerous in a practically
new town proves the large flux of negroes from country to town
since the war. The marvel is how so large a population, white
or black, has been gathered here in so short a time. "Northern
capital" is the general explanation given; and the Great Hotel
is constantly referred to as a sample of the grand effects which
"Northern capital" is destined to achieve in the Southern States.
The number of Northern firms established in Atlanta, and the
commercial prospecters flocking down from as far as Boston and
New York, attest the mark which Atlanta and the "H. I." together
have already made in Northern imagination. But the town is
mainly indebted for all the progress yet made to political influences. The capital of Georgia has been removed from Milledgeville, situated, like other State capitals throughout the Union,

as nearly as possible in the centre of the State, to this Northern town. The courts of justice, the annual sessions of the Legislature, and the constant residence of the Governor and other officers of State, give to Atlanta both traffic and *éclat*, and may render it more and more a place of general concourse from all other parts of the State. Poor Milledgeville has been left in widowhood and desolation, and the State buildings, as well as much private property, been rendered of no account, while Atlanta is expected to grow into a great city. Two brothers Kimball came down from Boston at the close of the war in a humble and unassuming character, but probably with ulterior ideas in their heads. They are types of a class of aspiring Northern men who have rushed to the South since the war, some to run plantations, some to open mines of coal and iron, some to build railroads, others to establish great hotels, and all to give a grand impulse to Southern progress, and show the "old fogies" in the South how to do it. Many of these enterprising men have already come to grief and left the country, while others are in full career to Fortune, or—her eldest daughter— Miss Fortune. The brothers Kimball appear to have seen the tide in the affairs of Atlanta sooner than almost anybody else, and seized it with remarkable success. They saw that Atlanta had an opera-house which was never likely to be finished, and could yield no return to anybody even though it were. They bought this building, it is said, for 85,000 dollars, and they sold it immediately to the "reconstructed" State at 350,000 dollars for a State House, to serve in room of the deserted building at Milledgeville. After this brilliant "spec," Mr. H. I. Kimball conceived the design of a grand hotel "to beat all creation," and in eight or nine months has reared a splendid structure, at an estimated cost of 600,000 dollars, to accommodate "some 1,000 guests, and an unlimited number of boarders."[1] The main front is 210 feet, and the sides 163 feet each. The dining-room is 75 by 40 feet, and the grand hall or ball-room is 103 by 46 feet, and 23 feet high. Besides the hotel proper, there are twenty-one stores and warehouses in the building. Two thousand labourers and mechanics have been thumping away in this mammoth caravansera since March last, and are still thumping. The estimated cost may very likely fall much short of the actual cost, but the peculiarity of the hotel as a speculation seems to be that the going expenses must for a long period swell the capital outlay. There is a French cook at 250 dollars a month. The gas bill alone would open half a dozen coal mines. Any one who desires to live well and handsomely could pray for no better caterer than "mine host" of the H. I. Mr. Kimball has naturally become a man of great influence in Atlanta. He is a

[1] *Atlanta New Era.*

H

munificent patron of State fairs, horse-races, and every good
work. His political influence is even thought, with probably a
little dash of popular superstition, to be supreme in the State. A
common saying in Georgia is that Blodgett, senator, controls the
Governor, but that Mr. H. I. Kimball controls Blodgett. The
old native citizens look with some distrust on the general briskness of trade and speculation in Atlanta. While willing to see
" progress " in it all, they doubt whether robbery may not be
going on. By an Act of Legislature passed this year, the Governor
is authorized to receive from J. H. James a warranty title to " a
city lot " for an executive mansion, and to pay the said James
100,000 dollars in 7 per cent. State bonds. The taxpayers are
shaking their heads, sometimes gnashing their teeth. The narrow
base on which the universal negro suffrage, " carpet-bag " qualification, and white proscription under the Reconstruction Act of
Congress, have placed political power, tends everywhere to
destroy confidence in the financial operations of the State authorities. There is a decided rumbling in the sub-political world,
and a great election to take place in Georgia towards the end of
December may decide whether taxation and representation—the
issue of State bonds and the property and substance pledged to
pay them—are to be brought into more satisfactory and inter-
dependent relationship.

The present position of Georgia in the Union is a little anomalous. The State started very fair for reconstruction and admission to the Union after the war, but the Legislature made a false
step by ejecting two negro Deputies after allowing them to sit,
vote, and take part in the proceedings of the session, and there
has been some difficulty or delay since in getting the reconstruction properly " fixed up." But there is no doubt that the status
of Georgia as a member of the United States will soon be completely arranged.

I was glad to find the Education Act of this year under
practical consideration in Atlanta, where in the present turmoil
some of the higher matters of the law are but too apt to be
neglected; and I attended a public meeting of the citizens, the
object of which was to urge the authorities to put the Act into
operation. The meeting was not numerous, but intelligent and
earnest as to the business on hand. There was strong advocacy
of a system of free public schools for the people at large, the
chief argument being one the force of which has been equally
felt in the large towns of England and Scotland—viz., that private
education is attainable only by the rich, and is too expensive for
the working classes. One of the speakers, a mechanic, said that
he and others would leave the town and seek a home in the
West unless their children could be better and more cheaply
educated, and he called upon the owners of property to consider

what hope there would be of attracting artizans to Atlanta to
build up the trade and wealth of the town if this privilege were
denied them. A small party of opposition insisted on the
financial difficulty, one of the number reminding the meeting
that the city bonds had fallen to 72 cents per dollar, and asserting that they would fall to 50 if more bonds were issued. The
whole assessment, he said, would barely pay the interest of the
city debt. But a quieter spoken and better informed gentleman
denied this assertion, and stated with authority that the annual
income of the town was 200,000 dollars, and the interest of the
debt only 50,000. The resolutions in favour of the object of the
meeting were at length passed unanimously. The Education
Act of Georgia does not contain any compulsory provision, but it
constitutes a State Board of Education, consisting of the Governor,
the Attorney-General, the Secretary of State, the Comptroller-
General, and a State School Commissioner to be nominated by
the Governor and confirmed by the Senate, on which Board the
central authority and responsibility rest; it provides for the
organization of County Boards; the division of each county
into sub-districts of not fewer than thirty pupils, and the introduction of ambulatory schools into thinly peopled parts; and it
enacts that the funds shall be levied by a tax on the "taxable
property" and on "the labour of the qualified voters" of each
district. The State Board prescribes the text-books, but it is
provided "that the Bible shall not be excluded from the public
schools of the State." There are to be separate schools for white
and coloured children.

The ladies of Georgia affect a Highland style of costume, wear
tartan plaids, tartan ribbons, and brightly striped mantles, and,
not to flatter them, are as gay and handsome as any other section
of the fashionable sisterhood. The gentlemen also seem very
fond of grey plaids, which they place in smooth fold round their
shoulders, losing one-half the comfort and all the picturesqueness
of that Highland garment. One of these grey plaids costs from
13 to 15 dollars. A lady's shepherd tartan plaid—72 by 144—
sells in the shops at 8½ dollars. The American manufacturer's
price, I believe, is 5·75 dollars, leaving the draper a profit of
50 per cent. One element of the high price of goods in the
Southern States is no doubt the ample scale of retail profits.
The shopkeeper expects a return of 50 per cent. on the staples
of his stock, while on minor and miscellaneous articles his profit
is almost anything he likes. Foreign goods in this region are not
abundant. Yet English earthenware and cutlery, and fine cloths
of England and France, are sold in Savannah, Macon, Atlanta,
and other towns, and a much larger direct trade with Europe
might probably be done, were anybody to take it up, notwithstanding the heavy duties.

The Atlantian who is fond of field sport, and chooses to keep a dog and gun, has abundant liberty of pastime. Partridges, turkeys, and sometimes deer, are shot freely in the wilds and woods round the town. One gentleman, on whom I called, had just returned from a day's hunting, and was able to show me his spoils, among which was a bottle of home-made peach brandy that had been presented to him at a farmhouse, and proved a much sounder kind of whisky than three-fourths that issue from the public distilleries of the United States. Peaches are superabundant in Georgia and all through the South. The people scarcely know what to do with them. They dry them, pickle them, preserve them, and distil them ; and after all, the hogs, I daresay, eat a great many.

There is seen from the upper windows of the Kimball House at Atlanta the most striking geological curiosity of Georgia. This is the Granite Mountain, rising sheer out of the plain to a height of near a thousand feet, and about seven miles in circumference. The primary rocks, though known to occupy a considerable area above the lowest falls of the rivers flowing to the Atlantic, are but rarely disclosed in the Southern States. An uprising of the Silurian formation appears in some places to have tilted the coal measures and the carboniferous strata to a considerable elevation, and to have given an anti-clinal deflection to what remains of the same deposits in the denuded valleys. But the primary rock seldom pierces the great mass of limestones which forms the common floor of hill and hollow. The Stone Mountain of Georgia is, therefore, a very singular phenomenon, and must be deeply interesting to geologists. It is a solid pyramid of grey granite, its massive walls smoothed by the washing rains, the huge boulders resting on its sides no more disturbing its pyramidal outline than if they were so many pebbles, and the tall forest trees growing at its base looking like shrubbery under its mighty shadow. The Stone Mountain, itself an abnormal development, may be said to mark the entrance from the south to a country of very different physical characteristics from the rest of Georgia, traversed by ranges of mountain, and impregnated with mineral treasures.

Cartersville is fifty miles north of Atlanta. By a convenient arrangement of the American railways a passenger on a through ticket can stay at intermediate places, and pass on at his convenience. I stopped at Cartersville. A branch railway is being made to Van Wert, twenty-two miles from Cartersville, and is about half opened. At Van Wert extensive slate quarries have been opened on the face of the hill—a fine dark-blue slate, which has hitherto been hauled in waggons to the railway at heavy cost, but will by and by, when the means of transport are completed, come into great favour for roofing. The branch line passes through a very lovely valley, well settled, and yield-ing grain, cotton, and lumber in abundance. The soil all round Cartersville is a red clayey loam, deep and fertile, with abundance of limestone. The aspect of the country an English or Scotch farmer would at once recognize as that of a fine wheat-growing country, and heavy crops of wheat as well as cotton it does yield. There are numerous lime-kilns about, which produce the finest white lime, capable of being made an article of extensive commerce. Among the slate quarries, deposits have been dis-covered of a character somewhat between sandstone and soap-stone, which are cut out quite soft from the bed, fashioned into bricks, and become very hard on exposure to the air. They take a fine, smooth surface, are cream-like in colour, and so far as yet known will prove most durable. The bricks, when dried, are very heavy. This seems superior material for dressings round doors and windows, and cornicing. Marble quarries are wrought in Pickens County adjoining, and in a marble-yard at Cartersville I saw fine marble columns, almost pure white as well as variegated, and pedestals the scaly grain of which revealed a hard but ordinary limestone. The marbles of this section are carried chiefly to Marietta, a station on the State railway, and a considerable traffic is carried on in them to all the various towns—some being even sent to the North. There is abundance of rock in this district for mill and grinding stones. But no coal, so far as I have learned, has yet been discovered, though iron ore has been wrought to a considerable extent, and pig is carried laboriously from the furnaces in waggons to "the State Road," twelve miles and more. No geological survey has, unfortunately, yet been made of Northern Georgia. The appointment of a qualified State geologist would be a measure of great public utility. The whole of this northern section of the State is evi-dently rich in materials of scientific observation and commercial interest.

The little town of Cartersville, rising up on either side of the railway—on both sides of which I lived long enough to find that there is a lively jealousy betwixt East and West, and the Big and Little-endians of the corporation—presented a quietly busy scene all day long. There was a crowd of waggons in the place, drawn some by oxen and some by mules, carrying their load of cotton or other produce to the depôt, and taking up at the stores their necessary supplies from the outside world. I stepped into the upper hall of a town house, which was being built in the front centre of the Big End, and found a bevy of young ladies and gentlemen whirling on "parlour skates" in a style which on ice would have made a great reputation. A young man "from the North" was presiding over a large assort-ment of the "parlour skates" for sale! The Americans are a most ingenious people in small things. Let a want, or semblance of a want, be felt throughout the circumference of the Union, and "a young man from the North" will immediately appear and fix it all up to satisfaction. Still it is difficult sometimes to find the Post-office. I had wished to put a letter in at Carters-ville, and the business men could tell me, with some slight variations, where the Post-office was the day before, while a larger number of witnesses had a distinct recollection where it was the previous week; but the whereabouts of the postmaster for the day being undiscoverable, I was drawn at length to the county building as the last intrenchment of official life, whither a spry, active little man, above middle age, in long light-blue coat and top-boots, driving a covered waggon with two mules, came at the same moment in search of "the Ordinary," a legal functionary, and one of much higher rank than the postmaster. We were alike unsuccessful in our object—indeed, there was nobody at all in the county building—and we dropped at once into the fellow-feeling "wondrous kind." He had sailed from Liverpool thirty years ago, and had now "hold of a water-power and factory" thirty-five miles from Cartersville or the railroad. "How many hands in the factory?" "Seven." "How long does it take you to go home?" "A day and three or four hours." "Then you camp out at night?" "Of course." This English-man of thirty years' American citizenship, with his "hold on a water-power" thirty-five miles from any centre of habitation, and no "Ordinary" to be found, seemed to me a deeply interest-ing study, and I looked a long time after him as he briskly jogged on with his mules. His great expectation was that the rail-way would soon be extended from Marietta to Pickens county, where his water-power and the marble quarries are. Yet the reins of authority are by no means loosely held in Cartersville. The Mayor had issued an edict in writing that barbers opening their shops on Sunday would be punished with the utmost rigour of law. The severity of this proclamation may hardly be estimated unless one remembers that few American citizens can really shave their own beards, and that "the barber" is as great an insti-tution in this country as he was in Spain four hundred years ago. The observance of the day of rest is marked all through Georgia. One sees many Puritan-looking countenances; and sturdy yeo-men, with straight hair and earnest aspect, come and go on ambling palfreys and in splashed boots in such a place as Cartersville from sunrise to sundown. The state of society, the kind of traffic, the country roads, and all the surroundings here, probably differ very little from many a rural district of England in the days of the Roundheads and Cavaliers.

CHAPTER XVI.

[CHATTANOOGA, TENN.—*Dec.* 2—5.]

CHATTANOOGA is situated on the extreme verge of south-eastern Tennessee, but, in point of local attributes, is more closely allied to Georgia and Alabama than to the State of which it forms part. It acquired world-wide notoriety during the war as the centre of important military movements, and has since been rendering itself famous in a more useful and enduring sense. The population, now 8,000, has largely increased during the last two years. The construction of the Alabama and Chattanooga Railroad, the new life given to the Rolling Mills by an enterprising and successful company, and the increased importance attached to the mineral resources of the district, have all tended to enhance the value of property and give great briskness to trade and labour. From a little nest of shanties, Chattanooga is struggling forward rapidly into streets of brick, with hotels, stores, and public buildings. The railways of North and South Carolina, Georgia, Alabama, and Tennessee have here a common point of connection, and "*viâ* Chattanooga" figures all over the North-Eastern States as the index of a great route for passengers and emigrants to the South and to the vast tracts of Texas and Arkansas west of the Mississippi. Chattanooga is cradled amidst mountains, the great Cumberland chain spreading its spurs into Georgia and Alabama on all sides of it; and it may be said to sleep and wake to the sound of the waters of the Tennessee, which here pursues a most serpentine course, and in scooping out its bed amidst the sand and limestone rock appears at various points to have missed by a hairsbreadth a much shorter cut to the sea. Though built on one of the loops of the river, and environed by rock and hill, Chattanooga has ample space for expansion valleyward. In the immediate vicinity the Lookout range of hills terminates in the bold and striking peak known as Lookout Mountain, which, as the country was inviting, I resolved to ascend.

Though near mid-winter, the day was bright, sunny, and warm as summer in England. A short canter across the plain brings one to the base of the mountain, striking it about the middle, where a winding road has been cut to the summit. On ascending, the hill appears as if built up of huge boulders bedded in red sandy clay, which, but for the boulders, one imagines would make a good crop-bearing soil. Great blocks of stone lie on the surface, worn by the weather into all shapes and forms. Solid masses, square or oblong, rise out of what seems a deep earth, as if they had a foundation far down, and were either still an integral part of the everlasting hill, or had been built in and carved by the hand of man. Pines, whose roots had struck the rock, and spread in strong ribs along its surface, and wound their tenderest fibres through its crevices,- have shared the fate of storm or landslip, which has wrenched great masses of stone from their foundations, and placed them topsy-turvy on the mountain-side. The abundance of soil gives root all way up to a great variety of trees and shrubs. Wooden shanties peep out from the trees like nests along the mountain-side, and the constant tinkle of the cow-bell gives notice that many poor families nourish themselves in this wilderness. The mountain is pretty steep from its base, but near the summit the sandstone rises up in a massive perpendicular wall, somewhat like the top ridge of the Salisbury Crags at Edinburgh, but three or four times as high, reckoning from the point where it rests visibly above the "millstone grit," limestone, and Silurian rocks which probably form the nether foundations of the mountain. This crest of free-stone, with its fringe of pines and other trees atop, when looked at from a distance, while the sun is wearing down to the west, bristles up and spreads over the horizon like the comb of a cock. The road at length approaches the Summit House, frequented by New Orleans and other Southern people in summer, and by invalids from the Far West in winter. The glass in the house stood at 60 degrees between 11 and 12 o'clock. In summer the heat is seldom more than 85 degrees. Pushing forward, over the finest white sand, and through older and more umbrageous timber than appeared on the mountain-side, to the very edge of the cliffs in which the mountain abruptly terminates at a height of 1,800 feet, and at the base of which the Tennessee is forced by the massive resistance to make one of its sudden but graceful windings, scenes of surpassing loveliness burst on the view. The houses of Chattanooga seem sprinkled about like snuff-boxes on the plain. The majestic river, sweeping out from well-threaded mazes to the north, flows in a smooth and gentle current westward, as if in mere kindness to Chattanooga, which otherwise it might overflow, and, passing behind a great ridge in that direction, emerges again in a broad and placid south-eastern curve round another side of the town, till, meeting this formidable wall of rock, it bends once more and flows in a western course past the base of the cliffs, and is finally lost to view amidst wooded mountains and gorges, almost as far north as the point at which it first comes into sight. The Tennessee, in describing this series of syphon-like movements, albeit rockbound, seems never to lose its sovereignty of action, or to wander anywhere save according to its own sweet will. The process of denudation by the deluge of waters that must have rolled over these parts, splitting broad mountains in two, and washing down their disintegrated materials into a slowly and far-receding ocean, leaving only this perennial watercourse, amid deposits of "drift," and sand and clay, and minerals, and mountain sections thickly powdered with its alluvium, as its final representative in all this present equilibrium of land and water, is written on valley and mountain-top in characters so plain that "he who runs may read." Broad vales stretch away southward on either side of the mountain. Sandy pine-covered hills, which look formidable on the plain, appear like little mounds over which the plough might pass. Towards the east, tier after tier of woody heights lift the eye step by step to the towering Cumberlands on the verge of the horizon. Southward the view is bounded by the hills of Georgia, and westward towards Alabama by a series of mountain ranges, thickly wooded, and bearing on their crown the same perpendicular wall of rock and comb of trees as the Lookout range. The outfliers, the tasselled rocky standards, of half a dozen great States, may be seen from Lookout Mountain. And here, on the topmost cliffs, the sandstone lies in great slabs, horizontal, vertical, and angular, forming pulpits and streets of rock; and topes of trees umbrella-like have grown up to give shade and shelter;—the scene erewhile of terrible commotions of Nature, followed by long ages of rest, and growth, and the silent spring and fall of vegetation.

The plateau of the mountain is of considerable breadth, though it is evident, from the depth of the adjoining valleys, that the denudation has been here extremely powerful, and has cut more deeply than on many of the other ranges. The only traces of the war visible are the sites of two or three batteries on the edge of the cliffs, and an earthwork in the centre of the plateau. Seven or eight thousand Confederates are said to have occupied this natural and impregnable fortress, but were surprised one morning by the Federals under Rosencranz, who stole in the night along the western base of the mountain, and, passing under the peak to the slopes on the eastern side, gained easy possession. Somewhile previous the Federals had struck the railway at Bridport, and the defence at Lookout had lost its importance. The evacuation of Chattanooga by the Confederates was followed by the great battles on Missionary Ridge, where the Federals encountered severe resistance, and Rosencranz lost his command.

The Rolling Mills at Chattanooga, which had done good service to the Confederates during the war, fell into the hands of the Federal Government, and have now entered on a new and promising career under an energetic and capable private company. General Wilder, whose campaigns had revealed to him the mineral resources of this section of country, is the active spirit of this enterprise. He has joined with him a partnership of capitalists, and is displaying a natural sagacity and aptitude in mining coal and iron, as well as in the mechanical operations of the Rolling Mills, that are likely to be attended with the most successful results. The company bought the old mill and 145 acres of land from the Government for 225,000 dollars, and are selling off the land in building lots at prices which will leave the actual cost of the mill and 30 acres of ground not more than 12,000 dollars. They have built a new mill in line with the old one, and are fitting up the necessary power and machinery, including twelve of Danks' patent puddling apparatus—a new invention, of which confident hopes are entertained. This is the first mill in which it is to be put to actual working test, and if it prove successful the saving will be about nine dollars per ton. The process of puddling is effected by steam-power turning a double circular chamber, in one section of which is the furnace, and in the other the bloom. One puddler will be able to attend two of these machines. A charge of from 600 lbs. to 800 lbs. of pig is put in, the chamber revolves, and the bloom, when perfect, is carried direct to the squeezer, thence to a furnace, and finally to the rollers.[1] It is computed that, when all the new appliances are in operation, the mills will be able to make 150 tons of rails a day. The company mine their own coal and iron ore on a property fifteen miles long farther up the Tennessee, on which they bring down the pig and coal in small steamboats, drawing from two to three feet of water, to the Rolling Mills. There is a fur-

---

[1] While these sheets have been passing through the press, Mr. Danks has appeared at the autumn meeting of the Iron and Steel Institute at Dudley (Aug. 30), and submitted a paper explanatory of his " Rotary Puddling Furnace," which gave rise to an interesting discussion on mechanical puddling. Mr. Fothergill, M.P., is reported to have said that " the effects produced by Mr. Danks' furnace were so startling that he could not refrain from expressing the greatest interest in it. In that furnace the breaking-down of the fettling proved highly beneficial. It was claimed for it that it produced a higher quality of iron, and did away with the labour of the puddler." A suggestion that a commission should be appointed to go to America to examine Mr. Danks' works was well received by the Institute.

nace in operation at the mines, which produces 20 tons of pig
iron, and is being extended to produce 40 tons, a day. The coal,
as is characteristic of the coal measures in the South, is found
in the face of the mountain, above the underlying masses of
limestone, in seams of four to ten feet thick. The beds of iron
ore are from six to fifteen feet. The company are working two
veins of coal and two of iron in such immediate juxtaposition
that the furnace is close to both and midway between them.
The cost of ore at the furnace is 2 dollars per ton ; the cost of
coal 1·40 dollars per ton ; the limestone 80 cents a ton; and the
fire-clay so convenient as to cost nothing. The company calculate that they will be able to make iron rails and lay them down
in Pittsburg cheaper than they can be produced in that great
centre of the Pennsylvanian coal and iron fields; and if this
should be demonstrated, the mineral resources of East Tennessee,
Georgia, and Alabama will command immediate attention.

The Alabama and Chattanooga Railroad, one of the great
railway works of the last two years, passes from this point
through the mineral districts of Alabama betwixt the Black
Warrior and Coosa rivers, and has been already opened for traffic
as far as Elyton ; while at the other end, from Meridian in Mississippi, the connection has been simultaneously advanced. Some
thirty-five miles on either side of Tuscaloosa at this date requires
only to be laid with iron in order to complete this great line of
communication. It is difficult to see how this road can pay in
the meantime ; but if it should facilitate the opening of the
coal and iron deposits known to lie along nearly its whole route,
it will be the means of doing great good to the State of Alabama,
and may ultimately develop a large traffic.

With the view of visiting some mineral properties already
operated upon, and of seeing the general indications of the
country, I passed down this line of railroad as far as Trenton.
Near to that place there is an estate of 2,500 acres, extending
across the valley from the top of Raccoon Mountain to Lookout
Creek, a small stream flowing near the base of the Lookout
range. This property was bought some years ago for 75,000
dollars by Northern capitalists, who formed themselves into a
company for mining and manufacturing iron. They erected a
furnace of 30 feet base and 34 feet high; put up an engine of
70-horse-power, with the intention of erecting a second furnace,
for which the engine would have been sufficient; and proceeded
to melt the iron ore abounding over the property. But, apparently from want of practical skill and efficient arrangements,
the company lost so much money—though it is difficult to see
how—and fell into such discouragement, that its operations have
for some time been practically abandoned. The property is in
the meantime under the care of Mr. M'Lean, one of the share-

holders of the company, who is cropping the land. Mr. M'Lean accompanied me up the Raccoon. Along sandy mounds near the base of the mountain he pointed out a series of pits where, a few feet from the surface, deposits of fossiliferous iron ore were dug out with great facility, and were found rich enough to keep the furnace, from which they are little more than half a mile distant, going while it was in blast. These surface deposits are found in various parts of the property athwart the valley. The furnace was fired with wood, cut down on the mountain, and hauled by oxen to the plain. There is a winding bullock-track up the steep which had been used for this purpose; and our horses were able to carry us far up towards the summit. The character of the mountain differs little from that of Look-out; and on glancing across the valley one is struck with the verisimilitude of the faces of the hills. It almost seems as if the two ranges had been sliced, and had somehow glided or been floated away from each other. Nature has here, over wide districts, acted with such uniformity that it may be safely concluded that what is characteristic of one mountain or valley will be charac-teristic of another. But though it has been known for fifty years to the blacksmiths of the district that there is coal in the Raccoon Mountain, yet there has been no thorough survey of it, or no thorough effort made to mine either coal or iron from its bosom. Mr. M'Lean first conducted me to a spot where, from the *débris* around, coal had evidently been picked out; but, owing to the subsidence of the superincumbent rock, it could not be judged how far the excavation had been made, or of what thickness the seam, though visible enough, might be. Farther up, a bed of fine hematite ore was revealed along several yards, and was at least two feet thick. Near this point the great wall of sandstone above had cracked, and fallen in masses down the mountain. This barrier seemed almost im-passable, but we dismounted, and, climbing over the sea of broken rock, landed on a shoulder, where we discovered, half hidden by bushes, a real coal-pit—a lateral boring into the mountain fifteen or twenty yards long, three or four yards wide, and about as many feet deep. The place was filled with water, and did not seem to have been entered for years; but the black and glistening coal was seen in unbroken lines, nearly three feet thick, on both sides of the boring. The probability is that these beds of coal and hematite not only run along the whole range of hill till the latter falls away or is intersected by cross valleys, but lie through the whole mountain to the other side; so that the comparative thinness of the seams may be compensated by their vast superficial area, and the ease with which they may be brought to the face, and shot down to the furnace.

A few miles farther down the valley there is another mining

property on which a large amount of capital was expended by the "Empire State Iron and Coal Company" just before the outbreak of the war, but which has never recovered from the collapse that ensued. The ground was prospected, seams of coal and iron found, and a furnace erected; but there operations seem to have ended. The property embraces the summits both of Lookout and Raccoon Mountains, with the intervening valley, or rather valleys; for the Silurian has been uplifted between the mountains so as to produce an anti-clinal structure in which the strata are found to dip in opposite directions from the centre of the valley. One peculiarity of the "Empire State" property is that the coal measures have been exposed on both mountains, and that seams of coal and iron have been traced on the elevations of the valley with a dip towards the base of the hills on each side. I did not see the seam of hematite ore here which I saw on the other place, but I am told that hematite has been found, and all analogy would lead one to expect such a result. From the "fix" in which this estate has been left by the war, it might not only be taken up on advantageous terms, but under practical and skilful management might become very productive. A coal mine is wrought in the same neighbourhood at a place called "Eureka." This mine was not doing much, but Mr. Staunton, the *entrepreneur* of the Chattanooga and Alabama road, called in the assistance of Mr. Miller, a retired Scotch coalmaster who has been spending a long holiday in this part of the world, and under his direction the "black diamonds" were brought out in more satisfactory quantity.

The characteristic of all these properties is that they are very valuable in an agricultural sense alone. The railroad runs through the middle of them. The property under the care of Mr. M'Lean is as compact and delightsome an agricultural estate as could be desired. There are at least 500 acres of superior arable land growing wheat, cotton, and Indian corn; a large dairy could be supported besides; and the terraces of the mountain-side, basking under a bright sun, seem well-adapted for the culture of vines. Wide tracts of herbage on the mountain-top would rear many cattle. Pleasant little bits of forest glade enhance the charms of the scenery, and from the farmhouse in the centre of the valley, an old seat of the Cherokees, the eye falls over the whole bounds. A populous town is rising in the immediate vicinity, and in the event of mineral development the valley lands round Lookout may be farmed with great advantage.

Two classes of emigrants pass and repass through Chattanooga almost daily. Lithe young fellows rushing to or from some of the new terrorities in the South-West, who carry their blankets and few *et ceteras* in a knapsack, and make their own coffee on board the cars—resolved to spend little and earn much—so hardy, eager, and impetuous that one would say that nothing less than a crop of gold could satisfy the burning passion of their hearts; and small farmers, with their wives and children and favourite pointers, moving westward to Texas or Arkansas, who arrive in covered bullock waggons loaded with their household gods from distant points in the adjoining States—from homes which were made with difficulty towards others which may only be found with more. The restlessness of the American people, their eager quest of new lands, and their proneness to fall under the spell of new dreams of fortune, are very striking, and impress a certain character of change and adventure on every branch of business and pursuit of life. The proper cultivation of the soil, the progress of arts, and the development and consolidation of society are retarded, meanwhile, by the very superabundance of the elements out of which all the blessings of civilization spring. It will require probably a hundred years to settle the Americans down to works of minute but all-important improvement.

The Tennessee is navigable to small vessels hundreds of miles above Chattanooga. There is some talk of cutting the shoals farther down the river, and opening a continuous waterway to the Mississippi. Congress has shown some favour to a scheme for spending four millions of dollars, and has already appropriated a hundred millions to carry out this purpose, which may have some beneficial consequences in the great valley. But Chattanooga is so well supplied with means of railway transit that it stands in but subordinate need of being made a shipping port. The railways in America are carrying all before them in inland traffic.

CHAPTER XVII.

The " Valley of the Tennessee "—its first Settlement by White Planters—
its Physical Features.—Present Agricultural Condition.—Competition
betwixt the Old and New Cotton Lands of "the West."—Marks of
Desolation.—Want of Labour.—Movements of the Negroes.—Division of
Estates.—Symptoms of Revival.—Progress of the Small Hill Farmers.

[VALLEY OF THE TENNESSEE, ALA.—*Dec. 6 to Jan. 5.*]

FROM Chattanooga and its mountain defiles to the great Valley
of the Tennessee is only a night's journey on the Memphis and
Charleston Railroad, but it is like passing from one country into
another—from Nature in her sternest and proudest to Nature in
her softest and mildest moods. Fifty years ago this magnificent
plain was in possession of the Indians, who called it by one of
the sweetest names in their language—*Alabama,* or "Here we
rest." In 1818, when the American Government, in pursuance
of its fundamental doctrine that " all men are born equal," had
advanced far enough in its wars and negotiations with the
Cherokees and other tribes to put up the partially evacuated
lands for sale, the Valley of the Tennessee was noted far and
wide, and pioneer merchants of the South-Western territories,
who had made little fortunes in trade and commerce, and gentle
families of agriculturists from Virginia and the Carolinas,
hastened down to the sales and bought up the estates. The
valley was then for the most part a great forest of oak and
cedar, broken only by natural glades, crystal streams flowing
through ravines of magnesian limestone, and broad spaces of
rich bottom land along the course of the majestic river. When
the settlers had built their log-houses on the picturesque sites
abounding in the woods, and gathered round them their little
communities of negro slaves—all the results of hard cash,
according to the doctrine of equality then prevailing—herds of
red deer would be seen of an early morning bounding across
the lawns, flocks of wild turkeys roosting on the trees, and
the Red Man, lingering in his much-loved haunts, would let fly
his arrow within the forbidden precincts, and assert his ancient
right of chase. The new life in the Valley of the Tennessee

was full of romance, of a rough but pictorial beauty, and of such difficulty only as was made light and easy by the excitement of new circumstances and the sense of growing affluence and security. It seemed philosophically to have only two drawbacks, inasmuch as it was founded on the dispossession of one race and the subjugation of another. But philosophy did not rule the world more in those days than it does now. The North is becoming every year more savage and implacable against the Red Man, and the South so much more indulgent towards the Black that he is already elevated into a sort of fool's paradise. After the Indians, there came white masters and black slaves in North Alabama; but there were only bridle roads from one plantation to another, no towns or pleasures of the ordinary civilized routine, and even bread and meat had to be imported. Yet cotton in those days was 25 cents per pound, and there was promise of money-making, with no one knows what El Dorados of territorial sentiment and splendour, snatched in imagination from the Old World to adorn the New. So the planters put their wives on pads behind the saddle, met at each other's houses, lived a merry and hospitable life; and the Valley of the Tennessee was soon occupied from end to end by lords and ladies of the land—men capable in business, and dames bringing both grace and wisdom from afar—who spread civility and plenty round them by degrees, and gave a tone to society that was spoken of from New York to New Orleans, and the impress of which, after all the havoc of war and revolution, still remains.

The Tennessee River, escaping from the mountain tangle in which it winds through many a ravine and round many a rocky bend and forest dell over hundreds of miles of its infant course, bounds at length into a spacious level country not far from Huntsville, a pretty little town of several thousand inhabitants, enclosed in an amphitheatre by the spurs of the Cumberland range, and possessing a magnificent natural water supply in a spring which sends forth a copious stream at the rate of 800 cubic feet a minute. The Tennessee, now at ease, flows in more majestic breadth without losing the air and dash of mountain freedom, or the will to wander in sweeping and graceful curves impressed by habit on its swelling waters. The valley first opens and extends towards the south over twenty or thirty miles, where the Tennessee bends round at Guntersville, and valley and river take a directly westward course to Bear's Creek, on the border line of Alabama and Mississippi. The Memphis and Charleston Railroad, which passes to the north bank of the river soon after leaving Chattanooga, approaches it again at Huntsville, and crosses to the south bank by an iron bridge at Decatur, twenty-four miles farther west. The river here seems full half a mile broad, and has the same aspect of mingled grandeur and beauty as impresses one at other points of its course. Cotton is brought in flat-bottomed boats and rafts from the plantations on the river bottom to Decatur, and is hauled up by mules to the railway depôt. The Valley of the Tennessee, thus stretching along nearly the whole northern frontier of Alabama, is fifteen to twenty miles or more broad. The line of hill country to the south, sometimes lost altogether, is at others visible only in a narrow blue strip along the verge of the horizon, which, as the sun sinks in the heavens, becomes more prominent, and, mingling its deepening blue and purple with the burnished gold of the western sky, gives form and limit to a scene of extraordinary glory. The mountain range on the north is in some parts bolder and more lofty, but, being broken by valleys and wide declinations sweeping down from the table-lands of Tennessee, presents an irregular outline. Many creeks flow down from the uplands on both sides to the river, and, fed by numerous branches that are almost pure springs, have worn themselves deep beds through the underlying rocks, and amidst soily banks clothed with tree and shrub, and scented by every species of wild flower. There is not only abundance of water everywhere for man and beast, but a facility of water-power for which the development of the country affords little or no present use. The soil of the valley is a deep reddish loam, almost dark in the bottoms, but of a lighter hue as the land ascends, till in the uplands, where the sandstones lie, the surface becomes almost white. Limestones of various qualities underlie the whole region, and form the bed of the river. On many of the lands a reddish sandstone is strewn in small boulders, not water-worn or pebbly, but apparently little pieces of broken rock, which are thickly marked with shell and other marine remains. On one plantation, where these fragments are more than ordinarily plentiful, the planter has them gathered in heaps on his clover fields, and built up in fences—the only stone fences I have seen in the Southern States. One cannot lift one of these stones and break it without being struck by the number of fossiliferous indentations. The Valley of the Tennessee would, no doubt, be deeply attractive to the geologist who abandoned himself for months or years to its study, but to the agriculturist it presents itself simply as "a land of Goshen" where every product of the soil may be grown and cultivated with rare success, where cattle may be reared and made fat and tender, and the produce of the dairy may contribute no unimportant item to the resources of the farm. In the meanwhile its agriculture has reached only a rudimentary and transitional stage, of which cotton was the beginning and is still the end, with little garnishings of "hog and hominy" as a collateral, but, so far, all too narrow basis of security. Whether cotton can be successfully cultivated as the

I

main crop in such sections of country as this, while at the same time full attention be given to other agricultural resources of the soil, is a question of deep concern, not only to the people here, but to the progress of cotton manufactures and the interests of the commercial world. If the production of cotton is bound to seek virgin soils and speculative fields, it is impossible it can attain the solidity and permanence so desirable and essential to one of the greatest branches of human industry and trade ever known. The Valley of the Tennessee is a favourable sample of countless acres of the older cotton lands of America on which this question is now forcing itself on the planter with all but desperate urgency and keenness.

It was hither that cotton culture made its first great stride to the West, and forty years ago the Valley of the Tennessee occupied the same relative place as the Mississippi bottom and the rich virgin soils of Arkansas and Texas do now. We are here on the border line of lands the maximum product of which is half a bale of cotton per acre, and lands where a bale to the acre may be gathered with nearly as much certainty. The competition is severe and crucial. It seems to waver in the balance whether the old cotton lands will be impelled at once or be forced gradually to let the new have it, and set against their greater mortality and social discomfort the larger pecuniary returns arising from a more prolific soil and a diminished area of production. An inspection of this valley does not at first view convey a very flattering impression of the regular and progressive extension of cotton cultivation. It consists for the most part of plantations in a state of semi-ruin, and plantations of which the ruin is for the present total and complete. They are mostly large plantations, 2,000 acres in extent or thereabouts, and retain very much the original division by the Government, according to exact lines of survey. The boundaries can usually be traced by the belts of wood which the old planters reserved round their possessions for fuel, fence rails, and other plantation purposes. A scarcity of timber is as great a disqualification to a cotton plantation as a scarcity of water on a grazing farm, or a want of fall and outlet on an arable swamp. The trail of war is visible throughout the valley in burnt-up gin-houses, ruined bridges, mills, and factories, of which latter the gable walls only are left standing, and in large tracts of once cultivated land stripped of every vestige of fencing. The roads, long neglected, are in disorder, and having in many places become impassable, new tracks have been made through the woods and fields without much respect to boundaries. Borne down by losses, debts, and accumulating taxes, many who were once the richest among their fellows have disappeared from the scene, and few have yet risen to take their places. But generally the old homesteads and the old families continue to be the centres of reviving industry and cultivation, and many valiant efforts have been made since the war to stay the advancing tide of barrenness and ruin. Fences have been rebuilt round not a few of the plantations, and the negro and the mule been once more set to work in growing corn and cotton. Yet in the best examples of this kind the restoration is incomplete, and a plantation, however firmly held and actively cultivated, has seldom more than one-third of its good arable soil in crop or grass, the balance being abandoned to broomsedge—a tall, grassy weed, which waves at this season in whitey rankness over immense sweeps of this fertile valley. Want of labour, and want of means of deep, rapid, and effective ploughing, are the chief immediate causes of this wide-spreading inutility of soil. When the Federal armies passed through the valley, many of the young and able-bodied negroes followed them to the wars, and few lived through the toils and sickness of the camps to come back. When the war ended, and the bond of slavery was dissolved, other swarms went off to seek new masters in the field of free labour, and after a season of trial, often bitter, are only returning by degrees to their old homes. There is a marked deficiency of labour in the valley for the cultivation and improvements which the planters would otherwise be willing and prepared to undertake. The patches of cultivation, under such a laborious crop as cotton, must follow slowly and patiently year after year the number of hands available. The general tendency of circumstances is to break up the large possessions of former times, since every proprietor feels that he has more land than he can profitably handle. Many of the planters would sell a portion of their estates were there any buyers; but I have been able to discover few new settlers or investments of fresh capital in land. In one instance an English doctor of medicine who came to this part of the world in quest of health, has bought a plantation in the neighbourhood of Courtland—a little village on the railway, that, in its general features and surroundings, may have reminded him of many a rural spot in his native land—and is so pleased with the result that he is bringing out his family and relatives. Upwards of ninety advertisements of real estate for sale are posted in the hotel at Courtland. The revolution that has passed over the soil has left many embarrassments, which time alone will clear away. One sometimes falls upon a great proprietor who came to the valley a working man, and made money, and added plantation to plantation, till he was richer than all the older planters or their descendants, and who now sits amidst his wilderness of lands without labourers, not knowing what to do with them, or at what figure to estimate his worth in the world. In such cases, as well as others in which

farms have fallen into Chancery, the soil, for some nominal
tribute or share of the cotton crop, enough to pay the taxes, has
been literally abandoned to the field hands, who still under
emancipation retain much of the nature of *ascripti glebæ,* and
cling for better or for worse to the soil on which they were
reared. I have seen more than one great plantation absolutely
deserted, and as void of fence or labour as it was at the end of
the war. This state of affairs has given rise to assiduous efforts
to rent out land to cultivators ; and a class of people called
" croppers," mostly whites, enter into annual tenancies of land.
But as the beginning and end of these engagements is simply to
raise a crop, they leave the country as it was, or a little worse,
and are, so far, of little or no account as a means of permanent
extrication or improvement. Yet behind all this difficulty there
is an undergrowth of wholesome influences at work that
promise ultimately a great revival and deliverance. The sceptre
falling from the hands of fathers is being grasped by vigorous and
stalwart sons, who are rallying labour round them, and, while
plodding in the cotton field, are also riding and hunting, courting
and marrying, and casting all the past behind them with hopeful
outlook to the future. The war has been terribly severe on the
old people. The long struggle over, they have dropped into
their graves, unable to support the worry and anxiety any
longer. When a father dies in Alabama, as in other parts of
the United States, his property is divided equally among his
sons and daughters, and this law approves itself so entirely to
the general sentiment that it is seldom countervailed by will
or testament. The wealthy classes hereabouts, indeed, have
almost a prejudice that it is a bad thing for any one to be born
to riches or large possessions. In slavery times, when a plantation, with its quota of human chattels, hung very much together
and could not be well divided, one of the family would buy out
the other members, and preserve the property. This is still
being done in some cases, but frequently a division of plantations
is being carried out; and by-and-by there will be three or four
flourishing farms where there was only one before. Pushing law-
yers in the towns, and thrifty storekeepers, are also eking together
good manageable farms, and cultivating them with fresh spirit and
intelligence. Modes of agricultural improvement are discussed
with animation in society and in the newspapers, and not a few
of the older planters are " walking encyclopædias " of all kinds of
geological and rural lore. Some of Gray of Uddingston's ploughs
are being imported all the way from Scotland, and if Scotch
ploughmen and land-stewards would only follow them, a favourable change would no doubt pass quickly over the soil. But
while recuperation can here be but slow and gradual at the best,
there are not wanting many signs of progress and vitality. The

population of the Valley of the Tennessee is too considerable and substantial to allow its great interests to subside. Though the reduced price of cotton this season has raised new forebodings of difficulty, and caused planters in the heyday of life to talk of selling out and emigrating to Texas or Colorado, yet to graver and more patient minds it has suggested ideas of a more diversified development of the resources of the soil, and more economic arrangements of labour and husbandry; and, in a greatly modified system of agriculture, the Valley of the Tennessee is likely, without eventually impairing its production of cotton, to find its way at no distant time to new prosperity and fruitfulness.

It is here, however, in one of the "gardens of the South," famous for the production of cotton, that one feels more and more the increasing wonder how all the large crops of late have been produced. The old plantations, indeed, have gone on extending their crop, little by little, year after year, since the war—the first year after which, notwithstanding the high price then ruling, was probably the most unsuccessful ever known. But, acre for acre under cultivation, the Valley of the Tennessee yields now a smaller quantity of cotton than in slavery times, while there are obviously large tracts once cultivated now wild and in a state of rest and neglect. Yet, in going back from the river bottoms and the large plantations towards the uplands, one explanation at least, amidst various others, appears. The hilly districts have long been inhabited by a poor white population, who have always produced more or less cotton. But the high value to which cotton was raised by the war, and the "labour difficulty" of the large plantations, have inspired them with new hope, life, and industry; and this class of growers have swelled considerably of late years the deliveries of cotton at the railway depôts. The fall of price is probably as disappointing to them as to others, but the extent to which they raise their crop by the labour of their own families renders the *per contra* of cost less distinct to them than to the large planters. They gin and bale their produce at common gin-houses; they spin and weave their own cloth; nourish their cows and hogs; and, when the seasons are favourable, succeed in raising a fair stand of cotton. There never have been better or larger crops of cotton in the hill districts than this season. These small hill farmers come down occasionally into the plain, looking for land to rent or buy; and it is not improbable that many of the better and more industrious class of families in "the mountains," as the gently swelling uplands are called, will eventually come down altogether, and help to renovate the waste places, and build up the agricultural prosperity of the Valley.

CHAPTER XVIII.

Routine on a Cotton Plantation.—The Surroundings.—Planting and Marriage.—A Ride " round " 2,500 acres.—Disposal of the Soil.—Organization of Labour in the Cotton-fields.—Cotton-picking.—Ginning and Pressing. —Need of White Labour.—Live Stock on a Plantation.—The Hogs.— " Killing Day."—Pauperism and Free Labour.—Shallow Ploughing.— The " Mussel Shoals " of the Tennessee.

[VALLEY OF THE TENNESSEE.—TOWN CREEK, *Dec.* 10.]

THE routine of life on a cotton plantation, though busy and engaging enough, does not realize all the pleasures and advantages with which imagination may surround it. There is nothing to which I can more aptly compare it than the life of a large sheep farmer in the pastoral districts of the old country. For while the occupation differs widely, there is often the same solitude, the same distance from town and market over difficult roads, the same want of society and of the smaller comforts and elegancies of civilized life, and the same general roughness of exterior circumstances. Save in the vicinity of towns, where the planters sometimes build houses and ride out to their plantations, or some famous old homesteads in the country where the wealth of a former generation has erected mansions and offices more in the style of the rural gentry than of the farmers of England, the planters for the most part live in plain log-houses, with a wide open hall running through the middle of it from a verandah in the front to a dining apartment and kitchen in the rear. The temperature is so mild in winter that all open arrangements for admitting air are tolerable, while in summer they are supremely desirable; and when the cold winds blow, or a brief spell of frost sets in, great log fires are kindled on the hearths, and blaze and glow as " in the brave days of old." The dwelling-houses, besides having more or less well-chosen sites, are usually surrounded by a spacious courtyard, snake-fenced on its four sides, with stable for saddle and buggy horses, smoke-house, cotton-shed, corn-cribs, and uncovered pens for feeding milch cows and other select portions of stock, ranged round the exterior of the yard, and giving rise to other little mazes of snake-fencing. Cabins for the negro domestic servants and other right-hand persons about the planter are also put up near the homestead, so that, with a kitchen garden and peach orchard at hand, the log-house becomes the centre of a considerable establishment. The planter has few white people about him. When he has talked, morning, noon, and night, with his overseer, or is visited by a neighbour, he has exhausted the conversational resources of the place; for the negroes, though most respectful and polite to their employers, and not without a humorous side, do not add much to "the feast of reason and the flow of soul." If the planter be a married man, the usual fountain of domestic joys opens to him in the wilderness of life, and new sources of economy and well-being spring up around him with marvellous richness and contentment. The planter may grow cotton, and some hog and corn, but it is his wife who makes the plantation flow with oil and wine, milk and honey. Matrimony and planting are linked together by indissoluble laws of nature, and herein probably arises one of the present difficulties of cotton-growing in the Southern States. Such is the progress of railways, towns and travel, and of a taste for luxury and gaiety, and all the effervescing pleasures and enjoyments of artificial society, that heroines willing to

"Scorn delights and live laborious days"

on a cotton plantation are not so plentiful as they were in former times. Both young men and young women here discover much fondness, if not ambition, for city life, and for some form of emergence into the great world without; and the one sex pull the other after them. The old couple, tottering on the verge of life, are often found struggling with the embarrassments of the time, and their sons far away from them in cities; while the younger bachelors, who have shown a good example in one respect, and are unable to do the same in another, spend on their plantations, as any one may imagine, a rough and hard time of it.

But with or without mistress, there is no idleness on one of these great cotton farms. As soon as a very early breakfast is over, the planter will have saddled horses in the courtyard, and ask you to take a ride "round" with him. A ride "round" a plantation of 2,500 acres is a good day's journey, but the weather at this season is here usually fine and invigorating, and an excursion on horseback, with everything new to look at, is very pleasant. On getting out from the labyrinth of gates and fences, it becomes a ride over open country and through bits of woodland, amidst wide-spreading patches of Indian corn and cotton, and undulating sweeps of long sedgy grass, broken here and there on the slopes by raw cuts and gaping blood-red wounds inflicted by the weather. These rolling tracts, when not under the plough, would be fine pasture lands on a farm in England; but they are here simply a measure of the insufficiency

of labour and inattention to stock.   A few stray cows belonging
to the negroes are the only cattle seen as one brushes through the
far-extending sedge.   Yet on this side and that, near the steading, one's eye does fall sometimes on bright green swards, where
some choice animals are feeding with· much zest.   These are
fields of rye or barley, sown in September, and now closely
cropped by horses and mules, to shoot up again with new
strength and tenderness in spring; or fields of clover in their
first or second year, on which the stole and blade of this finest
of grasses lie thick over the soil as a carpet.   There need be no
want of sweet and succulent herbage at all seasons on these
Valley plantations.   But corn and cotton, and cotton and corn,
as one rides on, throw everything else into the shade.   These
crops are grown in alternate lots over large spaces of ground
without intermediate fences, cotton one year and corn the next
—this being the prevailing idea of rotation.   But corn grows
anywhere, and requires but little labour, and there are favoured
spots for cotton down on " the bottom" where some creek flows
along fine marginal stripes, and round loops and semi-islands of
rich and dark-coloured land, where the favoured commodity has
the preponderance.   The negro " quarters " now begin to appear in
rows of cabins, usually placed on the edge of the wood forming
the boundary of the plantation, and under the system of free
labour rapidly becoming little farm steadings, with corn-cribs
and hog and mule pens of their own.   It was usual in slavery
times to concentrate the " quarters," and the cribs, and the mule
stables, near the homestead.   But under the free contract, by
which the negro field-hand has become a sharer of the crop,
and loves to have a mule of his own to ride on Sundays and in
idle times of the year, it is found convenient to spread him and
the necessary animal more about, near his work, where, if so inclined, he may protect both his own and his employer's property
—which arrangement, expedient as it seems, and on the whole
may be, has created a new difficulty to the planter; for the
negro is not remarkably honest, and has such obtuse ideas
generally on the precise relation of *meum* and *tuum*, that his
master's share of the corn and cotton, when stored widely round,
does not always appear to him anywise radically different from
his own.   But a man who has a large interest should be honoured
with a large confidence and responsibility, and this general
ethical principle has its sway here meantime too.   The negroes
toiled in gangs or squads when slaves, and they toil necessarily,
though under much less control of the planter, in the same form
still.   A strong family group, who can attach other labour, and
bring odd hands to work at proper seasons, makes a choice, if
not always attainable, nucleus of "a squad."   The picking time
is the testing-point of labour in the cotton-fields, and that time

is now, or ought to be, nearly over. One loses much of the charm of this cotton country towards the end of the year. It should be seen when the tall Indian cornstalk, still luscious, is nodding under the weight of its golden pods, and the cotton-shrub, still a mass of green, is bursting into white globules, which play and flash in the gorgeous sunlight like pearls amidst a frippery of leaves. But the third round in cotton-picking has now been made, on all plantations whose labour is well up to time, over the spreading areas of something red and brown, and dying under maturity and "snaps" of frost into a ground of colour undistinguishable from the earth beneath. Yet there are laggard squads on the cotton-fields, and the planter tells one that he "developed" two hundred pickers yesterday, and expects to "develop" nearly as many to-day (though, to one like me, looking at so much else over so large a territory, it seems somewhat difficult to find them out); and he rides on, telling Jerry here that it is not good to leave the newly-burst boles, for he will have to go over the space again if he do; and assuring Jemima there (a sonsy lass with a great profusion of bonnet), that the cotton shed on the ground may actually prove of some use, and be worth picking up. Cotton-picking is really a serious business in these Southern States. I have seen cotton-fields hereabouts that have not been gathered even a first time. But every second bole which Jerry and Jemima gather up is their own, and the force of motive to labour and to all manner of frugal husbandry can no further go. If the negro does not work well now, one must be sorry for him. The planter gives the land, his stock and implements, working capital and credit, his skill, and plodding care and watchfulness from day to day for the chance of half the cotton which his hands may be induced to plant and till, or may think it worth their while to gather when it is ripe.

Our morning's ride may have discovered 500 acres of cotton-field, and when at the gin-house, on our return, we ask what the crop may be, the estimate seems to run betwixt 180 and 200 bales—the overseer holding out (the weather being so fine) for the big outcome, and the dubious planter, however willing to be convinced, adhering meantime to the more humble figure. Half a bale to the acre, which has been given me all through the Atlantic States as an average crop, is rather the maximum attainable on any given acre than the actual aggregate result over a whole farm with all the contingencies of soil and season, and sluggard culture, with probably still more sluggard picking. The cotton gathered by the various squads is brought to the gin-house to be cleaned of seed and husk, and partially skutched and pressed into bales. The gin-house is a little embryo factory, in which there is a good deal of mechanical ingenuity. The wool, driven out from the gin like wreaths of smoke, is a sight to see. The ginning apparatus is sometimes, though rarely, driven by water-power; and the planter, having abundance of mule power in the ginning season, is not very anxious on this point. But the cotton from the gin is neither perfectly cleaned nor perfectly baled. The cotton bale of the plantation is about three times the size of the bale when it receives from steam power, with a touch as seeming light as a feather, its final squeeze in the seaports. If the bale could be despatched from the plantation as compressed as from the seaport, there would be much economy in bagging and in iron ties, and as great a reduction in inland as has occurred in oceanic rates of freight. Though I do not know that there is anything immediately practical in this remark, yet amidst all the buzz of the Southern people about cotton factories, and making yarns and cloths for the world, one cannot but think that, if the economical process is to begin, it had better begin at the beginning, and that any planter who made his bale of cotton the fittest for transport by land and sea, and pure enough for spinning almost right off, inscribing his name or trademark upon it as warranty, might probably become illustrious, and would certainly command 10 or 15 cents a pound more for his product than anybody else! But what a great stretch of imagination may all this be, when the planter cannot get his good land ploughed, or near enough of fence-rails made, or necessary housing put up, and has to content himself with the first rough bruise of the rich agricultural resources wasting around him for want of labour. Near the gin-house is a smithy and a carpenter's shop, where the mules are shod, and the waggons kept in repair; and there may be also a corn-mill on the place, with good grinding machinery which does valiant service to the neighbourhood. All these departments are filled by black or yellow men of more than common ingenuity. There is a nucleus of mechanic art and manufacture on all large cotton plantations; but it is obvious that, if progress is to be made, the planter will have to call in a great deal of special white labour, handy mechanics who can drive nails, make gates, mend ploughs and locks, work and right machinery, and put doors on hinges; and dairymen and dairywomen, and herdsmen cunning in stock, by coming South would find many comfortable openings, and rise probably in course of years to considerable fortune. So the planters begin to think and say.

The live stock on a plantation, with the exception of a few bred horses, still consists for the most part of half-starved cows, and small brown and white two-year-olds which look as haggard and shaky as if they were already threescore and ten—the property of the negroes, and pointed out derisively by the overseer as the "Durhams" of the place. The country lacks the aspect

of life and substance, therefore, which sheep and cattle give to
well-handled farms.   But there is one element of stock in which
a cotton plantation is really great.   The negro and negress, and
the pickaninnies, who are not nearly so numerous as they are said
to have been in slavery times, have not much comeliness to boast
of.   The mules, indeed, are handsome enough creatures, with fine
traces of blood and culture in their busts and limbs, a preter-
natural bigness of head, and a long, wispy queue of a tail, quite
in the style of a "girl of the period."   But for the merry and
lively beings of a cotton farm commend me to the hogs.   They
are of all sizes, shapes, and colours—a small, black, well-rounded
Berkshire being the predominant breed.   As we take a short
cut through the wood, great families of them spring up among
our horses' feet; they gallop in groups round the negro quarters;
they meet us in droves in the avenue and under the spreading
oaks, and are always cheery, "gleg," and on the move.   They
have so great an abundance of territory, and so inexhaustible a
variety of acorns—white, brown, and grey—to feed upon, that
they seem not to know where to settle down, and to be always
trotting on to some richer Texas or Colorado in a purely American spirit of adventure and speculation.   The whoop of a negro
boy, late in the afternoon, brings troops of them from afar to
various points of the plantation for a little feed of Indian corn,
which sends them contentedly to bed for the day.   But generally
this lively animal is the latest heard at night and the earliest
afoot in the morning.   And in this month of December, when
the air is cool and the previous night may have been a little
frosty, and "killing-day" comes round, what a gathering of the
lame, and aged, and dependent negroes of the plantation is there!
Old Sally, herself 20-stones weight, has hurtled down, and
has placed herself at the head of a dissecting table; a bright
brown woman, who would be comely but for very thick lips,
which she spreads out more unhandsomely still by smoking
a 'baccy pipe, and her blind man, who lost his eyes by a powder
blast many years ago in his master's service, and has been a
pensioner ever since, and all their children; poor old Bibb,
whose shoulders are up to his ears, and whose woolly head and
beard are quite white as if he were all coming out at last in
cotton; and many others who do no work now, all are down on
hog-killing day, when there is much fatness about.   Every plantation in possession of the old families has its incumbrance of
negro paupers, who are fed out of the produce of the farm, and are
treated with all kindness, which may last a generation, and then,
probably, disappear in the more sifting relations of free labour.

   The preference of the planters for hogs is easily accounted
for.   They require little tending, find most of their own " grub,"
multiply rapidly, and are the best meat, except, perhaps, bear,

yet found on this continent. The negroes are very fond of the
big fat porkers, while the finer pigs make delicious hams. I
have been several times asked of late, by tall drover-and-pork-
butcher looking men from Kentucky, whether I wanted any
meat, meaning hog, to which I have invariably replied, "No,
thank you—plenty of that;" and the planters are coming more
and more, since the war, to give the same answer, and to want
neither meat nor corn from anywhere save their own farms.

Yonder are those large tracts of sedgy weeds, dry and sunny,
and swelling wave-like up to the edge of the woods, which one
would like to see covered with herds of dairy-cows and cattle,
and flocks of sheep. But, they require to be torn up by deep
ploughs and clothed by much cultivation with finest verdure,
before they can produce the milk and butter and butcher-meat
which fetch exorbitant prices all through the South, and, if increased in quantity, as well as improved in quality, would be a
mine of wealth to the Southern farmer. His corn and cotton-
land and negro labour meanwhile seem to tax the energy and
patience of the planter to the utmost. Where the land is not a
deep level bottom, one sees the washing effect of the two or three
rainy months of the year in a poor stand of cotton along the
knolls and slopes, contrasting with the rich crop in the fattened
hollows. If the slope be anywise considerable, the rain cuts
deep channels and gashes in the soil, and, rushing down, makes
a terrible gurgle and commotion at some point where its various
courses meet, as if a kennel of hounds had been unearthing a
fox. These gullies are the plague and eyesore of the planter.
But, after all, they seem mainly the result of shallow ploughing.
The ploughs in use, with small shoe-shaped coulters, and horns
little bigger than a child's wheelbarrow, turn over two or three
inches of the surface, and leave a hard iron trail beneath that
frets the roots both of corn and cotton ; and, refusing to absorb
the heavy rain when it comes, forces it to fall into a passion, and
to act with all this violence. Deep ploughing would no doubt
cover a multitude of gullies, and probably double the crop on
every upland plantation.

The life of a cotton-planter, with all these cares and in these
times, would be barely supportable but for the abundant occupation it gives to the mind, the opportunities it affords for
wholesome exercise and field sport, and the ever fresh and
natural charms of the country. The farmers and farmers' sons
are all good shots, and they smooth many a difficulty by pulling
on their top-boots, and, taking their horse, gun, and pointer,
sallying forth to shoot partridges, which are found in coveys of
seven or eight in the corn-fields and the woods; or by starting
at early dawn to hunt wild geese and ducks round the islands
of the Tennessee.

The plantations hereabouts debouch on the famous Mussel Shoals, which are fifteen miles in length, and have a fall of about 90 feet. The broad river has cut a channel over the flinty limestone, which, following its natural strata on the land, forms a magnificent staircase, over which the great volume of waters descends in a series of gentle cascades. The wearing of the limestone in parts where it is softer than in others has formed what are called "chutes," through which boats pass, as through the eye of a needle, up and down. The roll of the river is heard all over the plantations, and from some points of the bluff the spectacle of what seems a sea of waters, studded with woody islets, swarming with wild fowl, and dancing in the sunbeams to its own shell-like music, sounding and resounding as it skips from one marble floor to another, is altogether exquisite. Many years ago a canal was made along the Shoals on the northern bank, but somehow has been allowed to fall into disuse and ruin. The Shoals are a complete obstacle to continuous navigation up river, and it would seem to be by a canal alone that this obstacle can be turned.

CHAPTER XIX.

The Town that Jones built.—Riot in a Liquor Saloon.—What the Planters complain of.—Pay and Privileges of the Negroes.—The Plantation Bell.—The doctrine of Equality run to Seed.—Planting discussions in Jonesboro'.—Bad Whisky and other commodities.—Need of Tariff Reform.

[VALLEY OF THE TENNESSEE.—JONESBORO', *Dec.* 19.]

JONES is one of the greatest founders of towns in America. The present borough of Jones must be the tenth or eleventh of the same name that have already passed under my observation without provoking a remark; but having wandered here more than once in quest of the postmaster, I may as well, were it only in respect to Jones, make a note of it.

Jonesboro' consists of ten houses, two of which—neat little frame stores—are in course of erection, and cause the people in the neighbourhood to say, when they meet to tell and hear the news, that Jonesboro' is building up rapidly. The ten houses are so arranged as to form a large square, of which the track and depôt of the Memphis and Charleston Railroad is one of the sides, with wings of streets from the corners to the right and left. The ten houses of Jonesboro' are disposed, as may be judged, with considerable effect. There are merchants in Jonesboro'—grocery, hardware, and dry goods—and one always finds half a dozen well-bred horses hitched in the square, and twice as many mules, saddled or waggoned, and, either way, having the art of standing still without the hitching process which, despite its "cruelty to animals," appears to be one of the institutions of the United States. Bullock teams crawl about with cotton or timber to the depôt; strong mounted men come and go, calling for the postmaster, with an air as if it were of little or no consequence whether they found him or not; and negroes are always dropping in on mules or afoot with little bags full of something, which they carry into the stores, and carry out again mostly empty. There are rich plantations round Jonesboro', but close on the other side of the railway track there are three or four thousand acres of as good and pretty land as one could wish to see, from which every vestige of fence and housing was stripped during the war, and all trace of cultivation has now disappeared; and how the taxes on it are paid no one seems to know or care.

But a great uproar arises in one of the ten houses, which, on being looked at, differs from all the rest, and has the appearance simply of an elongated caravan, raised on little pedestals of red brick that might be mistaken for wheels. The riot in the caravan at length bursts out through one of the ends in a rabble of men—backways, sideways, foreways, and on all fours pell-mell—yelling and whooping, throwing off their coats, squaring and drawing pistols at each other, and in a very high state of animal excitement. The scene was rather alarming; but I was assured by an "intelligent negro" that it was only a little bad whisky, the gas of which in the head must get off in this way every now and then, and that no harm would arise. Nor did there; for, though some shots were fired, nobody was killed or wounded, and in a few minutes afterwards the combatants were embracing one another in the most tender and affectionate manner possible, and in a minute or two more had all, greatly sobered and relieved, slouched back into the caravan. The bacchanalians were white men, of the class of "croppers," who had been trying their luck during the year in a crop of cotton on the waste and semi-ruined plantations about, and were taking the fall out of it in this fashion.

The planters who come to Jonesboro', though not in the most cheery mood just now, are men who take a philosophical and business-like view of their affairs and of the whole situation of the South. The fall of cotton does not profoundly disconcert them, for the rapidly enlarging crop had prepared them for a descending scale of prices, and the war in Europe is referred to as accounting in some measure for the depth and suddenness of the present decline. There is an opinion in the Northern States that the Southern cotton-growers are an inert, unskilful race. There could hardly be a greater mistake; and the idea that cotton can be grown, and the resources of the soil developed, more successfully than by the men who have been studying and practising these matters all their days, must be discarded as a vain hallucination. One requires only to meet the cotton-planters of the South, and to note the energy with which they act, and the care and diligence they apply to their affairs, to feel that strangers coming in to farm, welcomed as they would be, must be largely indebted to the knowledge and experience of the residents long engaged in the agricultural pursuits of the country.[1]

[1] Among the planters in this neighbourhood to whom I have been indebted for much valuable conversation, I cannot omit a tribute of admiration to Col. James Saunders, of Rocky Hill, a gentleman of the most extensive information—agricultural, scientific, and political—and whose vast stores of knowledge and experience are not more remarkable than their perfect systematisation, and

The emancipation of the slaves is accepted with remarkable
equanimity when one considers the overturn of personal fortune,
and all the bitterness of the war with which it was associated;
and an expression of gladness to have now done with slavery,
and to have touched some common ground of civilization, is
often heard.   But what the planters are disposed to complain
of is that, while they have lost their slaves, they have not got
free labourers in any sense common either in the Northern States
or in Europe; and, looking round here at Jonesboro', after a
calm and wide survey, one cannot but think that the New England manufacturer and the Old England farmer must be equally
astonished at a recital of the relations of land, capital, and labour
as they exist on the cotton plantations of the Southern States.
The wages of the negroes, if such a term can be applied to a
mode of remuneration so unusual and anomalous, consist, as I
have often indicated, of one half the crop of corn and cotton, the
only crops in reality produced.   This system of share and share
alike betwixt the planter and the negro I have found to prevail
so generally that any other form of contract is but the exception.
The negro, on the semi-communistic basis thus established, finds
his own rations; but as these are supplied to him by the planter,
or by the planter's notes of credit on the merchants in Jonesboro', and as much more sometimes as he thinks he needs by
the merchants on his own credit, from the 1st of January onward
through the year, in anticipation of crops which are not market-
able till the end of December, he can lose nothing by the failure
or deficient outcome of the crops, and is always sure of his subsistence.   As a permanent economic relation this would be startling anywhere betwixt any classes of men brought together in
the business of life.   Applied to agriculture in any other part of
the world, it would be deemed outrageously absurd.   But this is-
only a part of the "privileges" (a much more accurate term
than "wages") of the negro field-hand.   In addition to half of
the crops, he has a free cottage of the kind he seems to like, and
the windows of which he or his wife persistently nail up; he has
abundance of wood from the planter's estate for fuel and for
building his corn cribs and other outhouses, with teams to draw
it from the forest; he is allowed to keep hogs, and milch cows,
and young cattle, which roam and feed with the same right of
pasture as the hogs and cattle of the planter, free of all charge;

the readiness with which he keeps them in command for practical use. Col.
Saunders, who is advanced in years, was shot through the lung at the battle
of Murfreesboro', and, that stormy crisis over, has enjoyed very good health
since. He has been for some time conducting experiments in grape culture,
and having found in the "Concord" grape a quality congenial to the soil and
climate, is at present preparing several acres of new vine-ground. The
"Concord" grape is almost black, of rather thick skin, but juicy and sweet,
and possessing considerable native aroma.

he has the same right of hunting and shooting, with quite as many facilities for exercising the right as anybody else —and he has his dogs and guns, though, as far as I have discovered, he provides himself with these by purchase or some other form of conquest. Though entitled to one-half the crops, yet he is not required to contribute any portion of the seed, nor is he called upon to pay any part of the taxes on the plantation. · The only direct tax on the negro is a poll-tax, which is wholly set apart for the education of his children, and which I find to be everywhere in arrear, and in some places in a hopeless chaos of non-payment. Yet, while thus freed from the burden of taxation, the negro has, up to this period of "reconstruction," enjoyed a monopoly of representation, and has had all legislative and executive power moulded to his will by Governors, Senators, and Deputies, who have either been his tools, or of whom he himself has been the dupe. For five years past, the negroes have been King, Lords, and Commons, and something more, in the Southern States.

But, to come back to the economic condition of the plantations, the negro field-hand, with his right of half-crop and privileges as described, who works with ordinary diligence, looking only to his own pocket, and gets his crops forward and gathered in due time, is at liberty to go to other plantations to pick cotton, in doing which he may make from two to two and a half dollars a day. For every piece of work outside the crop he does even on his own plantation he must be paid a dollar a day. It may be clearing ditches, or splitting rails, or anything that is just as essential to the crops as the two-inch ploughing and hoeing in which he shambles away his time, but for all this kind of work he must be paid a dollar a day. While the landowner is busy keeping accounts betwixt himself and his negro hands, ginning their cotton for them, doing all the marketing of produce and supplies of which they have the lion's share, and has hardly a day he can call his own, the "hands" may be earning a dollar a day from him for work which is quite as much theirs as his. Yet the negroes, with all their superabounding privilege on the cotton field, make little of it. A ploughman or a herd in the old country would not exchange his lot for theirs, as it stands and as it appears in all external circumstances. They are almost all in debt; few are able at the end of the year to square accounts with "the merchant;" and it is rarely the planter can point with pride, and with the conscious joy of recording his own profit, to a freedman who, as the result of the year's toil, will have a hundred or two of dollars to the good. The soul is often crushed out of labour by penury and oppression. Here a soul cannot begin to be infused into it through the sheer excess of privilege and licence with which it is surrounded.

K

There is a large sweetly-toned bell in the courtyard of one of
the plantations here. I would have given a quarter-dollar at
any time to hear its soft and melodious peal sounding over the
great silent valley, the almost oppressive stillness of which is
broken only by the screaming railway engine ; but, save when
the overseer went out after the dinner-hour, and gave a tap or two
with his finger as a note of admonition to a few of his hench-
men at hand, the great deep bell of the plantation was voiceless.
It appears the negroes represented to " Massa " that the ringing
of the bell was too "like slavery times," and should pass away,
and so it has passed away accordingly. Poor "Massa" since
the war has been humouring and bowing obeisance to " Sambo "
in everything, till he scarcely knows whether anything of himself
is left. If the negro field-hand were to ask him for his breeches
and top-boots—nearly all that remains—there can be little doubt
that the indispensable garments would be surrendered !

Yet it must be observed that the negroes on the plantations
are by no means an exacting, violent, or menacing race. Their
present excess of privilege has been gained almost without an
effort on their part. They retain in many instances a genuine
attachment and fidelity to " Massa." Their predominant feeling
is "to live and let live," but such is their superstitious belief of
the power of " Massa " to live largely anyhow that they are but
too prone to carry their own living to a point of largeness which
involves his entire extinction. A negro servant hereabouts, on
approaching " Massa " to announce something, or ask for some
supply or other, turns round on his heels in the awful presence,
and with "bated breath and whispering humbleness" mumbles
out his message in a jargon which nobody but a negro or a
" Massa " can understand. The marks of servility are sometimes
too deep to be wholesome betwixt one class of fellow-creatures
and another. This external demeanour of the negroes, where
they have everything their own way down to the possession of
the land and its produce, is a considerable proof that they have
been elevated by some " patent hoist " unknown to ordinary
human experience, and that the complaints of influences and
agitations extending from Washington outwards, with which this
whole Southern country is ringing, have a substantial foundation.
The principle of Republican equality, which, in the days of
Washington and Franklin, had a broad and deep political significance, has been hammered out superficially in the United States,
till serving another by any useful kind of labour in serving oneself has become a sort of sin, shame, and disgrace. The inconvenience of this demoralization is deeply felt throughout the
Northern States. But here, among negroes in the South, where a
man will often neither serve himself nor anybody else, the great
doctrine of equality has palpably run to seed, and all industrial

organization and social progress become well-nigh impossible. The "labour contract" of the negro field-hand on the cotton plantations presents a serious obstacle to the employment of white labour, which is beginning to be recognized as an urgent industrial necessity. The negro, all in all, is the best labourer *in the cotton fields* the South is ever likely to have; but if the resources of the plantations are to be developed, and cotton is to be produced with profit at such a price as the world will give for it, the labour of the negro must be largely reinforced by the labour of white men, both in agricultural and mechanical departments, for which the black man has no specialty; and until the negro terms of labour be adjusted, how are the dairymen and dairywomen, the tenders of stock, the steam-ploughers and the artificers, so indispensable, to be placed?

The planters who come and go about Jonesboro', are deeply moved by such considerations; but as these spring up in their minds with a rush, and are deeply agitating, they generally take some narrow and intensified form of expression. The prevailing impression of the planter, who finds it doubtful whether he can live on his own free and rich land, seems to be, that enormous thievery must be going on somewhere or everywhere. That he is stolen from, every hour of the day, and through every fibre of his ways and means, by the negroes, by storemen and advancers of money, by local governors, legislatures, and officials, and by the Federal tariff and taxation, and by the very "free" but meantime "unequal" Government of the United States—all this is a sensation in the planter's mind rapidly hardening into an article of faith. There can be no doubt that the negroes first steal one another's share of the crop, and next the planter's by way of general redress. It does not readily occur here that the condition of slavery, in which the negroes were bred, was not the most favourable to the dawn of ideas of commercial right and obligation on wool-clad brains, and the negro propensity to steal is commonly attributed to natural inferiority and propensity of race. On this point, there is probably truth on both sides. But the negroes steal, and when the planter has put his feet on the stove, and commenced to "whittle sticks" with the merchant, and a negro passes by with his bag to the back-shop, he gives a poke with his stick at the rib of the merchant, half in fun and half in earnest, and would really like to know whose corn or cotton that may be. The merchant, with eyes down-cast and the slightest possible purple mantling on his face, makes a semi-poke with his stick towards the rib of the planter, and says that the large crop, and everybody now growing, account for all the difficulties betwixt them. But why, interpolates another planter, if the crop be so large, with not more than a quarter bale an acre on the average over our best lands, should Congress

maintain the same tariff-duty as when cotton wool was 70
cents the lb., rendering what was a protection of 40 per cent.
to the Massachusetts manufacturer equal to a protection of 180
per cent. now, and thus restrict, by the high price of cotton goods,
the consumption of cotton even here at home ? This bold inter-
rogator, when pushed to the wall, is prepared to swear that the
protected cotton manufacturers of the United States have been
struggling hard since the war to use a million bales of cotton a
year, and cannot do it, and that there is not a negro on his place
who has a cotton shirt to his back, the garment being too expensive ! These statements are astounding, but are nevertheless
well borne out by statistics ; and one has hardly patience left for
a third planter, void of all political ideas, and his shoulders bent
fully down to the ground, who talks of dividing his farms into
smaller allotments, concentrating the corn and cotton cribs
within arm's grasp, and trying post-rails instead of snake-fences
as a protection against the thieving and wasting propensities
of the negroes. When the planters at Jonesboro' have warmed
themselves with these discussions, there is one common comfort
in which they subside at present, and that is that Robert
Lindsay, of the Royal burgh of Lochmaben, in Scotland, has
been elected Governor of Alabama, and that the State Treasury
and State credit, thank Heaven ! are now safe. My own prepos-
sessions, I confess, are all in favour of the new Governor.[1] The
triumph of the Democrats in this and other States has been won
by hard battles against ignorance and corruption, and marks the
return of the white people of the South to a rightful and much-
needed influence in the management of their affairs.

Jonesboro' may grow into a considerable place, but it will
always be associated in my memory, I fear, with bad whisky.
The liquor sold under this abused name in the United States is
mostly bad, but in places like Jonesboro' it attains its maximum
of villanous compound, for which distillers and a class of people
here called " rectifiers of spirits," of whose rectitude the gravest
doubt may be entertained, should be called to dread account—a
dreary drug, in which there is little or no whisky, producing only

---

[1] Mr. Lindsay was educated in the parish school of Torthorwald, and after
studying in the University of St. Andrews, where he had gained a bursary
by competition, emigrated to the United States about the year 1845. He
taught a school for some time in Wilmington, N.C., but, qualifying himself
for the bar, removed to Alabama, and has practised as a lawyer in that State
for many years. A man of probity, as well as learning and talent, his
election as Governor is honourable alike to himself and to the people of the
State. It is worthy of note that in Alabama before the war, natives only were
eligible to the office of Governor. The Radical party, in giving new constitutional laws to the South, abolished this restriction, and opened the highest
office in the State to foreign-born citizens. Otherwise Mr. Lindsay could not
have been elected, and the Radicals themselves, perhaps, might have still been
in power.

vertigo, and ending, through all forms of violent disorder, in cholera-morbus. Its mildest effect is a little fizzle in the system, followed by an aching void of brain and stomach not to be supplied, and subsiding through the whole inner man in a sensation simply of general despair! Bad whisky, though seldom or never seen in private houses, presides at the stores in dismal eminence over bad salt, bad knives and forks, bad boots and shoes, and all the varieties of " shoddy," the inferior quality of which is only surpassed by their enormity of price.   One requires to live a while in this country to learn the fearful cost a nation pays for the insanity of " protected manufactures."   While cotton is bought in Liverpool at three or four cents per lb. above its price on the plantations, anything from Liverpool can only be bought on the plantations at 200 or 300 per cent. above its value there.   But there is one article of great repute among the Southern people—" J. & P. Coats' six-cord "—which is found placarded in the stores even of Jonesboro', as in general warranty that there is at least one sound thread left to hold by and to rally round.   Were British manufacturers turning their attention to wants in this market, and battling with all the tricks of tariff legislation as the Paisley firm has battled, the scales of monopoly, with which business here is so thickly encrusted, might be pierced as with a thousand guns, greatly to the benefit of the American people and the advancement of American industry and national wealth.

CHAPTER XX.

Town of Florence.—Traits of the War.—New Bridge over the Tennessee.—
The Cotton Factory.—Abundance of Water-power.—Tariff Duties on
Machinery.—Possibility of manufacturing Yarn in the South for Export.
—Cypress Creek.—Natural Beauties and Characteristics of its Ravines.—
The Dripping Springs.—The Plantations.—Opening for Dairies.—Severe
Spell of Frost.

[VALLEY OF THE TENNESSEE.—Florence, *Jan.* 5.]

FLORENCE, a fine little town on the north bank of the Tennessee, was a favourite point of occupation by the Federal troops
in their raids through the Valley during the latter years of the
war. A seat of courts of law, of churches, of schools and colleges,
and surrounded by many flourishing plantations and wealthy
families, it was in ante-war times a centre of learning, refinement, and prosperous trade, pleasant though rare to see in the
Southern interior. The country round having sent to the front
nearly every man able to bear arms, the Federals had a war,
more or less stirring, with the women; and much of Sherman's
famous march must have been as easy as a parade through
Broadway. The Confederates, in the weakness of their arms,
made the Tennessee for some time a dividing line betwixt them
and the invaders; and the great bridge which spanned the river
at Florence fell an early prey to the war. There was known to
be much cotton and other riches throughout the great Valley,
and a command in the Federal army in this all but unmanned
and defenceless section of the South opened the path to fortune.
The Confederates, as they fell back, adopted the usual war
policy, now acknowledged to have been a mistake, of burning
what was valuable lest it should fall into the hands of the
enemy. Such of the Federal Generals as had an eye to business
offered to purchase stores of cotton if the owners would only
show where they were, and commercial transactions were entered
into betwixt "the wolf and the lamb" on this basis; but the
general effect of the action of the opposing forces was destruction, and the darkness of night along the plain was often
wildly illuminated by the flames of gin-houses and cotton sheds.
Every rich planter's house became in turn the head-quarters of

some portion of the Federal forces, and the beauty of the site and the excellence of the water were greatly admired by big "Dutch-men," who came armed to the teeth, and stayed till there was nothing left to eat, drink, or steal, and the charms of scenery failed to detain these lovers of Nature any longer. The Southern people maintain, as a point of honour betwixt them and the North, that they were conquered by the Germans—by the same military "swarmeries" of King William as have all this winter been making mincemeat of the French—and not by the Yankees. Anyhow, the havoc of war hereabouts was complete, and often purposeless. Bridges over creeks, made at great cost and now much missed, were destroyed down to their lowest stone but-tresses for no military end that can be conceived, inasmuch as the advance of troops could hardly be arrested by streams that have been forded daily by the country people ever since. And bands of robbers, called "Tories"—deserters from the armies, and other loose and desperate men—whom neither Federals nor Confederates could control, formed in the hilly regions, and watching their opportunity, came down into the plain and com-mitted atrocities more cruel, foul, and bloody than all.[1]

Florence is gradually recovering from this reign of terror and desolation, and while impressions of woe indelible have been left in the hearts of families, one external trace of devastation after another begins to disappear. The Memphis and Charleston Railway Company, whose road passes along the south bank of the Tennessee, has re-opened a branch from Tuscumbia to Florence, and thrown a high bridge over the river, having a track for its trains atop, and another for the common traffic of the country underneath—one of the light iron structures by which Mr. Fink, engineer, of Louisville, has acquired much celebrity. The scene from this bridge is very beautiful. The Tennessee, calmed down from its merry dance over the Mussel Shoals into a deep channel a quarter of a mile broad, moves placidly round islands and jutting points of promontories wooded to the water-edge, past

---

[1] The following atrocious outrage, narrated to me by a lady of Florence, a relative of the victims, is one of numerous acts of lawless violence at that troubled period :—A band of these "Tories" or marauders from the hills came one night to the place of an old planter in the neighbourhood of the town who was reputed to be rich, and in breaking into the house shot one young man dead and wounded another—his son and nephew—and then held the old man over a fire till he should tell them where his money was laid. He described to them a spot in the garden where he had concealed some money and silver plate. They made a search for it at the place named, but failing to discover it they returned into the house, swearing they had been deceived, and roasted the old man to death. The Federals, who were in power in the district at the time of this horrible event, executed a boy of respectable parentage in Florence, who was proved to have held the horses of the marauders while they were in the planter's house ; but the principals in the outrage made good their escape.

massive walls of limestone, which it has worn but cannot move,
and round curving bays stolen from the fat and yielding soil;
but with the boundary of land and water always so cleanly cut,
and the river so ample, buoyant, and everywhere filling up the
view, one might almost cherish the illusion that it was not so
much the Tennessee that flowed as the islands and promontories
and polished walls of rock that were afloat. It requires only a
few yachts, with their white wings spread to the breeze, to give
the picture extraordinary loveliness and animation. But the
railway cars sweep across it several times a day, and steamboats,
except when stopped by low water at the shoals farther down at
Eastport, come up to the beach at Florence, where the land dips
down into a bottom, and there discharge the wares and take up
the cotton of the town. The Colbert Shoals near Eastport are
not nearly so formidable as the Mussel Shoals, and it is upon
them that the expenditure of the Federal Government is being
made. It was customary in old times to put the cotton into flat
boats on the Tennessee, and float it down to New Orleans at a
cost sometimes of not more than a dollar a bale. With all the
railroad facilities of the present day, transport is much more expensive; and so magnificent a waterway may be well worthy of
being opened and improved.

Behind Florence, which is situated on the edge of a fertile
upland country, flows the Cypress Creek, a stream of spring-like
purity and coolness, through winding ravines of great depth,
and, while of almost enchanting natural beauty, affording the
grandest water-power probably ever seen in the same space of
territory. Here, before the war, three cotton factories, of 23,000
spindles, and supporting a white population of 800 souls, were
established by a prosperous firm, which made money, and never
was more thriving than when the great thunderbolt of civil
strife burst over the United States. The Federal troops burned
down all three factories, leaving only portions of the brick walls
standing, and scattering the twisted machinery about as a
common prey. Heaps of iron rods are still lying on the ground,
and little bits of fine and curious mechanism are seen in the
courtyards of the plantations, and in all the negro cabins of the
neighbourhood. One reason of the prevailing desire in the
Southern States to set up cotton factories is probably the un-
sparing hostility displayed by the Northern armies to this branch
of industry. They destroyed instantly and without remorse every
cotton factory within their reach, and one can hardly harmonize
the pure anti-slavery professions of the war party in the North
with depredations so systematically directed against establishments employing only free labour. One of the three ruined
factories has now been rebuilt, and the business resumed with
laudable energy by the sons of one of the former partners, who

have furnished the factory with Tatham's self-acting mules and other English machinery. Duties amounting to 8,000 dollars gold were paid on this imported material, and yet with all this dead weight it was deemed cheaper than American machinery. The factory makes shirtings and other common kinds of cotton cloth, but its chief trade is yarn, which is sold in considerable quantity to the country people for domestic manufacture. Forms of old-fashioned industry, which in England would now be labour thrown away, are here the highest marks of thrift and economy. The yarns of the Florence Factory sell wholesale at 34 cents per pound, and pay the manufacturers better than cloth. They assure me that, with labour as cheap and efficient as in the factories of England, they could lay down yarns in Liverpool at about the same price per pound as cotton wool in that market. The saving clause in this statement is so large that one can hardly bring it to any practical test. But the Messrs. Martin at Florence are meanwhile getting twice as much for their yarns as the price of cotton at Liverpool. The English factory operatives have the reputation here of doing twice as much work as the Southern operatives, though the latter are paid two to three dollars a day, and are apparently the same class of persons as fill the factories in the old country, rather impressing one by their sharpness and intelligence, and the delicacy of their manipulation. While perceiving all the difficulty that besets cotton manufactures, and all other manufacture requiring much capital and labour, in the Southern States—the limited demand for sheetings and shirtings round a factory here, and the probability, in seeking a market outside and in retaining the necessary skilled labour on the spot, of losing much more than all the advantage in raw material—yet any one, knowing the great currency of yarns in the markets of Europe and Asia, must own that this question of the production of cotton yarn in the Southern States opens considerations of much interest. The Southern people have a hold of the cotton trade at the root, and the making of yarn runs naturally along the lower reaches of development, of which the first step is the production of wool on the plantations in the greatest manufacturing purity and perfection, which step once attained the other might be quite easy. Such commercial attainments are not realized without long, patient, and steady effort; but, were there a Sir Robert Peel at the head of affairs in this country, he might probably see in this direction a means by which the Southern States might be developed in twenty or thirty years with greatly more solidity than any Federal march to victory in the days of the war. Still what practical use just now of speculating on the chances of cotton manufacture in the Southern States, when labour has to be paid near a dollar for a shilling in order that the labourer may support a bare existence, and a small cotton factory of some sixty looms has to pay 8,000 dollars gold on its machinery as a bonus, ineffective even for its avowed purpose, to Northern iron and machine manufacturers? The same blindness of protective fallacy, that is wiping out shipbuilding, wool culture and manufacture, and other branches of production for the use of the Americans themselves, is, of course, rendering it doubtful whether, with the "cotton belt" in their hands, they can produce with any profit even the raw cotton so greatly needed by others.

The factory at Florence is driven by water-power, of which there is superabundance at all seasons. The dam of the other two factories remains intact beside their ruins, a little higher up the stream. Cypress Creek pursues so intricate a course through the winding ravines, and comes back so often to the point it has so lately left as if loth to leave such lovely sylvan haunts and be lost for ever in the waters of the Tennessee, that it is often difficult to say what part of it is up or down ; but through every successive ravine it flows in volume smooth and deep, forming natural reservoirs of water, which may be utilized to any imaginable extent. The only drawback on the lower reaches of the Creek is the backwater of the Tennessee, when it happens to be in high flood, as it was in 1867. Crossing in a skiff below one of the dams, one is pointed to a board nailed to a tree, marking the rise of the water in the memorable "spate" of that year, probably 20 feet above the usual level of the water. But this is a very unusual occurrence, and the mills and gin-houses do not suffer much damage when it happens. The stream is full of fish, and a "fresh-water salmon" of large size affords exciting sport to the angler, and is a luxury at table. On the warm summer evenings the factory operatives plunge into crystal pools floored with marble under green and spreading boughs, and the farmers' children frolic down the slopes towards the bed of the Creek, and under subsidiary rills have their shower-bath in deep grottoes where no eye sees them, and where all around seems a wilderness of foliage. Threading this maze of cypress ravines, one soon perceives their wonderful formation, and the manifold affluence with which Nature has not only built them up, but seems to lavish upon them her choicest decorations and sweetest caresses. Along the bed of the Creek, in many parts, the limestone rock is exposed in massive walls, a hundred feet or more in height, with their bedding planes and vertical joints as distinctly marked as lines of masonry, in some places smooth and square as hewn blocks of marble laid a-plumb, and in others carved and rounded from joint to joint like the towers of some Norman donjon. The opposite bank, whether flat or steep, is sure to be a little peninsula, covered with oaks, poplars, sycamores, walnuts, chestnuts, hickories, birches, ashes, maples, as if Dame Woodland had here shaken out her lap, and said, "There, now, take all." On the massive lime-stone bank of the Creek the same abounding wild wood prevails, and twisting its roots round limestone slabs that project far into the stream, besides issuing from crevices high above, sustains a lusty life on what seems all but nothing, and yet mounts up and mingles with the much lustier life of the table-land overhead. Here and there, on broad open spaces of the limestone wall, the springs bursting from their stony cells, and dripping down in myriad crystal drops, have gathered round them by mysterious chemistry a bejewelled verdure all their own. Numerous varieties of fern fold their feathery sprays, green as emerald, over pillows of velvet mosses, bright as cloth of gold, and " dewy with Nature's teardrops" lambent, as they fall from leaf to leaf, bosom in every opening bud, or form in sparkling rings round tiny buttercups and water-cresses, with the light of diamonds and precious stones ; while spicewood, honeysuckles, trumpet-vines, and countless wild-flowers love to come about these fontal shrines, to shed sweet perfume round their borders, and sport in careless festoons to. their tinkling music. The deep bed of the Creek in these fairy spots opens out sometimes in wandering glades, sometimes in steep lateral ravines, where the forest trees grow in all their majesty, and prepare one for the magnificent woodland on the higher ground, spreading out now in expanses of copse, and now in green lawns and parks where sheep and oxen browse under ancestral oaks. The oak, of which there are half-a-dozen kinds, flourishes in all splendour here. Some I have measured are 12 feet round the trunk. The parks are so thickly strewn with their leaves that these have to be gathered up and burned. But the pine, the cedar, the laurel, and other evergreens, impart perpetual colour to the woods, and shine with lustre at this season amidst the leafless and ashy branches of other trees. Flowering shrubs of various kinds—among others, " mountain laurel " and the " white fringe tree " (*Chionanthus Virginica*), so called from its white fringe-like flowers—spring up along the open banks ; mag-nolias, ever lovely in their glossy leaves, quite splendid when they send out their bunches of white flower, grow to a large size in the lawns ; and trailing vines are often met with in the woods. The muscadine, in particular, seems to take all the forest into rejoicing fellowship, and, looping its long arms round the lower branches of the great trees, hangs its fruit in tempting glee above the heads of the passers-by. Sometimes a muscadine, springing side by side with another tree, passes into a marriage-union in which the two become one, and, in return for the sup-port afforded to its leaping and blending branches, gives a new and often singularly fantastic grace to the whole form and figure of its spouse. The fruit of these wild vines is not without value. The planters' wives and daughters go forth in autumn, with a negress or two, and literally gather grapes from thorns, as far as any labour of culture is concerned, and make sweet wine that strengthens the heart of man and boy. I have seen this brilliant scene at the deadest season of the year, but it requires little imagination to discover the abounding fertility and fragrance of the land.

The plantations stretch down from the woodland to the Tennessee, and have many still rich and fertile bottoms; but much of the soil, though deep and genial enough at heart, has a hard and wasted look—the result of shallow ploughing and constant corn and cotton cropping, without manure, or subsoiling, or anything to restore exhausted elements. A large portion of the cotton-fields, therefore, yields an indifferent crop. Even in slavery times one bale to the three acres had come to be an average product, but it is very doubtful whether more than a quarter bale to the acre is now produced, taking the plantations of this section through and through. The land is not efficiently wrought, and the planters see many difficulties in getting it into a better system of cultivation. One often meets with signal instances of failure. On one plantation rented to the negroes for one-fourth the crop, with probably 600 acres under cotton, the proprietor will not get more than 25 bales. The season was too wet in the early part, but the weak culture and the weak system of labour, handed down from the days of slavery, are the chief causes of this poor production. Some of the planters are giving up cotton as a main dependence, and turning their attention to wheat and other small grain. The soil is a good red tilth for wheat, with limestone underneath; clover also grows luxuriantly, and dairy-cows might be fed and nourished with great advantage. The relative profit of wheat or cotton to the farmer, at present prices, may be briefly stated. The land, cultivated as it is, yields 20 bushels of wheat per acre, at one dollar per bushel, or 20 dollars an acre; cotton gives 150 lbs. an acre at 12 cents per lb., or 18 dollars; and Indian corn yields from 25 to 30 bushels an acre at 75 cents per bushel, or from $18\frac{1}{2}$ to $22\frac{1}{2}$ dollars. So that cotton, unless the product per acre be much increased, does not compare well with other crops requiring much less labour. It takes the gilt from cotton-culture as a money-making speculation to learn, further, that the plantations here were bought from the Government in 1818 at a price of 25 dollars an acre, and when put to sale do not bring so much now after much improvement and fifty years of cultivation.

It is to be regretted, when good butter fetches 40 to 50 cents per lb. in towns like Florence, and not very good is brought down from Northern dairies, that the planters do not give more attention to dairy produce. While this neglect goes on from year to year, the people are tickled and amused by Yankee inventors, who are always coming South with some patent mousetrap or other. One is just now pressing the sale of licences to use a patent for making eight pounds of butter out of a gallon of milk from the cow. He has found, in short, by some admixture, how to congeal the whole body of the milk into make-believe butter. Every plantation might have a dairy, and in cultivating grass and clover, and applying a deep plough and farm-manure, the planters would find new sources of profit, and speedily restore the old fertility in cotton which has so far sensibly declined. Along the Valley east and west from this point there are famous farming lands, all in the same state, and all capable of the same great things. It is deplorable that the country should want anything good to eat from any other place.

The Valley of the Tennessee offers little difficulty to European labour. The heat is not extreme in summer, and a beautiful and temperate fall, lengthening into December, is often followed by a winter bracing enough. Alfred, a gentle negro-man, who has crept noiselessly into my room at dawn, and lit up his huge log fire, one morning lately ventured up to the window, and arousing me, asked that I should look out at something wonderful. Snow, that would have been pronounced good snow in the Arctic circle, was falling thick, and to the question whether there were any danger of it reaching above the roof of the house, Albert replied only by a wondering face, and long before night all trace of snowfall had disappeared. But there has been a really Borean spell of frost since. It set in on the 20th, froze up the ponds at the rate of an inch a night, and driving the mocking-birds to the windows, the boys to their skates, and the *bon-vivants* to their " egg-nog," was really as intensely cold as I have experienced in very northern latitudes. The negroes, for two dollars a day, or as much whisky as they could drink, were persuaded in many cases to fill the ice-houses. As for the " Dripping Springs " on the Creek, they were as completely transformed as if they had been the subject of an incantation. Where the water flowed down in numerous thread-like rills there were now solid pillars of ice; where it distilled like dew there were broad and flashing surfaces like mirrors, resting on bureaux of rock chased as with silver, and windows looking into deep recesses like conservatories, where mosses lay stiff and stark in crispy winding-sheets, and leaves appeared like mere daubs of colour upon glass; while around were pipe-like instruments, with keys and convolutions—organs, it may be, of an " eerie music" that would almost justify the fable of Münchausen; but as I did not hear the tunes played either when " John Frost " was casting his spell, or when fairer Sprites came and blew a more genial blast, I forego the luxury of an imaginary description. The frozen fabric, at all events, quickly disappeared. The thaw came on the 27th, and the air of spring in two or three days breathed with balmy warmth over the land.

CHAPTER XXI.

[CORINTH AND OKOLONA, MISS.—*Jan.* 6–10.]

THE road from North to South Alabama is, meantime, somewhat indirect, the railways not having formed connections through the hilly districts immediately south of the Valley of the Tennessee; and the usual mode of turning this difficulty is to pass along westward to this point in the State of Mississippi, where the Mobile and Ohio Railroad intersects the Memphis and Charleston. I postpone, therefore, further consideration of the " Alabama claims," until, getting round through a very interesting section, including the famous " prairie land," of Mississippi, I can take them up at another stage.

Corinth was the scene of much strife during the war. The Federal and Confederate hosts surged and resurged round this railway point for several years; and though there was not much heavy fighting at Corinth—the great battle of Shiloh having been fought at some distance—yet the contending troops pushed each other in and out of the little place, and sat down all round, and ate and burnt up every green thing. The country over miles on every side is completely stripped of timber. There is abundance of fair good land, with an immense bed of greensand marl a few feet beneath the surface, thickly charged with fossil remains, and forming almost too strong a manure for raw use, save with the utmost caution. Many of the landowners have been ruined, and cultivation is carried on under more than the usual difficulties of a state of transitional chaos and embarrassment. Some of the plantations are rented out, but to little good account. The renters take a crop, do nothing for the land, and, indeed, not unfrequently burn up the fences before leaving, so that the owners profit little by the three or four dollars an acre, or the one-third or one-fourth the crop, agreed upon as rent. Other plantations are being broken up into small farms, occupied by white people, who are taking the cultivation in room of the negroes, less numerous in this neighbourhood than before the war, many having moved down to the richer lands of South Alabama and the Mississippi bottom. From 4,000 to 5,000 bales of cotton are delivered annually from the neighbourhood at the depôt in Corinth. The old planters, in trying to sell their lands in order to get extricated from debt, sometimes succeed. Two hundred acres, with valuable improvements, were recently sold at 15 dollars an acre, which were bought many years ago at 12½ dollars. But some of the owners near the town hold out for much larger terms. Every railway junction in this country with a dozen or two of houses is fondly believed, by those who have the deepest interest in so believing, to be the destined seat of a great city ; and, by putting up the price of land and houses, they may often indefinitely postpone the desired result.

A " North Mississippi Cotton and Wool Manufacturing Company," organized here about eighteen months ago, was to have a million dollars of capital, to be taken up in 100-dollar family shares over several adjoining counties, and subscriptions were made to a considerable amount. That in the most desolated districts, where the land cannot be brought into cultivation for want of capital and labour, a proposition should be made to leap at once into cotton manufacture with all its elaborate processes, is a remarkable proof how deeply the manufacturing idea has imbued the minds, and the iron of Northern Protectionist injustice has entered the souls, of the Southern people. It is with regret that one thinks—after all the Southern States have passed through —of the delusions to which this sense of wrong and fervour of feeling may lead, and the losses and disappointments with which it may be accompanied. The capital of the " North Mississippi Manufacturing Company " has been struck down to a quarter of the sum at first proposed, and this has not yet been wholly subscribed. A very neat building has been put up for an office, and the company is busy burning bricks for the future factory, and is in treaty for the supply of English machinery. The Colonel at the head of the enterprise has a notion that, by taking cotton in the seed, making cotton-oil, and using " Clement's patent " for cleaning the cotton-wool without ginning on the plantations, the company will be able to produce goods and yarns to beat the world. As there is no water-power here, the factory must do its work by steam, with an uncertain supply of coal from Pittsburg in Pennsylvania, at a monopoly price. The population in and around Corinth is only a few thousands. There is a Confederate Orphan Asylum in the county, in which there are 300 orphans—the children mostly of soldiers killed in the war, many of whom, as they grow up, it is supposed, would make good factory operatives. This institution derives its

revenue from voluntary subscriptions, and appears to have been
most laudably and liberally supported, though some of the
little inmates are taken round the country to sing at concerts as
a means of eking out the funds.

The country south of Corinth soon passes into the ordinary
woodland of the American continent, where clearings are going
forward, and comfortable homesteads, with fields of corn and
cotton, and mule and hog pens, are being chopped out of the
primeval forest. There is little swampy ground; the timber is
sound and stately; and the soil, in every opening of the forest,
has an aspect of fertility. The Mobile and Ohio Railroad, in its
straight track north and south, strikes at every ten to fourteen
miles little towns and villages, often prettily situated, whither
cotton is brought, where country merchandising goes on, and
country acquaintances visit one another at the end of the season
and tell how the "picking" has got on in their respective districts. But the forest here overshadows all until near Okolona,
seventy miles south from Corinth, where the train suddenly
darts into an open country, in which the woods recede and
all but vanish from the view, and the iron wheels roll with
a more airy sound over an elevated plain, which is the famous
"prairie land" of Mississippi.

Okolona was all but totally destroyed in the war. Only two
or three houses and a few gable-ends were left standing. The
whole place might have been bought for 5,000 dollars on the
surrender of the Confederate forces, but no one believed that
Okolona could be Okolona any more. It is now a well-built
town of two or three thousand inhabitants, with a long street of
brick stores, and many offshoots on the east, towards the railway
depôt, and a long avenue westward, with planked sideways and
elegant frame buildings, in which those who aspire to live respect-
ably in family know so well here how to reconcile taste and
comfort with the actual situation. Large courtyards behind
several of the stores are filled with cotton bales, and the space
set apart for hitching nags and mules is like a horse-fair on any
market-day in Okolona. One must take a few canters hereabouts in order to know something of the richness of the prairie
land of Mississippi.

The soil is a dry deep red loam—what is called, in the language
of the country, "a buckshot soil," with a good deal of lime in it.
When the overseers and negroes brush it from their pantaloons,
it has a tendency to go up instead of down, and always keeps
hanging about. Underneath there is a great bed of white and
easily pulverized rock, known as "rotten limestone." Every acre
is cultivated or cultivable. Little slips of forest land break
the monotony of a plain not quite level, but agreeably undulating, and, as one advances from point to point, there is usually a

rim of woods all round the horizon, but always at a respectful distance, and the landscape opens out freely from all entanglement into broad spaces of rich arable territory. This general character of country prevails over thirty to forty miles in length, and probably, as far as I have explored it, half as many in breadth. At Artesia, forty miles south from Okolona, the country passes rapidly into the "piney land" characteristic of so much of the Atlantic slope, and of the southern section of the Gulf States. The "prairie land" of Mississippi, however, is a great cotton region. From 10,000 to 12,000 bales are received annually at Okolona alone, but all the railway depôts of the district, and indeed of the whole Mobile and Ohio line from Corinth southward, I have found full of cotton bales. The railway company, while forwarding cotton northward with all despatch, seems to have difficulty in transporting the much larger quantity destined for the Mobile market and for shipment thence to Europe, and, sure of this freight, allows it to accumulate and lie exposed in the open air till the "more convenient season." One of the first settlers of this part of the country was Robert Gordon, an emigrant from the province of Galloway, in Scotland, some fifty odd years ago, who, anticipating the action of tho Federal Government, negotiated with the Old Queen of the Chickasaws, and became the purchaser of large and choice tracts of land on the "prairie," which he brought into cultivation. Mr. Gordon, before the war, was reported to be worth a million and a half of dollars. Like many other old people of mark in the South, he sank into the grave soon after the close of the great struggle, and was succeeded by his only son, Colonel James Gordon, who, though not so rich a man as his father, has still as much territory in active and productive cultivation as might satisfy a prince. One of his plantations, five or six miles from Okolona, is in fine order, and forms a favourable sample of the fertility and culture of the "prairie." It is 2,000 acres in extent, of which 500 acres are woods completely enclosing the great garden of 1,500 acres, rising and falling in gentle undulations just enough to spread it out to the sun and rains without being scorched by the one or washed and gullied by the other. This immense space is a uniform round of corn and cotton divided only by waggon tracks and a few long ditches, the main arteries of the plantation. Save the exterior fence, and the usual snake-fence labyrinth round the buildings, the corn and cotton fields are open, and succeed each other like the patches of various culture in a nursery, the drills being laid off with a sagacious eye to the fall of the ground, so as to let in the sun and secure a natural drainage when heavy rains fall. While the crops are growing, the cattle are kept back or penned in folds; but, when the Indian corn has been gathered, they are let loose, and enjoy

all winter an abundant pasture. There does not appear to have
been a bad patch of cotton on the plantation; the battle with
the grass had been fought with great vigour in summer, the soil
betwixt the rows being now clean and red as drills in a garden.
The consistency of large plantations with good cultivation is
well marked on this place. Some four or five hundred acres
only of the plantation had not been in crop during the past
season, but will be overtaken this year, the supply of labour on
this plantation being abundant. The old proprietors have an
advantage in this respect over new planters. The negroes seem
to prefer their employment, and, after various changes, come
back and settle down to work in their old places; while strangers
have often to hire labour from a distance without being sure of
its calibre, and are apt to get into dispute and difficulty with
labour contractors and overseers. It is a remarkable proof of the
progress made towards better management under free labour,
that Mr. Gordon lost 24,000 dollars by his cotton crops the year
after the war when the price was high, but has been making it
better every year since under declining values. The system of
paying the negroes by half-share of the crops prevails in this as
in other sections, and one negro on this plantation will have a
thousand dollars to the good at this time, after settling all claims
upon him. But this is a rare exception to the general rule, and
the negroes, with opportunities of money-making seldom enjoyed
by labour in any part of the world before, scatter all behind
them in a careless spirit, and more frequently close the year in
debt than with clear books. The " balance in favour," when
rarely made, is commonly but a ticket-of-leave for a longer and
more spendthrift holiday than would otherwise be possible. The
negro is one of the most liberal buyers in the world. Stores
exercise a kind of charm over him, and when he looks round on
the wealth of wares he is ready at once to fling every dollar out
of his pocket, and to open a credit account with boundless
faith in the future. The share system has one merit, inasmuch
as the gain of the negro is thoroughly identified with that of the
planter. When the negro field-hand gains nothing the planter
loses much, and the small, unwrought, and neglected crops that
keep the negroes in debt and raggedness utterly break him on
the wheel, and "burst him up." The planters have unusual
pleasure under the share system in pointing out the good hands
that have made a profit at the end of the year. Yet it is doubtful whether the share system will survive; and if it be swept
away, the result will be due to the folly of the negroes. One
objection to it here, as elsewhere, is that the negroes will do
nothing but the work immediately about the crops in which
they have a share, and that this line is more and more rigorously
defined. If cattle stray into the corn and cotton fields, the

negro will often only drive them from his own part of the crop into that of the neighbouring squad. As for fences in general, they are allowed without remorse to go to wreck. The planter, by a considerable extra expenditure on special labour every year, may contrive to keep them up; but where he fails in so doing, the fences go from bad to worse, till the plantation is in danger of being deeply embarrassed or of sinking altogether. The money required to fence a plantation is considerable, and many fine tracts of land have not yet recovered the total destruction of fences with which they were visited during the war. A staff of white mechanics and special outdoor labourers would be necessary to secure to the negro such a share of the crop as would keep him easy and affluent. The only alternative of the share system is payment by time wages, and under this arrangement every squad of negro labourers would require an overseer to keep them steadily at work, and get the value of the wages out of them. Otherwise, it is believed, the wages plan would be less profitable even than the share system. The best and most willing negroes seem to have little self-reliance, and never work so well as when they have a white man at their right hand to show them how to do it.

Old Mr. Gordon established his head-quarters at Pontotoc, a little county-town some twenty miles north-east from Okolona, where the Federal Government had its first office for the sale of lands in this State; and there, on a site which had been the residence of the Indian Queen, built a stately mansion of timber sawn from the pine forest by hand. There were no steam saw-mills in the country at that time, and it took three years to build the future house of this branch of the Gordons. It is a plain but spacious mansion of fourteen rooms, all very large, and having large cellars stored with the juice of "the hanging grape" —which, here abounding, gave its name in the days of the Red men to the country round—and stables and offices, garden and vineyard, and a burying-ground near by under a spreading red elm sacred to family remains. There is a Scotch style about all which strikes every visitor. Mr. Gordon was noted for hospitality, and the son in this respect is worthy of the sire. There is a large orchard free to all who choose to gather its luscious fruit, and a pack of foxhounds, the best in the United States, that lead many a "tally-ho!" over wide plains and through forest tracks where the war-whoop of the Indian rose on the midnight blast in former times. The Colonel is an enthusiastic sportsman. The walls of his shooting-box are covered with the skins of bears, panthers, wild cats, and other *feræ naturæ* of the prodigious sort, the trophies of hunting expeditions on his plantation in the Mississippi bottom. The glossy plumage of wild fowl serves to soften somewhat these barbarous elements, and huge deer antlers, while adding to the ornament of the cottage, form useful resting-places for guns and fire-arms of almost every pattern and device.   As if hunting bears and panthers in the cane-brakes of the Mississippi were not enough, I have found the Colonel meditating, well satisfied with the improved working of his plantation, a trip to South Africa, where a Gordon Cumming and a Chaillu have made themselves famous, and in gorillas and other monsters of the wilderness have discovered subjects of sport worth writing about. Old Mr. Gordon gave his seat at Pontotoc the name of "Lochinvar," in memory of the ancient seat of the Gordons, on the Solway, famed in song and story.   The same veteran settler of Mississippi founded the town of Aberdeen, several miles south from Okolona, with a branch road from the Mobile and Ohio.   Mr. Gordon would have called this place Dundee, but a neighbour, meeting him one morning, said, " Wall, Mr. Gordon, I believe you are to call this city 'Dundy.'"   "No, I am not," said the offended Scotsman, who saw at once that the pronunciation of Dundee would not transplant to American soil, and so he gave the more northern city the honour of a Transatlantic namesake. Aberdeen is a thriving town of four or five thousand people, and on Saturday—a market day—was astir with country people, hitching up their horses and buggies, buying and selling, and taking general possession of the stores and their contents.

One is struck by the number of active young men who have applied themselves manfully to the cultivation of the farms in this section of the country.   They move about in work-day attire over long distances, and display a confident and hopeful spirit. But they say that 15 cents per lb. for cotton is necessary to pay the expenses of cultivation as affairs are at present manageable.   The war is seldom spoken of, and sympathy for the traces of it, everywhere visible in amputated arms and limbs, may sometimes be carried beyond due bounds.   Southern gentlemen have a singular habit of wearing their coats without putting their arms in the sleeves.   I have caught myself several times in a full flow of tender feeling for the gallant fellows who had lost both arms in the war, when it soon after became clear that the generous emotion was wholly misspent and thrown away.

CHAPTER XXII.

[MERIDIAN, MISS.—*Jan.* 11-13.]

I ARRIVED at Meridian on Sunday morning at half-past four, albeit the train that brought us was due shortly after midnight. The fact is that, the night being somewhat frosty, the engine took a fit of wheezing, and finally stood still, two hours or more, in the woods about thirty miles north from this point. The scene, I admit, was very charming. The track ran along an embankment of moderate elevation, from which the land, on one side, rose in gentle ridges of Indian corn-stalks, and spread away, on the other, in a plain of woodland, thinned, grassy, and ornamental as a park. The moonlight was clear almost as noonday, and made the lamps in the cars blink like dissipated owls. When an hour or two had passed in this delightfully sequestered spot, a vague desire to embrace the shadows of the trees, and follow the unknown but all the more attractive meanderings of the brooks, stole over both mind and body. So a few of us stepped out on to the embankment. The head of the train was a long way ahead, and getting down on a railway track in moonlight scatters a vast amount of imagination and romance. The engine was obviously in a bad way. There was a large escape of steam from the valves, and the engineers had apparently cut several of her ribs out, and laid them along the track, and were now labouring to knock her shoulder-blade out of joint. The swearing at the same time was terrible, and I was glad to stride away from the natural beauties of the situation to my seat under the blinking owls, reflecting mainly on all the British army once did in Flanders. There is a peculiarity, by the way, in much of the swearing in this part of the world which one notes. The whole practice is everywhere abominable, but an emphatic oath under strong passion may command passing respect by its thunder, and, whether or not, immediately apologizes by the fact that it is **not to** be repeated; whereas a long and never-ending **drawl of**

profane interpolations, running not only into words but syllables
of words, as if the sacred name could not in sufficient contempt
be cut into too many pieces, is more revolting than impressive,
and as weak as it is utterly inexcusable. Fortunately, the great
majority of those who are doomed to hear do not understand a
word of it, and for my part I have been always glad to conclude
that it is a form of *patois* which the poor devils who utter it do
not understand themselves. How our engine on this occasion
got into working order I am unable to explain, but its exploits
thus far have been singular. When once fairly in breath, it
seemed to get on very well at a rate of five to seven miles an
hour; but at the stoppages, which were numerous, the process
of re-inflation exceeded the due licence even of a Highland bag-
pipe, and, besides the usual droning and snorting of that delicious
instrument, consisted in a saltatory movement backward and
forward, as if the train had to leap a series of five-bar gates one
way and to releap them all over again the other, before getting
under weigh at its normal and regulation trot. The Mobile
and Ohio Railroad is just now choked with cotton bales; the
freight trains, one a day, are long and heavy, and the rolling
stock inadequate to the occasion; but at a time when the vital
struggle of the Southern seaports is to hold a place against the
great steam-power suction towards New York, it must surely be
worth consideration whether a thorough renewal of their existing
lines of inland traffic be not paramount even to new schemes.
The Memphis and Charleston, and the Mobile and Ohio, are
equally splendid lines of communication. They are being crossed
by other lines at various points to their detriment, but their
original sweep and convenience of transit remain intact, and yet
they are languishing and, to the stockholders, unproductive
affairs. It is the part of Charleston and Mobile to consider and
be wise. The great advance of the port of Savannah is largely
to be ascribed to the ability and vigour with which the old
inland lines of Georgia have been conducted, and the judgment
with which their connections have been extended far and wide
into other States.

Meridian is a lump of a town, sprawling over sandy mounds
in a wide open bosom of the forest. The tufty foliage of the
yellow pines, covering the ridges, forms the chief ornament of
the place. But the town is growing up rapidly, and several large
brick warehouses have been recently erected on lines intended
to be developed one day into streets. A long row of stores faces
the railway, with ample space between for all manner of open-air
business. Meridian is the terminus of the Alabama and Chattanooga Railroad; and the Mobile and Ohio and the Vicksburg
and Montgomery lines also cross at this point. The construction
of the Alabama and Chattanooga, which was pushed on from

Meridian under a superintendent, while Mr. Stanton was busy urging forward the work from the other end, naturally brought a deal of labour, money, and traffic about the little town, and helped it over its early stages. The negro population is numerous, and much of the storekeeping business is conducted by sharp, active young men of Jewish aspect, who talk German-English, and make no secret of their little bill transactions on cotton liens at the rate of 40 per cent. per annum. These people are sent down by firms in New York and other large towns to sell goods at a profit of 100 to 200 per cent. to the more impoverished class of planters, and to advance money on cotton at the approach of the picking season at as much interest as they can extort. One firm in New York is said to make half a million of dollars in this lucrative business per annum, after giving, it may be supposed, a fair share of the spoils to the Hebrew agents, who live on the spot, and bear the heat and burden of the day. About 100,000 bales of cotton are annually passed on from this point, where so many railways meet. The Alabama and Chattanooga, though not completed and opened to through traffic, is working as far into the Alabama interior as Eutaw, and passes at this end through Sumpter and Green counties, and other rich cotton districts of the Alabama "prairie" land.

I went out several miles with the superintendent of the Alabama and Chattanooga Company here to see mineral traces supposed to be coal, and found them to be thin chips of lignite exposed by a little superficial digging across the bed of a rill trickling down a depression betwixt the deep pine-clad ravines which characterize this locality. Having fallen on the well-developed seams of coal and iron at the northern end of the Alabama and Chattanooga Railroad, I have felt some curiosity in marking the characteristics of the country at its southern extremity; but though this line passes direct through well-known mineral fields of Alabama over a large portion of its course, yet the aspect of the country down here in Mississippi differs entirely from the neighbourhood of Lookout Mountain, and the northern interior of the intervening State. The highest elevations are simply heaps of sand, clay, and drift. The ravines are of immense depth, and I have not been at the bottom of the lowest of them ; but, in the beds of the creeks we had to cross, no trace of rock was to be seen, and the lazy waters moved over the same sandy slime as was found on the tops of the highest mounds. As one nears the Gulf the rocky strata seem to lie deep out of sight ; and lignite and shaly deposits, while highly interesting in a scientific point of view, as showing in embryo how the great coal-beds were formed, do not promise much commercial result. In this same district copperas has been found, and was wrought to some extent for dyeing purposes during the war.

One of the Meridian newspapers has announced that the Federal Government has sent detective officers into Mississippi to watch the proceedings of the "Ku-Klux-Klan," and en-deavour to bring some of its members to justice. A secret organization under this name spread with amazing rapidity over the South soon after the close of the war, and for some time, by moving in considerable bodies at night, in a peculiar costume, and executing a "wild justice," spread alarm both among Federal soldiers and negroes. For a time the "Ku-Klux" enjoyed the respect, if not the confidence, of the "conquered population;" but nearly all trace of this mysterious league has now happily disappeared from the country, or, where still extant in any form, its *rôle* has been taken up by mere marauders, betwixt whom and the white people there is no manner of sym-pathy. One day lately three rough men sat round the stove of a lager-beer saloon in one of the towns of East Tennessee. By and by a man came in dressed in fine broadcloth, and with an air of great briskness about him. He was a member of the legal profession, and his talk with the three rough men, while most familiar and cordial, was all about the extent to which, in certain crises, he would serve a client. It appeared that the legal gentleman was prepared to be very loyal in getting off a thief, and his views of professional honour gave general satisfac-tion. "But what is the Ku-Klux-Klan?" asked one of the trio. "The Ku-Klux," said the man of law, "are the three K's of Greece," from which profound explanation the inquirer did not seem to derive much edification, and he asked again, "What are they? who are they?" The lawyer, dropping his voice into a whisper, replied, "They are Confederate soldiers killed in the war who cannot rest in their graves!" The secret society was, in point of fact, a kind of ghost of the Confederate armies. Its uniform, made of black calico, was called a "shroud." The stuff was sent round to private houses with a request that it should be made into a garment, and fair fingers sewed it up and had it ready for the secret messenger when he returned and gave his tap at the door. The women and young girls had faith in the honour of the "klan," and on its will and ability to protect them. The "Ku-Klux," when out on their missions, also wore a long tapering hat; and a black veil over the face completed their dis-guise. The secret of the membership was kept with remarkable fidelity. In no instance, I believe, has a member of the "Ku-Klux" been successfully arraigned or punished, though their acts often flew in the face of the "reconstructed authorities," and were not in any sense legal. When they had a long ride at night, they made requisitions for horses at the farmhouses, and the horses were often supplied under a prevailing feeling of assurance that they would be returned on a night following without injury. If a company of Federal soldiers stationed in a small town vapoured as to what they would do with the " Ku-Klux," the men in shrouds paraded in the evening before the guard-house in numbers so overwhelming as at once reduced the little garrison to silence. The overt acts of the " Ku-Klux" consisted for the most part of the disarming of dangerous negroes, the infliction of " lynch-law " on notorious offenders, and, above all, in the creation of one feeling of terror as a counterpoise to another. The white people in the South at the close of the war were alarmed, not so much by the threatened confiscation of their property by the Federal Government, as by the smaller but more present dangers of life and property, virtue and honour, arising from the social anarchy around them. The negroes, after the Confederate surrender, were disorderly. Many of them would not settle down to labour on any terms, but roamed about with arms in their hands and hunger in their bellies; and the governing power, with the usual blind determination of a victorious party, was thinking only all the while of every device of suffrage and reconstruction by which " the freedmen " might be strengthened, and made, under Northern dictation, the ruling power in the country. Agitators of the loosest fibre came down among the towns and plantations, and, organizing a Union league, held midnight meetings with the negroes in the woods, and went about uttering sentiments which, to say the least, in all the circumstances were anti-social and destructive. Crimes and outrages increased. The law, which must be always more or less weak in all thinly populated countries, was all but powerless; and the new Governments in the South, supposing them to have been most willing, were certainly unable to repress disorder, or to spread a general sense of security throughout the community. A real terror reigned for a time among the white people; and in this situation the " Ku-Klux" started into being. It was one of those secret organizations which spring up in disordered states of society, when the bonds of law and government are all but dissolved, and when no confidence is felt in the regular public administration of justice. But the power with which the " Ku-Klux" moved in many parts of the South, the knowledge it displayed of all that was going on, the fidelity with which its secret was kept, and the complacency with which it was regarded by the general community, gave this mysterious body a prominence and importance seldom attained by such illegal and deplorable associations. Nearly every respectable man in the Southern States was not only disfranchised, but under fear of arrest or confiscation; the old foundations of authority were utterly razed before any new ones had yet been laid, and in the dark and benighted interval the remains of the Confederate armies—swept, after a long and heroic day of fair fight, from the field—flitted before the eyes of the people in this weird and midnight shape of a "Ku-Klux-Klan." The negroes were "scared" by the apparition, and many of the "carpet-bag" agitators were run out of the country. Warnings were given, visitations were made in force, criminals taken in *flagrante delicto* were torn out of the hands of the sheriff and shot or maimed, and more moderate punishments were inflicted which, whether deserved or not, could only be considered outrages. One reign of terror began to rise out of another. But six years of peace have greatly changed all that state of things. The negroes are quiet and orderly, and comparatively industrious; and the white people, more sure of their position under the Federal laws of reconstruction, are beginning to resume their right of voting, and of controlling the administration of affairs through the ordinary legal channels. Scarcely a trace of the original "Ku-Klux" organization remains, or, if it still exists, it is very seldom brought into action. With the exception of Robison's county in North Carolina, where the midnight raiders are known by name and character to be a mere band of ruffians without any political complexion, crimes and acts of violence in the South have this winter been few and far between— certainly not more numerous than in any very large northern or European city.[1] In this State of Mississippi there has been an ordinary crop of murders arising out of private quarrels, and in one or two instances criminals have been rescued out of the too feeble hands of the sheriff. But the only cases of outrage passing under my observation, in which a trace of "Ku-Klux" origin is recognizable, are not more than two or three in number. When crossing Williamson's Creek, on my way to Macon in Georgia, the place was under much excitement on account of a barbarous murder, or rather murders, perpetrated a few nights before. A band of men, said to be in "Ku-Klux" mask, came to the store of Allan Creich, a grocer, when the inmates were in bed, and, on being answered by the shopman, said it was Creich himself they wanted. Creich at length came down, and was immediately seized, dragged some distance, despatched, and thrown into the creek, where his body was found. The assassins then proceeded to the house of Allan's brother, where they found only the man's wife and a little boy or girl. The wife declared that her husband was not in the house, but refused to say where he was. The inquisitors then interrogated the child, who was finally induced to tell them where the father was staying the day before. They found him in the house named, where he had been drinking, and forthwith dealt with him as they had dealt with his brother Allan.

---

[1] Since this was written, very serious disturbances have occurred in a county of South Carolina, the excited political feeling in which State, and its causes, I have indicated in passing.

Such were the accounts given of this atrocious transaction. It appears that Allan had long been blamed for resetting goods and produce stolen by the negroes, and had been often warned to desist without avail. The stealings of the negroes are a subject of prevailing and almost wild complaint in many parts of the South; and soon after the war some of the Radical-Negro Legislatures passed laws prohibiting the purchase of produce by storemen after dark. The Legislature of Georgia had, in its last session, repealed this enactment, believing probably that the necessity for it had passed away. About the same period a party of men in masks came to a farmhouse twenty miles from Chattanooga, where a robust negro man lived, who was in the custom of going about with a loaded gun, and saying he would shoot any white man who quarrelled with him. They waked him up in his cabin, made him deliver his gun, and broke it into pieces, but departed without doing him any bodily harm. Some nights afterwards a more numerous body came to the same farmhouse and demanded horses. The farmer, a Pennsylvania man, was not at home; his wife refused in his absence to comply with the order; and through the intervention of a guest in the house, the tall-hatted men in shrouds were induced to go away, somewhat dissatisfied and undecided. These are the only "Ku-Klux" traces I have found. The institution is dying fast, if not already dead; but it is the deep vice of all such secret leagues to survive, in a more degenerate form, the circumstances which could give even a colourable justification to their existence, and to pass finally into the hands of utter scoundrels, with no good motive, and with foul passions of revenge, or plunder, or lust of dread and mysterious power alone in their hearts. There is a tendency in the Northern press to make too much of "Southern crimes and outrages," and by exaggeration and perversion to keep alive the very disloyalty they denounce. It would be matter of deep regret were the Federal Government, by any new schemes of repression or reconstruction, to rekindle distrusts and animosities which are rapidly dying out. The great object is to secure a more efficient administration of justice, without respect to party or colour. The popular and partisan election of Judges, more especially in the present state of Election Law in the South, is a gross abuse, and tends more than anything else to countenance and support every form of taking the law into their own hands, much too prevalent among the people in most parts of the United States.

A Doctor—whether of laws, medicine, or divinity, I have not learned—has made himself famous in the columns of the Republican organ here by agreeing to become the teacher of one of the negro schools. It may be inferred from the extravagance of the praise bestowed on the Doctor, that the social position of a schoolmaster of the blacks is not high. It may be necessary, indeed, to train negro teachers, of whom there are yet only a very few—all the aspiring coloured men having become Senators and Representatives—ere the education of the masses of negro children can be overtaken. This is one of the many difficulties of the school question in this country. There is a greater demand for teachers of white schools than can be supplied, and the office of public schoolmaster has sometimes to be filled by any one who offers. Yet fairly liberal salaries are given.

CHAPTER XXIII.

From Meridian to Eutaw.—Mr. Stanton's failure to pay the Interest due on the A. and C. Bonds.—The Alabama " Prairie " Land.—Bridge over the Tombigbee.—Tuscaloosa.—Decline of Learning in the University.— River System of Alabama.—The Warrior and Cahawba Coal and Iron Fields.—The Chinese on the Railway Works.

[EUTAW, ALA.—*Jan.* 14—15.]

EUTAW is a considerable way into the interior of Alabama, approaching, as I have done, from the south-west border at Meridian, on the line of what is called the "Alabama and Chattanooga," or North-East and South-West Alabama Railroad. It is some thirty miles or more from Tuscaloosa, the former capital of the State, where the mineral and agricultural resources of Alabama have a common point of meeting, and where " laws and learning," following "wealth and commerce," at one time had their seat. The earthwork of the road has been completed fifteen or eighteen miles beyond this point towards Tuscaloosa; but the trains work only to Eutaw from the south-west end of the line, and to Elyton from Chattanooga in the north-east. This well-designed line is thus, at present date, an unfinished road. But by cars which push ahead from Elyton on one side and Eutaw on the other with railway material, and stages to Tuscaloosa that run twice or thrice a week, one can attain some knowledge of the deeply interesting country betwixt these points. There was much talk along the line as I passed as to the consequences of the failure of Mr. Stanton, the maker of the road, to pay the January interest due on his State-endorsed bonds, and what the new Governor and Legislature of the State would do in a matter which for the first time threatened to tarnish the spotless credit of Alabama.[1]

---

[1] The Legislature held an adjourned session at Montgomery in the end of January, and instituted a full inquiry into the Alabama and Chattanooga Railway bonds, the result of which was that there had been an over-issue of bonds to Stanton and Company, and that, in particular, the previous Governor and Legislature, when State endorsation had already exhausted or surpassed its legal limits, had issued two millions of direct State bonds to the company to enable them to complete the undertaking. These disclosures

The day is warm, almost hot towards noon, and the motion of
the train from Meridian is an agreeable fan as it passes through
a good agricultural country of mounds and hollows and natural
drainage, where, along the watercourses, the Alabama canebrake,
famed in negro song, springs in some luxuriance, and is crunched
at all seasons of the year with greedy zest by mules and other
"bestial" of the farms. The railway passengers are not numerous,
and some have to pay five or six dollars for stage conveyance
from Eutaw to Tuscaloosa. At Livingston, a considerable town
half-way between Meridian and Eutaw, we get on the edge of
the Alabama "prairie" land; and at Eutaw—a respectable little
place, spreading over a rising ground nicely embowered under
rows of trees, giving shade to many private residences and streets
of stores, and what seem hotels or boarding-houses, where outside
not a few blood horses are "hitched up"—the "prairie" land is
all around. The Alabama prairies extend across nearly the whole
breadth of the State from east to west, and are of varying widths
north and south of 60 to 100 miles, forming, with the bottoms
along the rivers, the richest agricultural region of Alabama.
They are of the same character and structure as the prairie-land
of Mississippi, of which they seem a lateral extension, but
spread out in much larger compass. The soil is deep and fertile,
and rests on beds of rotten limestone, which afford it elements
of perpetual renewal. The railway cuttings reveal the limestone,
white as chalk, up to near the surface. The rock throws off a white
powder under the slightest pressure of one's finger. The Tombigbee,
one of the many navigable rivers of Alabama, is here crossed by
a high wooden triangle bridge, and, as the train suddenly sweeps
along it, the scene draws forth exclamations in which delight is
mingled with surprise. The limestone cliffs on one bank rise 60 to

excited a great deal of public indignation, and for a few days the financial
integrity of Alabama seemed to be passing through a severe ordeal. The
resolution come to by the House of Representatives, after various animated
debates, was that the Governor be authorized to make provision, either by
temporary loan or unappropriated money in the treasury, for the payment of
the interest due on all bonds loaned or endorsed to the A. and C. Railroad
Company, proved to be in the hands of *bonâ fide* purchasers on the 1st of
January last, and to proceed to recover in form of law from the defaulting
company; and the interest accordingly, by arrangement of the Governor, was
paid in New York during the first week in April. Mr. Stanton has since
been completing the road. The abuse of State credit, and the imposition on
the financial world practised in this instance—an abuse and imposition
rendered all the more flagrant by a letter that has appeared from the pen of
ex-Governor Smith, arguing strongly that the bonds signed and sealed by
himself are illegal, and blaming the Legislature and the Governor for paying
the interest on them—have received an effectual check, and the railway
liabilities of Alabama will be kept in future to the limit strictly prescribed to
them by law. The total obligation of the State, when the various railway
projects to which State endorsation is pledged are completed, will amount,
I believe, to about 20,000,000 dollars.

80 feet above the bed of the river, and are carved by the action of the waters with almost sculptural art. Columns resting on chiselled pedestals, with ornamental capitals, and long lines of moulded cornicing over massive walls planed and coursed into regular blocks, are seen along the cliffy bank, as if fairy hands had, with wondrous cunning, erected temples of whitest marble in honour of all the goddesses of the river. The railway, after crossing the bridge, passes, on the other and lower bank, along a trestle 3,800 feet in length, and gets down again among the farms and plantations. Bales of cotton are lying on the bluff along the river-side, waiting for the steamboats; but the river, after the long dry fall, and a winter in which there has been a spell of frost, but hitherto little rain, is unusually low. The surface of the deep soil is not a dead level, but slightly swelling, and is free of swamp or other obstruction to uniform cultivation. Yet the watercourses are sluggish ditches, and at the farmhouses there are large bucket wells, dug down a great depth through the soft limestone to the springs. Slavery was dense in this prairie region in the time before the war, and now there is a great scarcity of free negro labour. A spirit of roving, and the demand for labour on the railways, have carried away the blacks in thousands. The planters have been able to grow but small patches of corn and cotton on their teeming lands. Hundreds of acres on every plantation of rich arable soil are lying idle, and enjoying a long fallow, which will probably make them richer and fatter still, against the time when they may again be brought into use. Yet this prairie land cannot rest, but must always be doing something. When the hand of man ceases to till and dress it, the strong and untamed soil begins to work and wanton in its own way, and is now sending up over large tracts a wild herbage, and, where ditches and watercourses have not been kept clear as formerly, displays a tendency to develop little germs of swamp. So that over wide areas of open land, which one can readily picture a garden full of wealth and people, an aspect of wildness and solitariness reigns.

Tuscaloosa, with its pretty Indian name, so much finer and sweeter than the "Jonesboro's" and "Smithvilles" of a more prosaic race, is as beautiful and spirited a country-town as one could hope to see anywhere. There is a style about it that is marvellous, when one considers how long it has been not only decapitalized, but shut out from railway communication, another word for "the world." Tuscaloosa is the seat of the University of Alabama, where upwards of a hundred students, the flower of the State, were wont to spend or misspend, as the case might be, their golden hours. But the professors, at the close of the war, were put under the ban of political proscription like all other highnesses in the South, and new men of inferior attainments

were set down in their chairs. The consequence is that Alabama
has still a University, with buildings and libraries, and professors,
and expenditure, but no students; and one wanders about this
beautiful arboury, asking, "Where is the fruit ?" The wise men
of the North and East attribute this lack of fruit to the deep
and inveterate disloyalty of the South, forgetting that while
"one man may lead a horse to water a hundred cannot compel
him to drink," and that three-fourths of the disloyalty in the
South is the result of a too prolonged course of political injustice.
This is a well-worn truism of the Old World, which the American
people will probably find out much sooner than it was found out
elsewhere. At Tuscaloosa, the Black Warrior River passes from
a fall, over its long upper course, of five feet in the mile, to a
descent of five inches in the mile through prairie land, and into
confluence with other great rivers which search out an ever-
deepening and concentrated course towards the Gulf. The river
system of Alabama forms a subject of study and interest in
itself. The Tennessee, diverted at Gunter's Landing, in the north-
east of the State, from its southward course by the "millstone
grit" and carboniferous strata which the force of the subsiding
waters would appear to have been unable to scoop out as at
Chattanooga and down the great valley betwixt the Lookout and
the Raccoon range of hills, flows westward over the softer sandstone and cretaceous rocks along the northern border of the State,
till it pours its great volume of waters with the Ohio into the
Mississippi. The low range of hills skirting on the south this
westward valley of the Tennessee forms a new watershed, from
which all the rivers of Alabama flow southward to the Gulf of
Mexico, and converge till they find a common outlet into that
Mediterranean of the New World. Within a few miles of the
Tennessee the Warrior begins to gather from numerous forks its
portly stream, till at Tuscaloosa, hundreds of miles from the
Gulf, it becomes a deep and navigable river. Farther west along
the Mississippi line the Tombigbee emerges into importance, and
is navigable by heavy-laden river-boats a long way above the
railway bridge betwixt Livingston and Eutaw. On the north-
eastern border of the State the Coosa comes down from its head-
waters in the hills of Upper Georgia, and is freely navigable from
Rome in the latter State to Greenport, fifty miles south from the
Tennessee at Gunter's Landing, where, amidst the hard material
of the mineral region of Alabama, that turned the greater river
westward, it takes a southward course over 150 miles of rapids
and other forms of navigable obstruction to its confluence with
the Tallapoosa, near Wetumpka, a town some twenty miles or
more above Montgomery, the Alabama capital, where it becomes
freely navigable again, flowing through rich agricultural lands
amidst deep banks of sandy clay, which, in its winding course,

it has moulded at various levels into lines of almost architectural exactness. The Cahawba River, in the middle territory
betwixt the Warrior and the Coosa, drains a distinct mineral
basin of its own. But all these rivers flow, south-eastward
on the one hand and south-westward on the other, through
mineral lands, prairie lands, and alluvial bottoms, to form what
is called *par excellence* the Alabama River, a great navigable
channel passing through the southern division of the State,
and with new tributaries swelling successively into Mobile River
and Mobile Bay, till they become one with the Gulf itself,
sweeping round the Mexican and Texan shore and the Western
Indies, and so mingling

> "With a' the pride that loads the tide,
> And crosses o'er the sultry line."

The river system of Alabama is thus singularly connected
and harmonized in all its wide-spread parts; and, with the exception of the thirty miles betwixt the Tennessee at Gunter's
Landing and the Coosa at Gadsden, forms in reality a complete
inland water communication extending far beyond the territory
of Alabama, and converging over vast regions towards a common
oceanic outlet. Two-thirds of the State of Alabama are traversed
by navigable rivers, that are not only parts of a whole within the
State itself, but by natural and easily opened connections might
be made to extend their power of transport far northward east and
west. A small fraction of the money spent to good effect for navigation purposes alone on twenty miles of the Clyde in Scotland,
and a still smaller fraction of the efforts in Pennsylvania to
bring coal and iron together, would have sufficed to open up all
the copious resources, mineral and agricultural, of this richly
endowed State, without the modern invention of railroads. But
the railway age is now upon the world here as elsewhere, and
great lines, two or three hundred miles in length, are being made
through the basins of the Coosa, the Cahawba, and the Warrior,
with supreme contempt of water communication; so that any
one may place himself in the cars at Euston Square in London,
and be duly delivered, if he has nothing else to do by the way,
at the foot of any of the numerous coal and iron mountains of
Alabama in three weeks, a few hours less or more. Tuscaloosa is
in the Warrior coal-field, and has been mining coal in its own
fashion for half a century. The railway is now coming to it, not
under the most auspicious financial circumstances, but it is there
within a few miles, and will probably modify in a few years, as
in other sections of the mineral region of Alabama where the
iron horse is pacing, the whole aspect of affairs. The Warrior
coal-field, extending from this neighbourhood to the north-
eastern corner of Alabama, between Lookout Mountain and the

M

Tennessee River, covers an area of 3,000 square miles. Over this wide district coal seams one to three feet thick abound. There are twenty-five localities in the basin of the Warrior where the coal crops out, and has been more or less imperfectly mined and made merchantable. They are scooping it out from the hill-sides, where it is deposited in horizontal beds of unknown breadth, gathering it on the edges of the roads, and diving for it, by a curious process, in the beds of the Warrior and its forks; and the accumulating material brought into Tuscaloosa in waggons is put on barges and floated down the river, and sold in Demopolis, Selma, Montgomery, and even as far as Mobile, at a price which puts the Pittsburg black diamond out of joint. It is for the most part a soft bituminous coal, but burns brightly, and can hardly be excelled for the generation of heat and steam. The production of coal in Alabama, by the primitive processes pursued without either skill or capital, amounts to about 30,000 tons per annum. The Cahawba coal-field, a little farther south, and in the centre of the State, is still richer in mineral deposits than the Warrior, though of much smaller compass, having an area only of 700 square miles. Seams of coal have been found there in five or six localities three to eight feet thick, and there also beds of red hæmatite iron ore have been disclosed in surprising richness. From Bibb county, a few miles south from Tuscaloosa, to Will's Valley in De Kalb county in the north-east corner of the State, the red fossiliferous iron is found deposited in nodules in the valleys, and seams of hæmatite look out from the sides, and appear to permeate the interior area, of the hilly ranges. The seams of hæmatite are at some points seven to fifteen feet in thickness. Over at Elyton, beyond the present gap in the railway, the Red Mountain, a long range of hill rising betwixt the basins of the Warrior and the Cahawba, and extending north-eastward till it seems to pass into parallel line with the Lookout range culminating in the great peak at Chattanooga, is charged with thick beds of coal and iron, and has long attracted eager attention as the backbone, so to speak, of the mineral wealth of Alabama, loosely scattered over 4,000 square miles of territory. Many furnaces had been erected along this coal and iron district before the war, and various ironworks, such as the Briardale and the Shelby, had attained considerable eminence when the great armed struggle broke out and threw every work of industry and useful enterprise into difficulty and confusion. Two or three new companies, with capitals of a million dollars each, had just been formed, had bought up mineral lands, and commenced operations, when the war came and reduced them to a state of collapse. The Confederate Government stepped forward, and in some cases, where there were working powers and appliances, bought up the property, or gave financial assistance. The ore at Briarfield, in Bibb county, was converted by a hot-blast furnace into pig, transported to Selma, and there cast into heavy rifled guns. But when the war languished on the Southern side, raiding wings of the Federal host forced their way even here into the mineral heart of Alabama, where, though slave labour had never penetrated, free white labour was beginning to raise its head, and blew up the iron furnaces and devastated the ironworks. Northern capitalists have since the war been attempting to repair this ruin with varying success and failure, but the furnaces for the most part remain extinguished, and ruin still spreads its sable wing over great and promising works, the resumption of which, with the railway facilities now extended to them, can only be a question of time.

Who should be here even now, in untrodden valleys where the negro has scarce shown his face, and where the white man, conscious all the while of the riches within easy grasp, trembles in his gait, and the steam-engine seems in fiery fury to have rushed ahead of all other elements of civilization, but our old and classic "citizens of the world," the Chinese. A band of Chinese labourers, 600 to 700 strong, drawn from California and the Pacific Railway, have been employed on this Alabama and Chattanooga road from an early period of its construction. They are lodged in tents at present over on the Elyton side, and are doing the earthwork *pari passu* with the negro, who is not so particular in the matter of tents, and is much more easily moved from one site to another. Anything in the shape of a sleeping-place satisfies the negro, and, if put to it, he will take the shadow of a bush or tree for a few nights, and build up his square box of frames without windows by degrees. The Chinée, who struts even here with a celestial sort of air, must have his tent all nicely fixed up and provided for him. The Chinese navvies are paid 15 dollars gold a month with rations, and the negroes 1·75 dollars a day without rations. The terms, as thus arranged, are considered pretty equal ; but as the rations of the Chinaman are not extremely expensive, save in the article of tea burdened with duty, the equality of Chinese and Negro wages can only be accounted for by the practical superiority of Negro to Chinese labour. The Chinese came in on this line of railway at Meridian, the southern end, and did not comport themselves to the approval of the superintendent. Their rations were in money-cost 75 cents a day. Their work done in "grading," or earthwork, cost the company 97 cents a yard, when the same labour could have been contracted for at 35 cents a yard. The superintendent at Meridian would not bear it, and the whole band of Chinese were transferred to the Chattanooga end of the works. The testimony borne there by the chief authorities was that the Chinese had not done so well as was expected, that they were not so capable of labour as the Negro, but that their hands were hardening, and they were now on the whole giving satisfaction. As regards the alleged saving and economical habits of the Chinese, it seems certain that on monthly pay-days at Meridian they spent their fifteen dollars in whisky, chickens, and whatever they could buy in the stores, as freely as any other spendthrifts. The Chinese are inveterate gamblers, and Sundays are spent about the railway cuttings in elaborate efforts of the Celestials to overreach the Infernals at cards or dominoes ; but the Negro, also an adept in play, is not supposed to lose much in these encounters.

CHAPTER XXIV.

The Vicksburg and Montgomery Railway.—Demopolis.—Despair of the Planters for Labour.—Negro Women.—Selma—its Cotton Mart.—Reform of the Municipality.—Claims of the Town to be a Railway Centre.—Free School System in Alabama.—The Negroes and the School or Poll Tax.—Distribution of the School Money.—National Banking.—Patent "Cotton Transplanter."

[Selma, Ala.—*Jan.* 15–16.]

Returning down the Alabama and Chattanooga road from Eutaw to the little station called York, one gets upon the railway from Vicksburg *viâ* Meridian to Montgomery, part of a great line to be carried to Brunswick in Georgia, the Atlantic seaport nearest the Mississippi. Every strategic point in railway communication is searched out in all this Southern country with a keenness seldom equalled. The old lines may be tolerably serviceable, and may not have traffic more than to make them moderately prosperous; but these considerations do not damp the ardour with which new lines are devised, if two or three hundred miles of distance are to be saved to the Atlantic seaboard, and new and fertile tracts to be opened up by the way. The point of departure may be Vicksburg, a small place rising into commercial importance on the Mississippi, and the point of arrival Brunswick, trying to become a seaport, one hundred and thirty miles south of Savannah, because it has three feet or four feet deeper water than any port, save perhaps Norfolk, on the Atlantic coast; but all this poverty of present resource is scarcely deemed a rational impediment, and though the difficulty of raising the necessary loans is great, and the difficulty of obtaining a respectable subscription of capital is greater, yet the idea of an "air-line" as direct as birds can fly seizes on the general mind, and, gathering up all the interests at either end, and piecing itself on to existing roads with the rarest ingenuity, gets itself lobbyrolled through the Legislature into a legal shape, and forthwith becomes more or less an accomplished fact. In a few years hence every salient point on the Mississippi will be connected by direct "air-lines" with the Atlantic seaboard, and the great draught by steam and capital to New York of late years, which would speedily become suffocating to the American continent, will be gradually modified and counteracted by railway enterprise, and by the desire of British and Continental manufacturers, in the natural course of commerce, to get into the most immediate relation with the producers of their raw material. On any narrower hypothesis the present railway making in the South would seem quite unjustifiable. But the interior and local interest of the new railway projects at the same time is very manifest. The great difficulty of the United States is country roads, and the want of stone and rock. The constant tendency to drop into ruts and puddles both wide and deep wherever wheeled vehicles can pretend to go, is observable from the suburbs of Philadelphia to this point. It is only by the iron track, liberally distributed, that the produce of the Southern States can hope to get to market; and over-numerous as the great lines of communication, made and projected, seem to be, they all pass through wide interior regions of country, thinly peopled indeed, but settled and in working order, and capable of much development.

The railroad from York to Selma passes through Sumpter, Marengo, Perry, and Dallas counties, fertile tracts, yielding heavy crops of cotton on a soil that is inexhaustible. At Demopolis, a pretty town founded by French refugees, and where the railway again crosses the Tombigbee after its confluence with the Warrior, the steep limestone cliffs seem even whiter and finer than near Eutaw. The chalky substance when touched whitens one's fingers, and a penknife cuts it as easily as if it were a piece of cheese. This natural "fertilizer" underlies the whole middle or "prairie" territory of Alabama from east to west, and enriches, mellows, and invigorates the deep upper soil of its own accord. But a great desolation has passed over much of these lands, which the vitality of free labour can but slowly efface; and external marks of wealth, and even comfort, have in many places for the present all but disappeared. Many of the planters have deserted farming in despair, and taken up their abode in the small towns, where they live on the profits of some house property, or of some chopping business of insurance or merchandise. Tough and weather-worn men, who adhere to their posts in the field, come riding through the depôts inquiring eagerly for hands to come and pick their stands of cotton, or drive their teams with the bales already made. A crowd of negroes—mostly girls and young women, not unconscious of certain charms, set off with various brass ornaments and glass beads—are always seen about the railway stations, looking up and down, wondering, and toying out their long holiday. Other negro women, modestly and tidily dressed, come in with little baskets of eggs, and chaffer greedily for the 30 cents per dozen.

The remark is often heard, that the old negroes, who retain some of the industrial discipline and habit of slavery times, are the only remaining life of the cotton-fields; and that when they are gone the rising generation will not be worth a cent for any useful purpose of labour.

Selma is a town of six to seven thousand inhabitants, and looks as large as if it had as many more. It is an extensive cotton mart. Upwards of 50,000 bales have already been received this season, and the merchants and brokers expect to draw 25,000 more—being within 15,000 bales of the highest receipts before the war. The railway must be helping Selma, for the neighbouring plantations have not recovered in this proportion. There are many fine buildings, several large yards for storing cotton, and two or three broad streets of shops and warerooms where most necessaries and many articles of luxury may be purchased. Two-thirds of the men of business are Germans, many of them of Hebrew extraction. The Jews have settled largely in Southern Alabama, and what with negroes and coloured people, and German and Jewish names, there is a foreign air about Selma. The weather is also, even at this period of the year, sometimes hot and sultry, as if one were approaching sources of perennial fire, which even torrents of rain neither quench nor cool. There is neither hill nor sea near the town, but the Alabama River winds past it in rather beautiful curves under deep banks of reddish sand, and steamboats call twice or thrice a week and carry down considerable cargoes of cotton to Mobile. The town has slipped for commercial purposes over the edge of the "prairie" and its underlying beds of chalk, on to the expanse of clayey sand, that billows over the southern section of the State; and it suffers some inconveniences in consequence. The negroes in Selma outnumber the whites; but though every man, however black or white, who loafs about the town for three or four months, has a vote, the Democrats, who are here the white and conservative portion of the population, gained by the recent elections the upper hand in the municipality, showing that the negro vote need not always be on one side. The new party in power have re-organized the police force, which consists of fifteen men, four of whom are retained negroes, because they are deemed efficient constables worthy of place and trust. The pretension of the Republicans and Radicals that the negroes can only be safe under their supremacy is gradually crumbling down in the South. There is much congratulation among the business people in Selma on the change of administration. The thieves and burglars are believed to have run away from the town when the Democrats obtained the direction of affairs, and the streets have not seemed so clean for a long time as since the new broom has begun to sweep.

Selma is struggling hard to become, and has become to some extent, an important inland railway centre. One does not readily see how, within so short a distance of the capital of the State, a prominent position of this kind can be attained; for, being on the same line east and west as Montgomery, the town is simply asserting an advantage which Montgomery possesses equally, and the facilities of any new project it may devise Montgomery may more or less equally share. But Selma is farther to the west than Montgomery, and the diagonal lines from north-east to south-west, and south-east to north-west, strike Selma as a point of vantage. Thus a railroad already in operation—"the Alabama and Tennessee" of the maps—passes from Selma through a large space of the mineral land of Alabama to Rome and Dalton in Upper Georgia, and thence goes into connection with the "Virginia and Tennessee," or Lynchburg and Washington route north. This completed scheme, of course, involves a direct extension from Selma to New Orleans, the greatest of all the Southern seaports, and the only worthy rival in the south-west of New York in the north-east. Selma, by another line of road, is being connected *vid* Marion and Okolona with Memphis, in order that Memphis, with its great present and future power of cotton seeking the directest route to the manufacturer, may get direct on the road eastward to Brunswick in Georgia, the nearest "air-line" Atlantic seaport. This road is promoted with much energy under the presidentship of General Forrest, and great efforts are being made to obtain liberal subscriptions in the various counties through which it passes. The "Selma and Gulf" road, another project, is designed to connect Selma direct with Pensacola, the chief timber harbour of Florida. These works are giving Selma an independent place in the railway system, and, having a large and rich country of its own, it will probably become a considerable seat of trade and population in the new era of prosperity calculated upon in Alabama. If the most ample means of communication can do anything to develop great natural riches, there should be a brighter future for this State than probably any other in the Union. The railways made and being made in Alabama open up and intersect the country in every direction. The Memphis and Charleston road sweeps the whole valley of the Tennessee along the northern frontier of the State. The Alabama and Chattanooga passes right across the interior, in the slanting line of the mineral valleys, from the north-east corner to about the middle of the western border line. The South and North goes up from Montgomery, through the same mineral districts as the Alabama and Chattanooga, which it crosses near Elyton, in the Red Mountain country, to Decatur on the Memphis and Charleston, and the Nashville and Tennessee lines. From Montgomery the same

South and North route is prolonged by the old line from the capital to Mobile, and by a new road recently opened for traffic is carried onward from Mobile to New Orleans. The Montgomery and Eufala, the Montgomery and West Point, the Selma and Dalton, spread out from the interior eastward to distant points along the frontier of Georgia, and form connection with all the Georgian railways ; while westward, the Montgomery, Meridian, and Vicksburg, the Mobile and Ohio, the Selma, Marion, and Memphis, penetrate by diverse routes the Mississippi border, and carry the means of communication to the levees of the great river, and to the northern and north-western roads through Kentucky and Ohio. A scheme, projected some years ago, to extend the New Orleans and Jackson Railroad to Decatur, in North Alabama, would traverse the only part of the State still shut out from the iron network; and in the northeastern counties, more especially Sanford and Marion, would traverse mineral districts where the abundance of iron ore is probably as marked as in any other part of Alabama. This State is thus in rapid progress of being thoroughly opened up in all parts, and as amply provided, when not only its railways but its almost unique river system are taken into account, with the means of transit as any country could hope to be, or as any country in the world probably is. It is surprising to see so many great public works pushed forward simultaneously where so comparatively little industry and commerce have yet been developed to support them, and their operation may be attended with some financial trouble ; but they are too far advanced to be arrested by timid considerations now, and when completed and opened to traffic they will afford an opportunity of drawing forth the mineral treasures of Alabama which have long been sought in vain.

The administration of the free school system is the subject of loud exclamations in Selma, as in many other parts of Alabama. At the close of the present fiscal year the finances of the town will show a deficit of 40,000 dollars, and the school expenditure gets the blame of most of it. There was a common school system, free to all white children in the South before the war, but the addition of the negro children has necessarily demanded more school buildings, more teachers, larger staffs of administrators, and a much larger expenditure of every kind. The difficulty of finding qualified teachers, more especially for negro schools, the doubt whether any good is being done commensurate with the expenditure of money, and the lingering unbelief of slavery times as to the capacity of the negro for literary instruction, combine with the impatience of taxation to render the free school system less popular than one would desire to find it. The system of administration seems also very faulty, if not corrupt. The late State Superintendent of Education embezzled or misappropriated the funds; and a county superintendent in North Alabama, following so good an example, ran away with several thousand dollars entrusted to him for the payment of the teachers. The schools in that county are being carried on in the interim on fees prepaid by the parents, but many of the children have left off attendance. The school assessment is also partially levied as well as singularly distributed. A poll-tax payable by every male inhabitant over twenty-one and under forty-five years of age, together with some small duties on insurance premiums, have been set apart for the support of the free schools as a supplement to old school funds and trust endowments which appear to have been mismanaged, but for the annual interest of which the State continues religiously to charge itself. The poll-tax, as assessed on the various counties, amounted for the past year to 162,819 dollars, the duties on insurance premiums to 13,327 dollars—in all, 176,146 dollars. But the total collection of this special assessment for schools is not expected to be more than, if as much as, 100,000 dollars. Nearly half the poll-tax is uncollected. The money thus levied in the counties is sent into the State Treasury, and thence remitted to all the counties in sums proportioned to the number of children of school age in each; so that defaulting counties, and counties that have many children of school age but do not teach them, get largely of funds which they do not contribute, and very probably abuse and squander; while counties that most honour the tax-collector get greatly less than they pay, and than they need and wish to apply to school purposes. The new Government of Alabama will doubtless proceed without delay to correct abuses and anomalies which are subjecting the cause of education to an unnecessary strain of public dissatisfaction. One of the most obvious means of alleviating the financial difficulty of providing at once for the education of all the negro children was to exact rigorous payment of the school tax from able-bodied negro men, whose labour is in urgent demand at high wages. The slave-holders paid taxes to the State for them as slaves, and when this fiscal resource was cut away by emancipation, it became on general grounds of finance all the more necessary that they should pay for themselves as free labourers. But when the poll-tax—the only tax to which the negro labourer is liable—was wholly devoted to the education of his own children, the obligation upon him to pay became sacred. Yet, in point of fact, the negroes cannot be got to pay this poll-tax for schools, or the collectors hitherto employed are unwilling to exact it from them. In one instance where a planter, when paying his own taxes, offered to pay the State dues of the negroes in his employment, the money was refused, because payment by substitute was a relic of the slave system, or on some equally frivolous ground, and payment has never since been asked of the coloured people in question in any more direct form. When qualified teachers, who are scarce, have to pass a board of examiners, composed wholly or in part of negroes who may not know the alphabet themselves, the education question here, with all its solemn sanctions and ennobling associations, seems to receive the last touch of ridicule, and common sense itself is struck completely dumb.

The National Banks authorized by Federal law, and enjoying the privilege of drawing the interest on their capital in Federal bonds deposited in exchange for 90 per cent. of their value in national currency—albeit a great field was opened for them by the crumpling-up of the old State Banks by the war—are not yet very numerous in the South. There is only one in Selma, having, according to an official statement just issued, a capital of 100,000 dollars; deposits, 241,000 dollars; and cash in hand, 119,327 dollars. The bank, following a rule which experience in Europe has defined as safe and prudent, has thus an unemployed reserve equal to about a third of its liabilities. There are no banking funds visible in such places as Selma adequate to the amount of trade; but the volume of business in cotton and other merchandise is transacted by credits established in New York, which are only banking in another form.

Our old friend "the patent inventor" is always turning up. I made the acquaintance of him and the celebrated " Cotton Transplanter " at night in the hotel, and on going out in the morning found him on a mound of sand exhibiting his machine in action to a crowd of negroes. The " Cotton Transplanter " consists of a little double-valved spade which is pushed by pedal force into the ground round the plant, and, closing convexly under the latter, lifts it up with as much of the earth as would fill a small flower-pot. The plant thus caught in a trap, may then be carried to a hole prepared for it elsewhere, with as little disturbance of the root as may be conceived. To amateur gardeners and lady florists this latest " Yankee notion " is as nice a little nothing as may be honestly commended, but it has no more relation to the cotton-field than a " B to a bull's foot."

CHAPTER XXV.

Progress of Trade and Population in Montgomery.—Opening of the Mineral
Districts by Railways.—Existing Ironworks.—Coal and Iron Seams in
the Cahawba Basin.—The Red Mountain—its Deposits of Hæmatite.—
Proximity of the Warrior and Cahawba Coal-fields.—Recent Survey of
Mr. Tait, F.G.S.—Analyses of Alabama Coal and Iron Ores.—Agricultural
Qualities of the Mineral Region.—Probable Geological History.—Relative
Price of Montevallo Coal and Pennsylvania Hay.

[MONTGOMERY, ALA.—*Jan.* 17-21.]

THE population of the capital of Alabama is about 10,000, being
the largest town population in the State, with the exception of
Mobile. Huntsville, in the valley of the Tennessee, ranks next
to Montgomery and Selma, in the number of inhabitants; but it
may not be surprising if—somewhere midway betwixt the
Tennessee and the " prairie " land, in the mineral region now
for the first time pierced by lines of railway, about Montevallo,
Elyton, Oxmoor, or Talladega—a populous place should arise to
throw all the interior towns of Alabama into the shade. The
capital is built on the Coosa—now, having received the waters
of the Tallapoosa, beginning to take the name of the Alabama
River—over a swelling surface of hill and dale, that gives a fine
picturesque sweep to the semi-rural avenues, shaded by the
China tree whose clustered berries are said to make the robin-
redbreasts drunk, and radiating from a central dial where the
hotels, the banking and insurance houses, and the business of
the town are gathered, and where Mr. Knock-'em-down, the popular auctioneer, round a large circular pond or fountain shows off
the paces of his mules to purchasing and other admiring negroes,
and by his switch laid across the backbone has an art, as he
rubs to sharp or flat, of making the animal strike out malignantly
from behind or pace gently forward, that seems more than
straightly human. Loud laughs burst from the dial of Montgomery, disturbing the bankers, merchants, and brokers in their
calculations, as Mr. Knock-'em-down plays his fiddle in this
fashion over the spinal marrow of the mules for sale. The
Capitol or State House, occupying a commanding eminence at
one extremity of the town, overlooks the scene, and from its
colonnade the eye wanders over a wide expanse of country, in
which breadths of " prairie " are lost to view under successive
belts of forest.

The low price of cotton at Liverpool does not much damp the business people of Montgomery, who are in good spirit, and speak only of the progress of trade and population during the last two years. Out from the central dial, along the business streets, an active country trade goes on all day long. The steamboats come to a high but sloping bluff near the warehouses and cotton yards, where the cotton bales are rolled down easily to the water-edge, and taken on board. The railway depôts are in the same vicinity, and carry off large quantities of cotton to Savannah and other seaports beyond the limits of the State. But the steamers continue to do a good amount of business from Montgomery and Selma to Mobile, at a rate of freight from a dollar to a dollar and a half a bale.

The superiority of Alabama as a cotton-growing State is well established, and so long as its "prairies" last can suffer little diminution. But that which gives unparalleled importance to this section of the South, and is at present exciting the deepest interest, is its mineral wealth. The Warrior and Cahawba coal-fields and iron beds are easily reached from Selma by the Alabama and Tennessee, and from Montgomery by the North and South, railroads. From Selma, a journey of forty or fifty miles in the cars carries one to the Briarfield Ironworks, in Bibb county, where there is a large establishment for mining and manufacturing iron. The ore is brown hæmatite, and is gathered over five or six hundred acres in sufficient quantities to keep eight furnaces going. The mineral industry of Alabama is still so entirely in its infancy that little or no attempt has been made, even in the largest operations, to work the seams of hæmatite in the hilly ridges. Enough of ore is found embedded in the low ground, and in fragments and outcroppings scattered about, to enable costly mining work to be dispensed with. Veins of bituminous coal, five and seven feet thick, are found within a short distance of the furnaces at Briarfield. A few miles farther, on the same line of railway, are the Shelby Iron-works, which, though not so extensive nor so completely re-stored from the devastation suffered in the war, command a large and easy supply of superior brown hæmatite. In the same vicinity are the Montevallo coal-fields, which are annually send-ing a considerable supply of bituminous coal into the local markets. Betwixt Briarfield and Shelby Ironworks are the Shelby lime-kilns, which first redeemed Alabama from the disgrace of importing lime from Maine, in the far North, while possessing inexhaustible supplies of the finest limestone for calcination in the world. Alabama lime is now in repute out-side the State. There is in this small district, therefore, a field of industry and wealth of the deepest interest. The railway has here brought us full on the Cahawba coal basin. The river flows through Shelby, Perry, and Dallas counties, till it joins the Alabama at Cahawba. Over a series of low hilly ridges, within a short distance north-westward, is the much larger coal and mineral field of the Black Warrior. At Centreville, in the heart of Bibb county, where the limestone projects from the banks of the river, and the older fossiliferous rocks of Alabama seem to find their southern extremity, the Cahawba coal-field may be said to terminate, though traces of the coal measures have been found in Perry county, south of Bibb. From Centreville the coal-field of the Cahawba extends north-eastward over a long anti-clinal valley to Murphreesville, upwards of a hundred miles, and spreads eastward over Shelby and Clair counties towards the Coosa river, which has a very interesting mineral development of its own, and for more than twenty years has been sending down coal and iron to Montgomery and Mobile. From Centreville to Murphreesville, along the course of the Cahawba, numerous beds of hæmatite ore have been disclosed, of varying thickness, in some places fifteen to twenty feet, and in others thinning down to one or two feet. At the lime-kilns betwixt the Shelby Ironworks and the Montevallo coal mines, the Alabama and Tennessee Railroad passes eastward to Talladega on the Coosa, where, on Talladega Creek, as well as on Cane Creek at Polkville, furnaces were in operation as long ago as 1849, and a large amount of iron has been made without really opening the seams or doing more than gathering up the superficial and fragmentary deposits of ore. But, dropping at Lime Station into the cars of the North and South Railroad from Montgomery, which there, in its direct course north to Decatur, intersects the "Alabama and Tennessee," one is brought in a few minutes to Elyton, where the greatest wonder of all appears in the Red Mountain, so called because of the beds of red hæmatite found in great thickness both on its north-western and south-eastern sides. The Red Mountain is a long range of heights traversing the eastern border of Jefferson county, and passing out north-eastward into St. Clair county, till it fades and loses its name in the Lookout range, stretching down from Chattanooga through De Kalb county in the north-eastern corner of the State. It is broken at various points by gaps and cross valleys, and is flanked by parallel ranges of lower heights, called Sand Mountains, which are in reality composed of the "millstone grit," so closely allied here with the coal measures. Murphrees Valley, at the head of the Cahawba coal-fields, opens upon it from the north; and it trends north-east towards a long tract of valley ground, through which the Alabama and Chattanooga Railroad takes its course, called after "Jones," or "Roup," or other celebrity, at various stages, till it becomes "Will's Valley," some miles of which I travelled from the Chattanooga end.

Over all this district the records of iron ore are as numerous as they are authentic, and rude furnaces appear to have been erected at every few miles, and to have bloomed for a season, and then perished, under the difficulties of communication and such seasons of stagnation as have often brought the great iron districts of England and Scotland themselves into straits. But the name of " Red Mountain " is more strictly applied to the hilly range from where it approaches Elyton, the small county town of Jefferson, and extends some twenty or thirty miles into St. Clair county. The development of hæmatite is here very rich. At Gracie's Gap, near Elyton, ironworks were established during the war, and two furnaces erected and put in blast, but they are silent now, though the iron ore is on the spot in large deposits. Eight miles farther north-east, the Irondale Works were begun in the second year of the war, and made a great deal of iron, but were burned down by the Federal troops, and have since been taken up by a Northern company, who are building a new furnace and a rolling mill and machine shops. The red hæmatite is at this point also in great quantity. The beds of hæmatite in the Red Mountain, and appearing on both sides of it, are in some parts ten to fifteen feet in thickness, though this cannot be pronounced uniform. The aspect of the country is that of mild volcanic upheaval, followed by a long course of denudation, in which the loosened materials have been swept away by the receding ocean and by the erosive action of the rivers, leaving a wavy and irregular stratification, in which the coal and iron beds are often cut and wasted, and, while traced over considerable spaces along the withstanding ridges, are deposited in fragments through the valleys, and reappear in the channels of the streams and branches. The dip of the strata at Red Mountain is southeast, and the ascent on that side is gradual ; while on the northwest the face of the ridge is more sharp and abrupt. The geological formation is much the same as at Lookout. There is the same crown of sandstone along the ridges above seams of red and brown ore, resting on beds of yellow clay, with the Silurian limestones uplifted in the valleys, and passing under the carboniferous strata and millstone grit of the hills. The sandstone and carboniferous limestone are often dyed red by oxide of iron, and strata of silicious conglomerate are met with, in which innumerable pebbles seem to have been blended into a tough and compact mass by metallic influence. I have not discovered that seams of coal have been opened on the face of the Red Mountain, immediately under or above the hæmatite, as I found on the Raccoon range near Chattanooga, but the striking peculiarity of the Red Mountain is, that it divides by a narrow strip the Warrior and Cahawba coal-fields, stretching over hundreds of square miles on either side of it, and approaching so close together that the coal measures of the two basins bound some of the narrow valleys. The Cahawba coal mines and the Southern coal mines are in operation within a few miles of the Red Mountain. A company, called "The Red Mountain Iron and Coal Company," was organized before the war, with a capital of a million dollars, and acquired a large tract of the Red and Sand Mountains and the Cahawba coal-fields. They formed a little town settlement at the base of the Red Mountain, called "Oxmoor," where the iron stratum is very rich, and proceeded to open veins of coal on their coal-field. Seventeen veins of coal have been discovered on the company's property, eight of which are two to four feet thick. But the war paralysed the operations of the company, and left it disorganized and impoverished to an extent from which it has been unable to recover, though coal continues to be produced from the out-crops in considerable quantity. This property, which remains in the hands of some of the most substantial men of Alabama and Georgia, could probably be purchased at a fourth of its cost ; or the proprietors would take an interest to that amount with any practical mining company who would bring an equal value to the development of the coal and iron. The lands of the company are about 8,000 acres in extent, all accurately defined in the Government survey. Mr. Tait, of Montgomery, a Fellow of the Geological Society of London, proceeded last fall, at the instance of the North and South Railroad, to survey the section of country on both sides of the railway from Boyle's Gap, where it cuts the Sand Mountains, to where it crosses the Warrior River. The average distance from the Sand Hills to the Warrior River is about fifteen miles. Mr. Tait had only the most ordinary means of excavation at command, and he explored chiefly along the channels of the creeks, and cleared and measured wherever practicable the seams of coal observable to the eye. His conclusion was, that there are five distinct coal-beds in the upper portion of the area, varying in thickness from thirty to sixty-six inches, and at no considerable depth below the surface. The bed of the Warrior, where the railway crosses, he found composed of carboniferous shale, which he supposes to be the roof of coal strata occupying a lower position than those found along the channels of the smaller tributaries. The seams of the Warrior basin, examined by Mr. Tait, have a slight north-west dip, seldom exceeding ten degrees ; whereas the seams of the adjoining Cahawba coal-field have a south-east inclination of forty-five degrees. The "strike" of the seams, however, is the same in both areas, and Mr. Tait's opinion is, that the volcanic force passing on its anti-clinal axis along the Jones Valley, betwixt the two coal-fields, where the Silurian rocks out-crop in uniform ridges, exerted a lateral force in a south-easterly direction, and raised up the Cahawba strata to the high angle at which it is found; but that the two basins were originally one common plain, having the same general geological formation. Mr. Tait pronounces all the coal seen by him to be an excellent semi-bituminous coal, without any iron pyrites or visible trace of decomposition when subjected to the microscope. The coal and iron ores of Alabama have undergone many chemical analyses. In the coal of the Warrior there is a little sulphur, while in the Cahawba there is none, or only the slightest trace. Professor Mallet, who now occupies the Chair of Chemistry in the University of Virginia, and who probably knows more of the mineral resources of Alabama from a scientific point than any other person living, found the coal of the Warrior, near Tuscaloosa, to be composed as follows :—

Volatile combustible matter	40·60
Fixed carbon	54·07
Ashes	1·09
Moisture	1·18
Sulphur	1·06
	100·00

The Cahawba coal, according to the same analyst, has the following elements :—

Volatile combustible matter	36·68
Fixed carbon	57·23
Ashes	5·30
Moisture	0·79
Sulphur	Trace.
	100·00

In a table drawn by Sir Charles Lyell, Alabama coal occupies the front rank of coals for producing steam.

Analyses of the Alabama iron ores show from fifty to eighty parts of peroxide of iron, with varying but usually small proportion of lime, alumina, magnesia, and phosphoric acid. Their production of metallic iron is from 36 to 58 per cent.

The country in which these mineral treasures are found possesses considerable agricultural value. The soil produces corn and cotton, is well adapted for wheat and other small grain, is watered by numerous streams, and in its agreeable blending of hill and valley would form not only a temperate and wholesome place of residence, but might be made to produce abundance of bread and meat and milk and fruits. Yet it is still, over a great part, practically a desert. There are no negroes, little population of any kind, and the hunter often finds wolves and other wild animals which have disappeared from other parts of the State. While this absence of population involves the necessity of im-

N

porting labour—an operation which, considering the industry to
be pursued, would be necessary in any circumstances—it has the
advantage of obviating all social entanglements and antagonism.
The mineral settlers would be free to create a society of their
own, and as rapidly as bands of miners and iron workers invaded
these mineral solitudes of Alabama they would be followed by
a white farming population to cultivate the soil and minister to
their wants.

The coal and iron deposits of this State are now, when the
railways have cut through them in all directions, by far the most
deeply interesting material fact on the American Continent. Of
the extent or depth of these deposits I should be loth to speak in
any exaggerated terms. The seams, so far as revealed, are not
of any remarkable thickness, and the slight and superficial degree
in which they have been mined, as well as their geological pecu-
liarities, forbid imaginary estimates from a business point of view
of their cubical contents and probable commercial outcome. But
they everywhere obtrude themselves on the most cursory observation over thousands of square miles, and coal and iron are
found in such immediate juxtaposition, and are raised from the
bowels of the earth into such elevations of surface, as must render
their commercial development much more easy than coal and iron
can be developed in most other parts of the world. The coal of
Alabama is marked by impressions of *lepidodendrum* and other
magnificent flora found in the coal measures of Europe, and
there can be no doubt that a high tropical vegetation at one time
flourished over all this mineral region of Alabama, and was submerged and covered with deposits of sand, since hardened into
rock, under which, save for a volcanic force that has tilted up the
underlying rocks, and broken as on a wheel an arid sandy plain
into hill and valley and fertilising streams, and the alluvium and
mould of a later world, both the coal and iron would have remained for ever concealed, or could only have been extracted with
enormous difficulty. All this subterranean wealth, exposed to
the eye, is now brought within easy reach; and not only the
railways of Alabama, but the great lines of road which are being
pushed with extraordinary energy through the vast States and
territories of the West to the shores of the Pacific, as well as
into Mexico and Central America, and the growing steam marine
of the Gulf, are opening an almost boundless demand on the
spot for both coal and iron. I take with me specimens of
hematites from the Red Mountain district, of manganese from
the neighbourhood of Chattanooga, and of the coal of Montevallo. The hematite yields 56 per cent. of metallic iron; and
having seen the finest hematites of Cumberland and the North
of Spain, I am mistaken if the Alabama ore does not compare
favourably with them all.

Montevallo coal is sold in Montgomery at fifty cents per 100 lbs. The coal of Philadelphia cannot be laid down at less than a dollar per 100 lbs., and is no doubt a richer coal. The coal of Alabama is lighter and more bituminous than the similar coal of England and Scotland; but it is pure and bright, and if efficiently mined could be profitably sold at probably not more than five dollars per ton, or one-fourth the value here of the coal of Pennsylvania.

The dependence of the South on the North extends to commodities even more strange than coal and iron, of which there is here in their raw state such abundance. Though Montgomery is surrounded by the prairie land of the State, bales of very coarse hay are transported all the way from Kentucky, Pennsylvania, and Maine, and fetch two cents a pound, or four times more than the price of the Montevallo coal. The Southern planters know little of rearing and feeding stock, or saving grass and fodder; or knowing and feeling the necessity of developing such elements of economy and profit since the negroes have ceased to figure as property in the balance-sheets of the plantations, they experience no common difficulties of capital and labour in introducing a new system. Such stock as existed on the farms, including even the hogs, was swept away in the war. Planters who had a thousand swine on their lands were left in some cases almost without one. Recovery in such circumstances can only be a gradual process, even where there are the best intentions and the greatest energy. Mr. Ross, a Scotchman who had spent the early part of his life in a tropical clime, bought a plantation thirty miles south of Montgomery, a year or two ago, at twelve dollars an acre. He complains of the difficulty of cultivating his land by negro labour, of the inferior quality and high price of goods and articles of ordinary consumption, and the danger of falling into lawsuits with overseers and labour-contractors. Since the war, husbandry has been playing chiefly on the old string, and the abundance of the cotton crop shows that this string has been played with surprising success. Some say it has been played out. The receipts of cotton in Montgomery in 1869-70 were 75,000 bales. This year nearly as many bales have been received already, and a great increase on the crop of the previous year is anticipated before the end of the season. The failure of the planters to make any profit at present prices of cotton will most probably give a great impulse to other strings of husbandry which have so far, under free negro labour, been too much neglected.

CHAPTER XXVI.

[MOBILE, ALA.—*Jan.* 22-24.]

IT is only by actual travel in the United States that one attains
to any adequate conception of the vastness of the territory.
Figures, however deep and large, fall flat on the imagination;
but when new tens of thousands of square miles spread out before
one's eyes weekly, as they have been doing steadily before mine
for several months, the impression of magnitude becomes real,
lasting, and all but overwhelming. I have been working in and
round the State of Alabama since the beginning of December,
often taking long stretches of a hundred miles or more at a time,
and at Montgomery the labour of travel in Alabama might have
been supposed to be about finished. Yet, from Montgomery, the
capital, to Mobile, the seaport of the State, is one hundred and
eighty miles, or from twelve to fifteen hours by railway. The
total area of Great Britain and Ireland is 122,091 square miles.
The area of Alabama is 50,272 square miles; so that this one
State alone is nearly equal in superficial extent to one-half of the
United Kingdom, and is divided so comprehensively and almost so
equally into stock and agricultural region, cotton region, mineral
and manufacturing region, and timber region, as to constitute, in
natural resources, a little empire in itself. Whatever the future
of Alabama (and it seems most promising) may be, it is certain
that the increase of its population in the ten years before the war
was greater than the increase of population in Massachusetts,
about equal to the increase in Pennsylvania, and double the increase in Virginia in the same period. The census of 1870, so far
as it can be relied upon, accredits Alabama with a somewhat larger
population than in 1860; and if the development of the great
resources of the State should now take a fresh start, there can
be no doubt that Mobile will share its prosperity. This city is
the common point to which all the southward river communica-

tions converge on the Gulf; and, besides, is well dovetailed into the railway circle. The railroads east and west draw off a great portion of the produce of Alabama to Savannah on the one hand, and to New Orleans on the other; but Mobile, while capable of sharing much of this traffic, must always be the point of import to Alabama from Mexico, the West Indies, and South America, and the outlet of coal and iron to the Gulf.

Having taken a night journey from Montgomery to Mobile in the "Pullman Sleeping Car"—all the comforts of which seem comprised in one relief, viz. horizontal position—I found myself at dawn in fine but heavy pine woods—the "timber region" of Alabama extending deep into the southern region of the State along the whole Gulf Coast—remarkably free from swamp or underwood, and with a green, dry sward under the trees. The railroad stops at a few shanties on the Tensaw River, whence the passengers and goods are meantime carried by steamboat twenty-two miles to Mobile. The Tensaw is in reality a bayou, issuing by one or more of its affluents from the Alabama River, and flowing back again into the same waters at the head of the Bay of Mobile. The boat moved down smooth waters, spreading and opening into various channels, and amidst tongues of land covered with heavy white reeds, till definition became lost in the *embouchure* to the bay. A good breakfast was spread on board the steamer for the people, among whom was a considerable number of emigrants from the wide and pleasant but poor lands of Georgia, bound for the still wider, probably less pleasant, but, alleged to be, much richer lands of Texas. They had already travelled hundreds of miles. From Mobile to New Orleans is upwards of a hundred miles more, and from New Orleans to Texas is five hundred or a thousand or two miles, just as one may be inclined. They were working country-people, the same kind of folk as one sees passing from all parts of Europe through the British seaports to New York. This movement from east to west goes on constantly. Nothing stops it. Among these groups, but not of them, I espied a sturdy, sandy-haired young man, whom I fancied to be a countryman of my own. He told me he was from "Aberdeen awa'," and was the son of a small farmer. He had been working on a farm in the State of New York, and, after making some little money, was now emigrating in general. He had no point of arrival. Soon after breakfast, a Georgian youth, much more weather-beaten than the Aberdonian, roamed round all parts of the floating castle in a state of semi-distraction. The ambition of this young man seemed to be to have a whole county, somewhere in Texas, all to himself.

The stockades driven into the approaches of the harbour of Mobile to ward off Federal gunboats during the war still remain, and steamers have to thread warily a zigzag course through little forests of piles before getting alongside the wharves. It might have been supposed that the Federal Government, so zealous hitherto in reconstructing the South, would have long since effaced these marks of rebellion. Only the lighter class of sailing vessels come up to the city, the navigation being obstructed not only by such effete warlike defences, but by the natural bar at the mouth of the bay. The heavy cotton ships, that must have 3,000 bales with *et ceteras*, lie off, and receive their cargoes from lighters, twenty to thirty miles from the city. Yet the captains like this distance from port, as a protection from the demoralisation and "skedaddling" of their hands, who for the most part are engaged out and in. The office of the British Consul, Mr. Credland, is thronged at this period with skippers in search of runaway seamen; and Captain Semmes, of the Alabama, who is settled here as official attorney of Mobile, has often to give legal advice and assistance in captures of a totally different kind from those to which in his more heroic days he was accustomed. "Jack" does not like to be deprived of his land frolic by the dodge of anchoring twenty miles from port, and gets up scuffles at night on board ship, and, in the darkness and confusion, jumps overboard and pretends to be drowned, when, by a boat at hand, he has made ashore. The captains, judging from the frequency of such escapades, reason how much worse matters would be were their ships nearer the city, and rather like the wise provision Nature has made by the bar. But if "Jack" were more at liberty in port, he very probably would have less tendency first to drown himself, and then to run away. Mobile is not a place one can easily escape from, unless prepared to undertake a very long journey. It appears that foreign seamen in this free country cannot be arrested for breach of contract, but if they steal the ship's boats, or maim or kill the mate, they may, when caught, be made amenable to law and equity in some degree.

The chief topics of interest among the merchants, keenly alive to the necessity of keeping abreast of the movements in other ports, are the opening and deepening of the harbour, and the extension of the railway connections of Mobile with the interior. There is a prospect of the former being attended to ere long, and though the present railway communications of Mobile are by no means contemptible, a meeting of citizens has just been held to promote a great new line, to be called the "Mobile and North-Western." There are already three lines of railroad in operation, viz. the Mobile and Ohio, extending to Columbus on the Mississippi River, and there falling into connection with other roads north and west—the Mobile and Montgomery, and the Mobile and New Orleans; and there is in process of construction the Mobile and Alabama Grand Trunk, which will place this seaport in direct communication with the mineral region of the State on to Chattanooga. But the line at present obtaining the suffrages of the citizens is different from all these, and is proposed to go to Jackson by a route twenty-four miles shorter than the road from New Orleans to Jackson, from Jackson into the Yazoo Valley in the heart of the most fertile region of Mississippi, where large quantities of cotton are involved in annual difficulties of carriage by boat and bayou, and from Yazoo one hundred and twenty miles farther to Helena in Arkansas, where it will connect with roads giving a shorter run to St. Louis and Missouri than any meantime available. Mobile is fired, like so many other places, with the ambition of being the eastern terminus of the great Pacific lines, which will probably begin to be of some commercial value a hundred years hence, but is keeping a wakeful eye all the time on more local and attainable advantages. The splendour of conception with which railway lines are mapped out in this part of the world exceeds belief; nor can one declare, considering the deplorable circumstances of the interior in the matter of common roads, and the facility of railway construction over a soft and level surface with superabundance of timber, that the splendour is without a strong basis of practical utility, albeit there is a wide difference always betwixt conceiving and executing. The "Mobile and North-Western" involves a distance of some four hundred miles, and is estimated to cost four millions of dollars, though a million or two more may perhaps be safely added. Mobile engages to subscribe half a million of dollars, and the undertaking is legitimate enough both for subscribers and lenders; but the promoters must be aware that the resource of State bonds is for the present played out in Alabama, and that an ample subscription along the proposed line cannot fail to prove a condition-precedent of its success. The merchants of Mobile feel that the question of interior communication is one of vital necessity to them. Savannah, by the great railway activity in Georgia, has been encroaching largely in what was wont to be their fields of operation both in Alabama and Mississippi, while New Orleans, with its vast waterways, always turns up on its feet; and it is only by pushing new roads into productive territories hitherto unvisited by the iron horse, and thus obtaining a control of cotton and other country produce, and of the return trade of agricultural supplies, that Mobile can hope to maintain its old place. The exports of cotton from Mobile exhibit considerable fluctuation since the close of the war. From upwards of 400,000 bales in 1865-6, they fell to 251,000 bales the following year, when there was a general failure of production under the new system of labour; rose to 358,000 bales in 1867-8, and fell again to 247,000 bales in 1868-9. The total exports last year were 298,523 bales, and, judging from the receipts up to this date, are expected to amount this year to 375,000 bales. The exports of lumber from this por last year were 3,859,000 feet. The importation of foreign goods direct into Mobile amounted to 1,350,000 dollars, being probably not a thirtieth part of the value of its total exports, though comparing very favourably with Savannah in direct foreign trade, where, notwithstanding the great traffic in cotton, direct transaction with the sources of foreign supply appears to be reduced to the lowest ebb. As an instance of what mercantile energy might do in many various forms to revive trade and independence in the Southern seaports, the importation of coffee from Rio to Mobile has increased in two or three years from 8,000 to 75,000 bags, and is likely to go on increasing, as the trade, of course, is much more direct and rapid and the charges of transportation much less from Mobile to the North-West, than from New York or Baltimore. But Mobile, like the other Southern seaports, labours, after the huge losses of the war, under a disability in want of capital. There are only three banks, and these of very limited means, in the city—the Bank of Mobile with a capital of 500,000 dollars, the Southern Bank of Alabama and the First National Bank, with capitals respectively of 300,000 dollars. But for the insurance companies, which have prospered greatly since the war, and which invest their surplus means in commercial paper to an amount exceeding the total capital of the banks, trade would have been much more crippled than it has been ; and, of course, a commodity, so scarce in proportion to the work to be done as money here, is only obtainable on very high terms.

There are no manufactures of any consequence in Mobile. If a cotton factory may thrive anywhere in the South, one would suppose that it must be in a town like this, of 40,000 inhabitants, among whom there is always a large class of white people to whom indoor labour is of vital consequence, and where the most active agencies of sale and distribution are to be found without cost or seeking on the spot. Paper is made in the neighbourhood, but the water on the deltas of the Gulf is too turbid for this manufacture, and there are many places of natural water-power and pure running streams in this State where paper, which, unlike cotton, fetches three times the price of the raw material, might be manufactured with much greater success. There is a vast amount of cotton waste in every gin-house which a paper mill would gather up at little cost; and, not to speak of much other fibre wasting in the fields, there is a tall plant almost peculiar to Alabama called *Okra*, which I have seen growing in the gardens, and which is capable of field culture, that makes excellent paper pulp—root, stem, and branches. Very good " news " has been made from *Okra* in a mill at Tuscaloosa. Rags are among the few things to which the tariff of the United States extends the privilege of free import, and the American paper makers, with a continent in their hands overflowing with paper fibre, and trusting to every device of law and taxation rather than exercise their own ingenuity, and gather up the wealth profusely growing at their feet, have been poaching on the raw material of paper, all too scarce, of other countries, and throwing upon other countries, of course, an amount of brain work and commercial activity in the discovery and development of paper material which is neither equal, republican, nor even, on the most indulgent theory, commonly civilized. They have verily been trying to import Esparto grass all the way from Spain, as if the United States did not contain within themselves the resources of this kind, ten times told, of all the Spains; and because it does not pay to make paper for the intelligent and reading people of America from grass grown in Spain, they would immediately inflict a much higher duty, already from 20 to 25 per cent., on all foreign paper, and, of course, an equally increased amount of disgrace and despite on all American grass and American paper manufacture. The Southern people, who have heretofore suffered deeply from this system, and are crushed to the ground under it still, with the further bitterness, war-born, of being proscribed and misgoverned from Washington as "rebels," have no sympathy with the suicidal and incomprehensible follies of tariff legislation; and one cannot but think that were the North once weaned from the lust of protection, misdirecting and perverting all its great commercial and political energies, and making Republican institutions themselves a hollow sham and imposture as regards true material development, American spirit and ingenuity would soon search out the ways and means, and places too, for making paper as well as much more besides, not only enough for the United States, but to spare for export to less favoured countries.

One branch of manufacture established at Mobile since the war is worthy of notice. The "Mobile Cotton Oil Mills" is a large establishment, employing a good many hands, and having, in buildings and machinery, probably near a hundred thousand dollars. Cotton seed, forming the larger bulk of the cotton fruit, was in the old times deemed of little or no account. The planters seldom took the trouble even of returning it to the land as manure. It is now bought up from the plantations at from 10 to 12 dollars a ton, and is manufactured in this Mobile mill, and in similar works rapidly extending in the Southern towns, into cotton oil, cotton-seed cake, and cotton-seed manure. It is first carefully separated from the hull and wool in which it is encased, the latter being gathered up and baled as merchantable cotton. The pure seed is then ground into meal, which is put into little narrow rectangular bags of a strong and peculiar texture. These are next placed in the pigeon-holes of a powerful hydraulic press, which expresses the oil. The bags are then drawn, and their contents are the cotton-seed cake. The oil flows down from the press **into** tanks, whence it is pumped into an upper story, and undergoes a regular process of refining. When manure is to be made, the seed-cake is ground by the same stones as grind the seed, and the meal is mixed with bone-dust or other preparations of lime, treated with chemicals, and becomes a "fertiliser" as good, some say, as Peruvian guano. It is sold to the farmers at 50 to 60 dollars per ton. The seed-cake is also exported in hundreds of tons, chiefly to England, for feeding cattle ; and large quantities of cotton seed of the Southern States pass by the mills on the spot to the same destination, where it undergoes a similar process of oil-making. The cotton oil does not seem to have yet established any very legitimate place in commerce, and fluctuates some-what mysteriously round olive oil and linseed oil. It is be-lieved that cotton-seed oil is beginning to figure largely on our tables under a certain veil as "first-rate salad oil." It is a very pure and beautiful oil as refined in the Mobile mill, and there can be no doubt of its nutritious qualities. A good agriculturist must demur to so much valuable material being taken away from the soil with so little chance of its ever returning to it. The manufacturers, of course, afford every facility to planters of exchanging cotton seed for seed-cake and manure, and whether their trade is to be an enduring one or not, there can be no doubt of the valuable lesson they are reading the planters as to the economisation of the materials about them. If the seed-cake with the oil expressed be good for fattening cattle, the seed, with all the oil in it, must be a much richer feed, and go much further in admixture with other stuffs ; while it is certain that there is no part of the world where there is so much room for profitable stock-feeding as on the cotton plantations of the South. There are little machines, to be bought for 150 or 200 dollars, by which any planter may separate the wool and the hull from the seed, and realize in his own farm-yard nearly all the economical results of these elaborate and extensive oil mills.

The citizens of Mobile, taking the bull of misrule by the horns, have in the late elections rooted out the traders on the negro vote from the Municipal Government, and aided the general movement that has given a Conservative-Democratic Governor and House of Representatives to the State. By the singular device of putting fish-hooks, when passing the ballot box, into the coats of the "repeaters"—as the hired negroes addicted to voting several times over in the various "precincts" are called—an effectual check was given early on the day of the poll to a practice that had formerly perverted the elections. The white people are in great heart at the change made in their government ; and, among other advantages of their political situation, boast of having in Mr. John Forsyth, editor of the *Daily Register*, one of the ablest writers in the United States. The Mobilians, remarkable to say, own a pride in their " able editors " as in any other pillars and ornaments of the city.

The people of Mobile exhibit a little nervousness on the subject of the public health of the city. They have had this season a visitation of the old plague of yellow fever, which, owing to the lateness of the first frost, had a more than usual protracted rule, and retarded the return of the cotton-buyers and the progress of business. The number of cases was certainly very large—at one time as high as 1,500—and yet the total mortality from yellow fever proper is stated to have been not more than 216. But there is no thorough health organization in Mobile, and no systematic vital statistics, which is a mistake, even in the lowest point of view ; for the effect of the strictest supervision and registration has always been in such cases to diminish, rather than increase, alarm. There is nothing so terrible, nothing so sure to run riot in the imagination, as the unknown. The people who stay all year in the city think but little of this scourge, and the British Consul, who is one of the " can't-get-aways," considers it very capable of successful treatment. There is much swampy and un-wholesome ground along the head and eastern shore of the bay about the delta and bayous of the river. But the town is built on the western shore outwards to a more pleasant country. Government Street is a magnificent avenue, two or three miles long, of pleasant residences, and grounds adorned with magnolias and other Southern plants which here bloom and flower in all their perfection. Farther out and round the edge of the forest there are also many fine houses, built on firm dry soil, under the shade of the trees, and open to the sea-breezes. And now, when business is again in full progress, and health and pleasure seem to meet, the Mobilians are as gay and lively a community as one could wish to see. The " Can't-get-Away " Club, which has greatly distinguished itself by its philanthropy in the history of Mobile, and is said to have spent 30,000 dollars in the late epidemic, had an amateur performance the other night in the theatre, for the purpose of recuperating its funds ; and what a gathering of beauty and fashion was there ! In five minutes after the opening of the doors the whole pit and boxes of the theatre were filled with brilliant ladies, who more than shared with the amateurs on the stage, I suspect, the admiration of the male portion of the audience.

CHAPTER XXVII.

The New Road from Mobile to New Orleans.—Singular character of the
Country.—The "Iron Horse" crossing Bays, Lakes, and Lagoons.—
The "Rigolets."—First Impressions of New Orleans.—Goods on the
Levee.—The Custom House.—The Streets and Avenues.—The Shell Road.
—Weather in January.—Vegetation.—Sunday in a City of "All Nations."

[NEW ORLEANS, LA.—*Jan.* 25 to *Feb.* 14.]

THE opening of the Mobile and New Orleans Railway has not
only reduced the journey betwixt the two cities to less than one-
half the time consumed by the steamers, but opened a most curious
country to observation. The road sweeps diagonally across the
tract of Alabama, between Mobile Bay and the Mississippi State
line, along the edge of an evergreen forest, where the yellow
pine, as in its home and birthplace, grows tall and strong, while
straight and taper as a fishing-rod; and where the number of
little shanty towns growing up, and steam saw-mills puffing
their white smoke into the bright sunny air, shows that an
increasing lumber trade, with the iron track so near, is being
carried on. The narrow strips of land, cleared of wood, are also
being brought into cultivation, and the negro and the mule are
following close in the wake of the woodsman with his axe and
teams of heavy oxen. The railway, after crossing the Mississippian border, dips down to the shore of the Mississippi
Sound, with its many long and narrow strips of island shutting
out a view of the Gulf, and seeming as if it were no Sound at all,
but merely an extension seaward of the bays, lagoons, and
shallow oozes of many-mouthed rivers, in which the road now
becomes enveloped as in an undefined maze of land and water.
Pascayoulas, Beloxi, and Bay St. Louis are points at which the
rails are carried by trestles across arms of the Sound, on which
over long distances one never seems to lose hold of land, and
yet is always above water, as if the country for miles round
were under some temporary inundation. Yet the white sails of
vessels are seen on both sides of the line, like the wings of sea-
gulls that have wandered far from both sea and shore. Several
rivers, flowing towards a common embouchure, produce in the

low flat land this labyrinth of channels and marshy pools, and are met half-way by the salt waters of the Sound. At Bay St. Louis the train crosses over at least two miles of deep water on a strong but open trestle, of which the iron rails are the topmost lines, and on which the cars seem to hang as by a thread that the first tornado perchance may snap, and what then? Yet in fair weather the passage is very pleasant, not in anywise alarming, glides rapidly once more upon expanses of dry land, where there are sweet-orange groves and bounteous orchards, and where Ocean Springs, Mississippi City, and other watering-places of fantastic names afford summer shade and recreation to citizens of Mobile and New Orleans; and then bounds into a broad savannah—dry and deeply grassy plains—on which a thousand herds of oxen might pasture, so far extending that the forest at length disappears, and only becomes visible again on some elevation of surface like a vapoury battlement in the distant sky. There is little human or animal life on this savannah, which is a mere bagatelle to the far greater " prairies " of the West, and it is easy to perceive that the American Eagle, in the universal spread of its wings, is but pecking feebly with its bill at the vastnesses round its borders. But, though by what agency or for what purpose is not to be defined, this savannah has at various points been set on fire, and the flames, licking up the long grass, and glowing scarlet-red even in the sunlight, with their smoke and trail of blackened soil and ashes, form a striking feature in the landscape as the train sweeps past. Then come the " trembling prairie," and new watery mazes spreading on all sides, till they seem to block the way, and render advance a mystery. The cars up to this point have been going at the rate of nearly thirty miles an hour, with a smooth and easy motion, as of wings rather than of wheels; but the palpitating track of the " trembling prairie " brings the prudent engine to a more temperate speed. Over many miles the road on this section has been made by excavating the soil on either side, and throwing it over among heavy layers of timber on the track. But as rapidly as the dredging machines scooped out the earth the broad ditches thus made filled with water, so that the narrow iron road passes along parallel canals now on this side and now on that, and sometimes on both sides together, and ever and again comes to places where lagoons expand over miles of territory, and rivers seem to lose themselves in unseen channels amidst the weltering waters. Little bits of land and human habitations appear in the distance above the flood and marshes, and one looks abroad with curious wonder on the scene at the stations whither floating houses have penetrated by patient navigation from some dry shore with goods and groceries, powder and shot; and where men and boys are always jumping into

canoes half-filled with wooden ducks, and paddling their way in
all directions, no one knows where by name, for their game. The
train passes on, and as one glances ahead along the shining rails,
with their flanking canals, it seems to be running direct into the
sea, which appears to swell up into communion with the sky on
the bright horizon; and over parts of the sea, sure enough, it
has oftentimes to pass on crutches; but as it dashes on, the sea
retires, and stretches of "trembling prairie" reappear, and one
begins to look for the spires of New Orleans. Away to the
north-west a speck is seen on the sky, and the glass brings out a
flag-staff and pennon. It is Fort Pike, on Lake Pontchartrain,
and in a few minutes more, while one is looking eagerly for
Pearl River, and thinking that it must have lost itself somewhere,
the train bounds upon the bridge over the Rigolets, a deep
channel in which a strong current flows from Lake Pontchartrain
to Lake Borgne, in the Sound, swallowing up the waters of the
Pearl in its course, and forming the line of navigation from
Lakeport in Pontchartrain for the New Orleans steamers and
coasters trading with Mobile and other Gulf ports. The railway
works span the Rigolets slantwise, and have a drawbridge in the
centre for the navigation 100 feet wide, complained of as not
being large enough. Yet still more lakes and serpentines! What
a country for duck-shooting! Animated nature here consists of
amphibious beings, with ducks at one end of the scale, and men
bent on their destruction at the other. On crossing by a trestle
work farther on the southern end of Lake Catherine—one of
those smaller fresh-water seas, but considerable lakes, that fill
up more than one-half the space betwixt the great Pontchartrain,
the Sound, and the Mississippi River, and would seem to show,
if experience did not establish the fact that the deluge is subsiding, how easily all might blend into one, and the whole
country be placed under sea once more—the surface of the water
is covered with myriads of wild ducks, and many shots are fired
at them from the cars, but being from pocket-pistols do very
little execution, though many of the ducks are quite within
range, and do not appear to be anywise alarmed by the noise of
the train. They are so numerous, indeed, that one does not see
very well how they could get away even if they were scared.
Leaving lakes and ducks behind, the railway now passes into a
scraggy country, where the wheels of the cars have a firmer
ring, and where hoary cypresses stand in pools of water covered
with miasmal moss, hanging like gigantic beards from every
branch and twig, and giving to the melancholy trees most
melancholy and weird-like shapes, with undergrowths of cane-
brake twenty feet high, and lowly palmettos growing in fan-like
tufts along the shallow swamps. The species of orchis seen
depending from the trees in all marshy places in the South, when

gathered and skutched, is found to consist of a bright tough fibre, the finest imitation of horsehair ever seen, and now coming into use in upholstery.

At length the engine slows, the train-bell tolls, and the cars, as the familiar fashion of American railways is, pass through suburban streets, round markets and vast warehouses, and along the levee, amidst acres upon acres of sugar barrels and cotton bales on one hand and a forest of ships on the other, to the axis on which all the whirl of life in the city of New Orleans revolves.

Formerly the merchandise of New Orleans used to be piled on the broad open levee, and probably did not come by much harm. The cotton bales, as soon as landed from the river boats, had to be drayed to the cotton·yards and steam-presses, and were not moved again till the ships were ready to take them as cargo. The molasses, barming under a hot sun, probably suffered most. But of recent years a company has been incorporated, with compulsory powers, to erect sheds, and place all produce intended to lie and be sold on the levee under cover, and has already exercised its powers to a large extent, not without murmurs of dissatisfaction from the merchants, ill at ease under this innovation on their ancient freedom and habitudes of business. The barrels of sugar and molasses newly landed on the levee have a tendency to be the first sold, and those in the sheds to become old ·stock; and, moreover, the shedding process adds to the charges on imports and exports, which have increased, are increasing, and, if the prosperity of the port is to be regarded, must be diminished. It may be remarked, by way of dismissing a wide subject, that in the great burst of enterprise and temptation to "grab" since the war in many parts of the South, powers of improvement have been seized and engineered through corrupt Legislatures by private companies, which are essentially public and municipal powers, and that a city corporation or river trust, carrying out the same in the public behoof, while imposing a new charge, would dissolve a host of discontents by reducing from the accruing profits either this or various other charges of a like kind. The Mississippi River is here the largest commercial interest; and, on stepping down from the levee to have a straight look at the "Father of Waters"—the drainage of 3,000 miles of territory in length, not to speak of breadth—one sees that he is only a little broader than the Thames betwixt Westminster and Blackfriars, and really flows in a calm, slow, majestic current, as if he did not mean to overflow anybody or sweep anything away. But when one inquires the depth of the Mississippi at New Orleans, the answer is "160 feet!" New Orleans is built on one of the great loops of this enormous volume of water. It has the Mississippi in front, the Mississippi on both flanks, and lakes

or seas Pontchartrain and Maurepas overhanging it in the rear.
The builders have gone quite methodically to work, and have
erected streets behind streets across the segment of a circle along
the river front—great marts of cotton, sugar, hides, tallow, oil,
and groceries—and as rapidly as they have built behind, the
Mississippi in its grand and silent way, without negro labour or
charges of any kind, has been forming for them new land and
sites in front.   Streets which, no farther gone than thirty years
ago, were No. 1 on the levee, are now No. 3 or 4, so busily has
the Mississippi been working out the fortune of New Orleans,
while New Orleans herself may not have been turning it all to
the best account.

Shooting straight up from the levee into the loop is Canal Street
—a broad, noble thoroughfare, with ample carriage ways and banquettes for pedestrians on either side, and a dais in the middle, partly
carpeted with grass, on which all the city cars have a common
rendezvous—a street of fine stores and warerooms, where any
stranger has a key at hand to all parts of New Orleans.   At the
corner of Canal Street, close on the levee, is the Custom House
—an enormous pile of Maine granite, imposing, but somewhat
out of character with the place—Custom House, Post-office, and
Law Courts all in one, with a gaunt and vacant interior, an
unfinished roof, and settling down under the weight of its
granite blocks on its soft foundation.   Even in the matter of
colour, mottled grey and red, it is not in harmony with the light
and aërial structures or the "floating castles" around it.   The
architecture of the Custom House seems a mistake at once of
taste and finance.   But there are many other grand buildings in
New Orleans, which it is scarcely my province to describe.
Branching off from one side of Canal Street are narrow but fine
old streets, bearing royal French names of the ancient Bourbon
era, with an air of Gallic tidiness about them, and all the choicer
wares of France in their shops—the original town of New
Orleans when Louisiana was a French possession, and still
largely the French quarter of the city.   On the other side are
Magazin Street, where the latest literature is doubtless on sale;
St. Charles Street, where the magnificent St. Charles Hotel is to be
found; Carondelet Street, where large business is done in cotton
and tobacco, and Shylock and Antonio meet together on the
plain-stones to negotiate a great variety of loans; and Baronne
Street farther on, where a Legislature of negroes and political
adventurers, sitting in the Mechanics' Institution, are popularly
supposed to be legislating in the most stupid fashion, and selling
the community all round.   In the same locality is the Medical
College—an institution of a different kind—that, with all the
stability and humanity of science, and the social fame of wise
and skilled physicians whom Pro-Consul Butler, though he tried

imprisonment, could no more shake from their orbits than he could blot out the stars, holds on its benign course amidst revolution and commercial convulsion, as if it were an angel from heaven sent down in infinite love and mercy to suffering mankind. The streets branching out from the "all-nations" side of Canal Street extend a long way across the loop, and at the end of every block have their busy and almost equally prominent intersections; but owing to the old custom in Louisiana of taking possession by "arpents" from the river front, as well as to the semicircular character of the river, definition, it has been impossible to give to New Orleans the parallelogram formation so fondly cherished by the planners of American cities. Yet, by a gentle twist or curve, the "all-nations" streets of New Orleans do, with a shock of the city cars affecting slightly the spinal curve of the passengers, get into new and long suburban avenues —named after the nine Muses, and other heathen goddesses to boot—rows of fine sweet timber dwellings, with verandahs and balconies, flower-plots, and tower-like cisterns, and sometimes a whole acre of white clover, with plum, peach, and fig-trees all round, where the family life of New Orleans blooms in no common quietness and natural splendour. These avenues—albeit New Orleans is much better paved in its business parts with broad dressed blocks a foot or eighteen inches square than the imperial city of New York, save, perhaps, on the levee, where after rain there is a curdled depth of ooze, in which Sambo and his mules are in momentary danger of losing themselves—stretch away into mere wilderness and swamp. But running across the head of the loop to Lake Pontchartrain, is the famous Shell Road, seven or eight miles long, straight as an arrow, hard as flint, and smooth as a backgammon board, along which the "bloods" of New Orleans drive their fine horses and buggies with marvellous celerity. Many quiet parties also take advantage of this splendid drive. The racecourses of New Orleans, where the fastest horses are put to their mettle twice a year, are on its side, and half-way houses invite a halt amidst the swamp on plots of sweet verdure, and under fragrant bowers, where a score or two of buggies are always hitched up, and cocktails and sherry-cobblers are dispensed to thirsty souls *secundum artem.*

The weather in New Orleans, in the last days of January, is warm, bright, almost fiercely sunny; but when the air is clear, and the heavens high, one basks in it with all the delight of contrast to some other parts of the world at the same time of the year. On the other hand, when the clouds, vapoury exhalations of sea and lake, gather over the city, the atmosphere becomes close and sultry, and one prays that the leaden heavens may crack, and that Sol, though it were in hottest anger, may show himself again. And, by and by, the prayer is heard—the rain falls in a plump, peals of thunder roll along the sky, and sheets of blue lightning flash through the darkening air ; but the sultriness does not abate yet a little while. One goes to bed amidst peals of thunder and heavy splashes of rain, and towards morning, dreaming of a railway train, is startled by a tremendous crash, as if the engine had exploded, and the rails, turning up on end, were tearing the cars into ribands. Throwing open the casement, the street is seen to be several feet deep in flood ; the square slab-laid gutter on either side, that seemed large enough to admit a Liliputian flotilla into the city, is buried under the deluge, and a smooth canal-like surface of water overspreads the avenue from croup to croup. But the rain is falling more gently; the artillery of the heavens has discharged its last round ; a current becomes perceptible to the eye, and it is evident the waters are flowing away somewhere ; the sun breaks out, and in a few hours all the streets of the city are dry, clean, and sweet, and the solar rays falling with golden splendour on tower and spire, and lighting up the nooks and crannies of a crowded town, New Orleans becomes loveable again. The drainage of this curiously situated city flows back from the river towards the interior of the loop, where it is helped on by steam-pumps into the swamp—imperfect, but as good as can easily be devised. The deposition of moisture in the intervals of rain and sunshine is very heavy, covering the lobbies, staircases, and all the interiors with a clammy sweat as of oil. At the same time vegetation is endued with extraordinary force. The blooms of early fruit-trees unfold themselves with a motion almost visible. But in the gardens there is a curious worker in the dark. A crawfish raises a little tumulus, with a hole in the middle of it, that grows night after night, till in its spiral formation it becomes a small Tower of Babel ; the cunning artificer of which, however, is unseen, retiring on its line of retreat to the depths beneath with masterly skill. I have put the question whether, under all the phenomena, New Orleans may not be a floating island ; but this supposition is stoutly contested in argument, and only by force of humour, in geography no force at all, is an admission obtained that " New Orleans does mayhap swing a little ! "

Sabbath morn, after the traffic and amusement of the week, nightly balls and operas, pleasant card-parties, and masked assemblies, dawns over New Orleans with sacred calm and serenity. Every place of business is closed, labour is suspended, and, save the quiet trot and jingle of the city cars conveying visitors from the centre to the circumference, and worshippers from the circumference to the churches and chapels in the centre —the Presbyterians, unmincing Calvinists, next to the Roman Catholics the most prominent—peace and quietness prevail. It is remarkable, considering the mixture of races and nationalities, with their widely different up-bringing and temperament, how becomingly, and with what mutual esteem and respect, all creeds and denominations here proceed on the Sabbath-day to worship God in their own forms, and to sit devoutly under their own vines and fig-trees. The Scotch Presbyterian can observe the Sabbath as calmly and undisturbedly in New Orleans as in his native glen; and were it possible, setting aside all sceptical "gallimaufry" on the one hand and all austere mechanical formality on the other, to enter fully into the Divine idea of the day "made for man," what a sublime rest—what a refreshing and composing draught from the fountains of Eternal Truth and Knowledge—would it be to all bodies politic!

CHAPTER XXVIII.

Population of New Orleans.—Natural Resources.—Revival of Business since the War.—Cotton.—Sugar.—Tobacco.—Rice and Grain.—Financial Disability.—Disproportion of Imports to Exports.—Great Decline of Imports of Coffee and Internal Trade.

[NEW ORLEANS.—*Jan.* 25 to *Feb.* 14.]

NEW ORLEANS, when one has seen round it all, is a large city, large not only as it is, but large also because it might be so much larger. The population, according to the census, in which no one here or elsewhere implicitly believes—such is the chasm betwixt public confidence and the simplest acts of administration—is 140,920 white, and 50,499 black and coloured persons. But I am informed by a statist of some authority that 40,000 or 50,000 may be added to this result of a lackadaisical enumeration with some confidence. The number of voters polled in New Orleans in great election times is within a few hundreds of 40,000, and since the adult males can hardly be more than one in five or six, New Orleans on that criterion may be taken as having, in round numbers, a quarter of a million of inhabitants. Yet it is not extent of population that strikes attention so much here as the great compass of rich territory, with rare and varied resources of production, and the easy and abounding means of transit by an extraordinary combination of navigable rivers, seas, and lakes.

The late war fell with as severe a blight on New Orleans as on other parts of the South. Though the early occupation of the city by the Federal forces saved it, as well as Louisiana, from much of the mere powder-and-shot devastation of war, that in the case of a more obstinate defence, simply impossible, might have fallen upon it; and though General Butler, while busying himself in domiciliary visits to the houses of planters and other wealthy "rebels" with no strictly pure intent, employed the negroes, clamorous for food, in making a branch way to the Shell Road and cutting one more canal through the city, with sanitary results which, however largely reported and believed in the North, must be accepted *cum grano salis* on the spot: yet the normal life of New Orleans was as completely suspended as if its throat had been cut; its most vigorous men were drafted a thousand miles away into the Confederate Army; little or no cotton was brought to market, and the cultivation of the sugar-cane was almost totally abandoned; mercantile capital and bank and insurance stock were consumed as in a furnace; and much of the solid house property, worthless for the time, rotted where it stood, and passed like furze under the harrows of a general destruction and decay. It must ever be a wonder how rapidly New Orleans, after this terrible ordeal, has become what she is now.

The rapid re-establishment of business in New Orleans is in no branch more marked than in cotton, and to understand the full significance of this fact it must be borne in mind that New Orleans is a full geographical degree south of the Cotton Belt, and that little cotton is grown within a hundred miles of the Crescent City. But in virtue of its commanding situation on the Mississippi and its tributaries, flowing through the richest lands, penetrating east and west to every cultivated field up to the northern limits of the cotton region, and yet so near the mouth of the great river as to give rapid export to the Gulf and the Atlantic, New Orleans has been enabled, in face of intersecting lines of railroads giving power and reach to other markets, and rendering this magnificent water-communication, as might be supposed, of less and less account, to become again the mart of about one-third of all the cotton grown in the United States. The export of cotton from New Orleans in 1860-61 reached the enormous total of 1,915,852 bales, which was somewhat exceptional, but still showing, when a large crop comes, where its overflowing is sure to be. As soon as the war closed, the accustomed pre-eminence of New Orleans began to appear. Her export of cotton in 1865-6 was 768,545, and last year (1869-70) it increased to 1,185,050 bales, of which half a million went to Liverpool, a quarter of a million to Havre, 115,000 to New York, 53,000 to Boston, and 70,000 to Bremen, with smaller quantities to nearly every manufacturing centre from St. Petersburg to Vera Cruz. This year already, with only one-half the season gone, 850,000 bales of cotton have been landed on the levee. The great flow of cotton New Orleans-ward has all the more probability of continuing, seeing that the tendency of increased cultivation is to shift from the East to the West, bringing the bulk of the product more and more upon the Mississippi and the Western rivers, by which its transport to New Orleans is so natural and easy. The finer and longer stapled cotton grown in Mississippi and Louisiana has naturally made New Orleans a special market for this description, and the classification here has hitherto not only been very minute, but always a grade or two above the cotton bearing similar titles in Liverpool. The general deterioration of quality, however, since the war, remarked elsewhere, is also complained of here; and orders from Continental spinners for New Orleans "middling" and upwards can with difficulty be filled this season. The relaxed control of labour under negro emancipation, consequent slovenly cultivation and untimely picking, and the large number of sporadic growers with no permanent interest in their farms or even in cotton-growing as a life-industry, are no doubt the chief causes of a downward tendency of quality, under which "ordinary" becomes but the "low ordinary" of former times, and the highest grades are more and more scarce. The general belief is that the best-conditioned cotton, both upland and bottom land, is grown by small white farmers who plant a few acres as a mere element in their general system of husbandry, and cultivate and pick the crop with the labour chiefly of their own families. The change passing over the cotton-planting industry affords a fair opportunity for adopting a common standard of quality, and making the Liverpool classification, with probably some little extension at either end, the general rule, whereby all purposes would be met, and transactions be greatly simplified and assured. A new Cotton Exchange Board, being organized in New Orleans, may aid in introducing this and other desirable improvements in the system of dealing. The merchants and cotton-factors of New Orleans, on resuming business after the war, adopted the old system of making advances to cotton planters at a great distance from their centre; but, under the serious difficulties of disorganized labour and want of capital, did not find such a policy to answer, and a new class of houses are springing up, mostly Jews, who, by establishing stores in the little towns near the plantations, are becoming middlemen through whose hands the cotton passes from the growers into the market of New Orleans, and whose conditions of advance are almost necessarily marked by a degree of rigour that was unknown in former times, and that will probably grind and impoverish the mass of poorer cultivators, white and black, for a long period to come.

While New Orleans is thus holding its old place so well in cotton, it is very striking that in sugar, the chief staple of Louisiana, the leeway of the war should be very slowly and feebly recovered. The exports of sugar and molasses from New Orleans do not afford any criterion of general progress as in the case of cotton, because the sugar of Louisiana goes chiefly into domestic consumption, not in New Orleans and Louisiana alone, but by "up-river" traffic in all parts of the West where New Orleans has natural and indisputable commercial relations. The consumption of sugar in other parts of the United States is supplied by the raw sugars of Cuba and the West Indies, brought into New York and other Northern and Eastern ports to be refined, and thence distributed to all parts of the Union, the Western field of Louisiana included. The exports of sugar and molasses from New Orleans are thus only such fragments of the native product as, in the eccentricity of commerce, find their way into the Atlantic seaports, and are not suggestive of any general result beyond the fact that they are there saleable, and take a place beside the sugars of the Northern refineries. In 1866-7 there were thus exported 2,529 hhds. and 2,199 barrels of sugar, and 21,893 barrels of molasses; and, in 1869-70, 1,805 hhds. and 4,094 barrels of sugar, and 42,212 barrels of molasses. But from a report, published here with the acceptance of the trade,[1] I am enabled to give the following results, which let one see down to the roots of sugar production in Louisiana before and since the war. The produce of sugar in 1861-2 under the "old process" of open kettles was 389,264 hhds., and under the "refining and clarifying" process, 70,146 hhds.—or in all, 528,321,500 lbs. In 1869-70, the produce of sugar under "old process" was 73,471 hhds., and of "refined and clarified" 13,619 hhds.—or in all, only 99,452,946 lbs. So that while the production of cotton in the Southern States has in five years about reached the level it had attained under slave labour before the war, the production of sugar is still barely one-fifth what it was in 1861-2, and had almost been, with some fluctuations, several years before. The contrast is so remarkable, and so clearly not to be accounted for by any "free labour difficulty," as to indicate some special obstacles affecting this branch of production in Louisiana, and requiring to be carefully investigated.

The tobacco market in New Orleans, though with more apparent reason, also recovers but slowly the position it held before the war. The receipts of tobacco at this port in 1859-60 were 80,955 hhds. In 1867-8 they had, from almost total disappearance during the war, risen only to 15,304 hhds.; in 1868-9 they increased to 28,026 hhds.; and they again fell in 1869-70 to 19,093 hhds. The receipts and exports of tobacco at New Orleans remain lower than, with the exception of the war years, they have been at any period for half a century. The merchants of New York, by pushing their capital among the Western growers when New Orleans was closed by the blockade, obtained an ascendency which they continue to hold with tenacity; and Louisville, profiting by the same state of things, has become one of the greatest tobacco markets in the United States. But the merchants of New Orleans are giving due attention to this ancient branch of the trade of the city; the official inspections are conducted with great efficiency; and there is much confidence that by a good regular market and reduced charges New Orleans will win back, in course of time, a great portion of this almost lost traffic. The tobacco of New Orleans is drawn chiefly from

[1] "Statement of Sugar and Rice Crops," by L. Bouchereau.

Kentucky, Missouri, Illinois, and Tennessee. Very little is said of Louisianian tobacco; and the production of the State, I imagine, must be very limited. But the soil of Louisiana yields prime tobacco, and any keen smoker who has had a course of the " hay and stubble " of the inland towns of the South relishes with almost Elysian fervour the " perique " of New Orleans, so fine in flavour, and yet so strong in all genuine properties. There can be no doubt that were tobacco steadily cultivated in Louisiana, the trade of New Orleans in this commodity would take all the sooner a fresh start, and that the native product would come to be in large demand for export, more especially to England and Scotland, where there are no Government monopolies, and where people who smoke like to get, with as little circumlocution as possible, at the *Nicotine* in its best and highest form.

Rice is a rapidly increasing product in Louisiana since the close of the war, and is declared in fifteen parishes, where it is now successfully cultivated as well as prepared in first-class mills, to have reached during the past year 100,748 barrels of 200 lbs. The receipts of flour at New Orleans are very large, amounting in 1869-70 to 1,641,477 barrels, of which 556,323 barrels were exported; but the efforts made during the last two or three years, including the erection of a patent elevator after the style of Chicago, and forming a prominent architectural feature on the levee, to divert some of the many millions of bushels of wheat of the North-West, destined for Liverpool and other British ports, by the southern river route to the seaboard, have so far been attended with only partial success. The exports of wheat during the past season were under half a million of bushels.

It is obvious that whether in recovering trade lost or diverted by the war, or in conquering a share of new trade that may be more naturally and economically directed from this point than from anywhere else, New Orleans must labour under great disadvantages from the destruction which passed over its mercantile and banking capital in the disastrous years from 1860 to 1865; and this fact meets one at every turn in the survey of the commercial situation. Where New York, travelling out of its sphere, supplanted New Orleans by large and free capital, and by naval and military power during the war, the " Imperial City," of course, continues to hold the new relations thus established by force of its superior monetary resources, and by a pressure on canals and railways, carried to the last degree of stringency, nay even to theft,[1] in pursuance of purely local interests, and in disregard of the only patriotic idea, viz. an equally developed and perfectly harmonized Union; and if New Orleans, by straining her utmost means, can with difficulty and but partially recover lost ground, with how much greater difficulty, or where-

[1] Erie Railway.

withal, shall she be able to take her proper share of the new sources of wealth and commerce always being developed? The prosperity of New Orleans, so far, consists in the handling of the raw products, commanding world-wide markets, of extended and fertile regions of which she is the natural and unavoidable emporium; and, more than likely, it is only because the great demand for cotton is outside the United States, where the commercial interests are rich and strong enough to operate, without any roundabout, in all the chief centres of supply, that the Crescent City has been so rapidly reinstated in this branch of commerce. Wherever the Northern cities successfully took up the trade of New Orleans during the war, they have continued more or less to prevail; and from the start thus made are the better able, with their conserved capital and profits, to make fresh incursions and conquests even now when New Orleans is again free and at work, but with greatly dilapidated resources. The magnitude of business here is seen only in the export of domestic products: in the import of foreign commodities, whether for domestic consumption or for re-export, as well as in all branches of manufacture, or partial manufacture, for which New Orleans has any peculiar advantage, it dwindles into marked disproportion. The value of domestic products exported from New Orleans to foreign countries last fiscal year was 107,658,042 dollars; but the value of merchandise imported from foreign countries was only 14,992,754 dollars. The duties collected on foreign merchandise in the same year amounted to 5,441,825 dollars, considerably more than a third of the value of the goods, showing the severity with which the tariff of the United States represses all reciprocal exchange. The great bulk of the Customs duties of the United States is collected in the modest building in Wall Street of New York. The imposing Maine granite Custom House of New Orleans must have been designed when different ideas and interests prevailed, and when New Orleans was both presently and prospectively one of the chief sources of this branch of revenue, which, no doubt, under a wise polity, she might still become. As it is, New Orleans cannot be supposed to supply direct the extensive countries from which she draws her immense quantities of cotton, sugar and molasses, hides, and other raw products, with more than a tithe of the foreign merchandise they consume, of which she is the proper and most economical port of entry. A considerable proportion of her limited imports consists of commodities which must be almost reckoned exceptional. Looking over a list, in the office of the British Consul, of vessels entered, about one in every four or five was a vessel from Cardiff or some other port in Wales with English rails, rendered necessary by the great pressure of railway projects; and a still larger proportion in ballast. Steamers and sailing ships, after discharging their foreign cargoes in New York, come round here for cotton in ballast—an incumbrance which, in some phases of the market, might present itself to American protectionists as a little spoiling of the Egyptians in Lancashire, but which in the meantime can only be an aggravation of the withering effects of present prices on the Southern planters and negroes. The foreign commodities re-exported from New Orleans, amounting in 1869-70 to only 446,418 dollars value, exhibit as strongly as anything else at once the maimed condition of trade and the great opportunities which under better auspices might present themselves. The immediate proximity of this Southern port to Cuba, Mexico, and Brazil gives it peculiar facilities for an intermediary traffic betwixt these countries and Europe; while of their staples—sugar, coffee, and other produce—it is the pre-eminently qualified *entrepot* for all the southern and western regions of the United States. Yet in this lucrative field New Orleans has lost ground. In the ten years before the war she imported 3,293,881 bags of coffee—a full third of all the coffee imported into the United States; whereas in the four years after the war she imported only 444,115 bags, or less than one-tenth of the total import of coffee into the Union. While of the sugar of Cuba alone New York imported last year 219,713 tons, New Orleans appears to have taken of Cuban sugar and molasses only 58,195 boxes, barrels, and hogsheads, and from other places than Cuba her imports of sugar and molasses were insignificant. Beyond the native product of Louisiana, New Orleans supplies or refines little sugar for any part of the country. The immense trade in foreign sugar and molasses in the United States—about six or seven times more than the home product—has gone round to New York, Philadelphia, Baltimore, Boston, and other north-eastern ports. The volume of New Orleans trade with the interior, north and up-river to the west, is no doubt, apart from foreign commodities, immense. Yet even here the weak side of the Crescent City appears; for in all the return traffic of dry goods, hardware, boots, and other articles of consumption, the merchants of St. Louis and Louisville, strong in purse and enterprise from the safety which covered them during the war, are making their hand largely felt, putting steamboats of their own on the Mississippi, and not only passing over Memphis and trading up the Arkansas and Red Rivers, but shooting over the head of New Orleans itself hundreds of miles into Texas, and selling to the furthest south-western limits of the Union not only American manufactures, but foreign goods imported at New York, and thence passed with cumulating profits through many hands, which could be quite as conveniently laid down on the levees of the Mississippi as on the shores of the Hudson, and hence distributed to the consumers with much less cost and trouble. There does not appear to be any want of perception of this, or of the necessary energy and determination to correct it, among the merchants and business people of New Orleans. It is to be ascribed mainly to the laming effects of the war upon this as upon other Southern seaports, and to a South-destroying system of import duties; and the tendency, however slow, must be for it to pass away. The natural laws of trade, superior to temporary misfortune and even to fiscal impolicy, will in course of time assert their power; the products of human industry will find their best channels of inlet and outlet; and while this happy consummation may be brought about more rapidly by wise and impartial legislation in the United States, it cannot fail to receive an impulse also from the general attention and observation of the mercantile world.

CHAPTER XXIX.

Grievances.—Review of the Tariff—its baneful Effects on the Producing Classes.—Deficiency of Mercantile and Banking Capital.—The "National Banks."—Severity of Taxation.—Importance of a Revision of the Fiscal System of the United States.

[NEW ORLEANS.—*Jan.* 25 to *Feb.* 14.]

THERE are various grievances, affecting deeply the commercial prosperity of the Southern States, and brought into striking prominence in New Orleans, which it may be well, before going out into the country among the sugar plantations, to refer to as concisely as so extensive a subject admits. Remarks on this head may be conveniently arranged under Tariff, Deficiency of Capital, and Excessive Taxation with Misgovernment, an "ill-matched pair" of which the evils are noisome and prolific.

The Tariff of the United States, always more or less protectionist, has, under the financial exigencies entailed by the war, attained a prohibitory and vexatious rigour which is without parallel, and gives the United States the curious distinction of being—China or Japan scarce excepted—the most anti-commercial country in the world. It is strange that a great people, falling heir from its British stock "to all the ages"—carrying forward year by year its great destiny by large accessions of European capital and labour, and called as it were by Providence to solve on a new and splendid field many knotty problems of human government and polity—should put forth in its Acts of Congress this intense hostility to commerce, which is not only its own soul and vital spark, in the most natural sense, but among material forces operating on the progress of humanity is now generally recognised as the most pervading, transforming, and benignly moral and social of all. There was a period in the history of the American Republic—when its foot was newly on the ice—when its "Declaration of Independence" sounded almost in its own ears as a kind of treason, and when the resolution to live within itself, to cover the workmen and manufacturers who came through much difficulty to its shores with all manner of protection, was not unjustified in reason, and was fortified by precedent in practice; but now, when it is great; when it has not even a supposed enemy in the world; when the inventions in arts and mechanism, the science and literature, and the surplus capital and labour of Europe are at its command; when the Atlantic itself has been bridged by the ocean ships of the "foreigner," skilled and ingenious artisans abound in its territories, and great cities and rural farms have grown up over the vast continent to vie with those of any part of the world, this tariff-enmity to reciprocity of trade—this narrow, exclusive, and self-degrading war of the American Republic against foreign commodities, seems, in the light of economical science shining so brightly everywhere else, to obscure and dwarf its otherwise resplendent greatness. It is impossible, in the nature of things, that such rooted infidelity to one of the first principles of modern progress should not inflict its own punishment; and the result is seen in the gradual withering of all commercial enterprises in the United States save that of spreading European immigrants over vast spaces of wilderness, where hopes of distant independence are, alas! too often buried under a load of social discomforts and infinite personal regrets. The question of free trade is here, as all the world over, the interest of the consumer, who is everybody, against the interest of knots and "rings" of monopolists who, despite their questionable gains and law-made importance, are in reality nobody. But Congress, in its Tariff Acts, has, with considerable ingenuity, supported the notion that its fiscal intentions cover a really substantial groundwork of American prosperity.

The Tariff of the United States is arranged alphabetically, and is nearly as large as a Johnson's or a Walker's Dictionary. Commencing with A and the "Acetates," one finds that the United States have a solid antipathy to chemicals, weighing from 20 to 150 cents per lb., and extending, on turning over the pages, to Z and the "Valerianate of Zinc" which is strange enough, considering the great need in this country, in all its nascent manufactures, for the elaborate scientific products of older and wealthier lands; but what is almost as strange, there is one exception to this universal proscription of chemicals, and "arsenic" —arsenic of all things—is declared free, surely an ominous exemption, and typical, were one to go no further, of the poisonous and suicidal properties of the whole document. Yet there is one feature of the Tariff which cannot but strike any student who looks into it—a feature, however, not peculiar to the South, but equally marked in the West, and indeed over nine-tenths of the whole American soil—and that is, that, with a single exception to be mentioned presently, there is no interest of any account in the South which enjoys its so-called protection, while it robs and maims all interests in the South, giving every

Southern man a direct blow in the face under the several letters of the alphabet, and falling in its totality from A to Z like a sledge-hammer on the whole Southern region, with a cruelty of oppression enough to "raise the stones to mutiny" among any people less loyally American than the Southern people appear to have aways been. The same unjust and one-sided legislation tried, say on Pennsylvania and Massachusetts, would in twenty-four hours convert these hives of Northern patriots into nests of rebels, ready to break up the Union and the Universe rather than submit. It was only lately that cotton was exempted from an internal tax of three cents per lb., without precedent even in the United States, and inflicted at a crisis when the plantations were in a state of desolation, without fences or stock, and when the planters, rich and poor, were harried and impoverished by the war. But taking the Tariff as it stands now in all its relations to the South, what does it show? A closely manipulated system of Custom duties, repressing trade and industry and the development of capital—the sources of all revenue—over the entire South and West, in order that "rings" of people in the Northern towns, inflated by indefinite ideas of American fertility, may extort from the industry of the fields a thousand-fold more than passes into the Federal treasury. Second letter of the alphabet, for example, boots and shoes, the last things which makers think of exporting anywhere, 35 per cent. of duty. Leather, for the protection of which there is no excuse—the United States having more than enough of the best hides and skins in the world, with hundreds of thousands of acres of oak woods, which rise and fall without being of use to their owners —35 per cent. On blankets there is not only the usual 35 per cent. *ad valorem*, but from 20 to 50 cents per lb. in addition, for which monstrous aggravation there is no discoverable reason. The wool and goat-hair business, raw and manufactured, in the United States has fallen into deep perplexity from sheer excess of protectionist stupefaction; for the wool-growers, seeing that the woollen manufacturers were so profusely protected, petitioned to have a share of the plunder, and were at once gratified with duties on foreign wool of 11 per cent. *ad valorem*, and 10 cents per lb. in access, with special provisions that wool of sheep, alpaca, or any other like animal, when mixed with "dirt or any other foreign substance,"—all dirt of any kind being legislatively pronounced "foreign,"—be subjected to twice the amount of duty otherwise exigible. It does not seem to occur to the legislative wisdom of this Republic that when "dirt," foreign or domestic, is mixed with any commodity, the dealers on the spot are infinitely surer detectors and punishers of the same than any number of Solons, with probably little commercial experience, can pretend by any general enactment to be. The result of the double attempt to protect the wool-growers and the woollen manufacturers has been to reduce both to discomfort, for the wools of Buenos Ayres, Australia, and New Zealand being placed under embargo and forced to seek a more free and open market, foreign woollens are cheaper than ever, the woollen manufacturers are in a state of distraction, and the wool-growers do not find even so good a market as they had before.[1] Passing from B and blankets to C and cottons, one is thrown into a thicket of details hard to understand. Cotton wool itself, to begin with, is declared "free," for which the poor ryots of India and fellahs of Egypt are doubtless thankful. But on cottons, when unbleached, with large exceptions there are five cents per yard, when bleached with ditto five-and-a-half cents, and when coloured or printed, with ditto again, five-and-a-half cents, and 10 per cent. *ad valorem* thrown in as a crusher; and so this Holy Inquisition against the freedom of commercial exchange goes, every new turn of the screw racking the joints of South and West to the very marrow, till at length at 7½ cents per yard, and 30 cents per lb., and 20 to 35 cents *ad valorem*, the poor, hateful, and worthless thing called "cotton trade" may be supposed to die, or to fly to other realms where, if it do not happen to receive more friendly treatment, one-half of the United States to-morrow may not be worth the price of an old song. After this, D and "Dowlas," E and "Essences," F and "Feather Beds," G and "Glass Bottles," H and "Hats," I and "Inkstands," &c. &c., are an utter weariness of the flesh. But, to be short, and passing over the duties on iron manufactures, which no iron manufacturer probably in the world would trouble his head in attempting to follow, suffice to say that all linen, muslin, paper, shawl, silk, and woollen goods are under import duties in the United States of from 35 to 100 or more per cent. That European manufacturers should dream of studying the needs, tastes, and fashions of a market so barred against them is one of the passing popular delusions which help to countenance and support all the monstrous enactments of the tariff. The matchless fabrics of Glasgow, Belfast, and Bradford, and the silks and broadcloths of England and France, are seen in some of the great warehouses here, but save at second-hand and in clothes actually made in London, Paris, and New York, they make but a small figure in the vast trade of the place. It is one of the incidents of high Customs duties that they not only discourage all enterprise and ingenuity on the part of the foreign producer as regards any special market, but burden the foreign product itself in the first exchange with double the amount of the

---

[1] See Fourth Report of Mr. Wells, late United States Commissioner on Revenue.

impost. I have it on good authority that dry goods, not much
proscribed beyond the "constitutional" 35 per cent. duty, are
seldom cleared at New Orleans under 70 to 80 per cent. duty and
charges. Then, there are the profits of jobbers and retailers
before the goods get to the consumers, which are not only rated,
of course, on the duty and charges paid as well as the value, but
are often carried much beyond any fair or reasonable line. The
Federal law having set the example of proscribing foreign goods,
and rendering them as difficult to get as possible, the retailers,
when they have them in their stores, are tempted to do like-
wise, to fondle them as precious rarities, and make a great thing
out of them. The foreign liquor trade, which I mention because
it is supposed to be overdone, is an example of the enormous cost
thus heaped on the consumer—the price per bottle being usually
about what a gallon might be sold for, duty paid, with fair profit
to all parties—to the end only of stimulating the worst practices
of domestic distillers and "rectifiers," whose frauds and trickeries
give the Inland Revenue department and Congress a world
of trouble, without any correction of the pitiable evils, personal
and social, arising from a profuse distribution of the most dele-
terious drugs. The robbery of consumers in mere dollars under
this system, extended alphabetically through the whole sphere
of commerce, is manifest though incalculable. Foreign goods
cannot be excluded in this quick and lively community of Saxon-
Celtic people, and if they could be more effectually excluded than
they are, the internal evils would only be so much the greater.
The earthenware of Britain and France is imported direct into
New Orleans and other Southern seaports, though subject to
duties, from "brown and common" to "white and cream-coloured,"
of from 25 to 40 per cent. European fabrics and tissues of clothing and dress find a market whatever their price may be. But
while the trade of the South in foreign goods is reduced
to the veriest minimum, the robbery does not end with the
actual consumption of these forbidden wares, but is carried
on through every article of domestic manufacture which any
one here, however rich or poor, may need, from an anchor to a
needle, from a plough to a paletot; and the people who have
to sell their products abroad become the down-trodden thralls
and slaves of those who sell theirs at home. All owners and
cultivators of the soil, all who hope to live by their own
fair means and industry in these Southern parts, are literally
mobbed by Tariff Acts of Congress, knocked down in every
purchase they make by Federal "knuckle-dusters," fleeced
when down of every cent in their pockets, and when sprawling
up again are told to "G' long for rebels, or it will be
much worse for them!" People in Europe, when they
consider all this, will begin to perceive how it is that

the present prices of cotton,,which seem to them so handsome, are here simply ruinous, and that to grow wheat, cotton, tobacco, *ramie,* or any other vegetable thing conceivable for export on this virgin and sun-brightened soil of America, with any profit or satisfaction to the grower, is becoming a most doubtful issue. As for New Orleans itself, the operation of the Tariff can only be likened to a stroke of paralysis, smiting down through the whole half of the organic frame from the brain to the big-toe, and leaving both sides, whole and smitten, in an almost indistinguishable state of peculiar disability.   How the great town wags on in this paralysis, sunning itself all the while under the bright Louisianian skies, with no end of cotton and molasses, is quite wonderful to any observer of nature.   But there is one interest in the South. as already hinted, which enjoys a full breeze of Tariff Protection.   The sugar of Louisiana has an advantage of two to four cents per lb. over all Cuban and other foreign raw sugars; but as if to point conclusively the argument of "Free-trade *versus* Protection " in the United States, the sugar-growing interest in Louisiana is the only interest in the South that has made little or no headway since the close of the war, and would seem now, like other much more heavily " protected interests," to require almost boundless public largess to keep afloat in this chartless sea.   The United States have had, since the war, to levy annually immense sums of money, but it is bad policy in the name of public revenue to extirpate root and branch the sources of private revenue, and, a large Customs revenue being indispensable, the only just and wise course is to select a few general branches of indirect taxation falling equally on all parts of the community, without affording any section of the country or class of citizens an opportunity of plundering the rest, as under the progress of economic knowledge has been and is being done in other parts of the world.   Great Britain, while purging her tariff of the last dregs of monopoly and protection, has never seen her Customs revenue declining, but, on the contrary, flourishing more and more every year.

The deficiency of capital in New Orleans for the commercial demands and resources of the port can only be referred to with a certain reserve ; and it must be remarked, both in justice to the relative merits of the case and in legitimate reduction of a too inflated idea abroad as to what Northern capital and enterprise may now be expected to do in the South, that *deficiency of capital* is written over all parts of the Union as well as the South, and that, save in some few localities where a long course of almost fanatical Protectionist policy has developed an outlay of hard money and entailed a perennial public sacrifice disproportioned to their natural value, there is scarcely any section of this immense continent in which

P

land, labour, and productive resource are not greatly in excess of the capital necessary to employ and cultivate them. There has never been any great country so hostile in its commercial legislation to other countries, while so dependent on other countries for its most essential means of progress, as the United States. But in the South, so lately desolated by war, the deficiency of capital is more marked than elsewhere. The British and other European houses that deal in exchange, bring great resources to bear on moving the cotton crop. The effective purchasing power at the other end overcomes all obstacles to its purpose. Yet it is observable that from September to January, when this movement is at its height, the pressure for funds is usually severe, and in the course of the present season, aggravated somewhat probably by the war in Europe, as much as two per cent. per month has been paid on good mercantile paper. It appears from an official Bank statement just published that there are eleven banking companies in operation in New Orleans, of which the total paid-up capital is 7,497,182 dollars, or about a million and a half sterling; and the total deposits 15,039,499 dollars, or three millions sterling. The banks of New Orleans are constituted on different foundations, some, like the Citizens' and Canal Banks, being of old corporate standing, and others being of more recent formation under the "free banking law," or as "national banks" under the Federal banking polity since the war. But their mode of business is much the same. Save some small portions of old outlying notes, amounting in all to little more than 200,000 dollars, they have no "circulation" of their own, and use wholly greenback or national currency, which has come, from its uniformity and stability, and in contrast with the multiform and sometimes worthless currencies of past times, to enjoy great public confidence and to be much liked, so that it may really be regarded as a particular advantage accruing to the United States from a great national debt. The banks in New Orleans all observe the rule of retaining a reserve in "specie and current funds," equal at lowest to one-third of their liabilities. Thus, while the total "movement" liabilities shown in this statement are 17,598,035 dollars, the "specie and current funds" in hand are 6,807,978; but, if the capital of the banks were added to the liabilities, the reserve would be as 7 to 24. The total liabilities, exclusive of capital, are 17,597,935 dollars, and the total assets 26,944,732 dollars, giving, with the capital of 7,497,182 superadded to the liabilities, a clear surplus of 1,849,615 dollars. But this surplus is very unequally distributed. The old institutions represented by the Citizens' and the Canal Banks have 815,523 dollars of it, the remaining million being divided among the other nine—the Bank of America, which enjoys the largest run of business and popularity, and pays the largest dividends, sailing closer to the wind apparently than any of them, its total liabilities with capital being 4,055,857 dollars, and its total assets 4,066,617 dollars. There is no interest paid on deposits, and until banking institutions and society in all its parts attain a more firm consolidation, this stimulus to the economisation of monetary resources by the general community, urban and rural, in the United States is only tentatively practicable. But it appears in the aggregate that a banking company in New Orleans can always calculate on deposits without interest equal to double the amount of its capital. Banking is consequently very profitable, without having more than, or probably even as much as the ordinary risks of banking transactions in other parts of the world. The Citizens' Bank divides 16 per cent., the Bank of New Orleans 15, the Southern Bank 9, the Bank of America 30 per cent. per annum. The Bank of America, with a capital of half a million some odd dollars, has three millions and a half of deposits without interest, which are the source of its extraordinary profits. The Germania "National" Bank, the most prosperous of that class, divides 20 per cent. per annum. "National" banks, based on a small capital, are increasing in New Orleans; but though enjoying much privilege in the legalised deposit of Federal bonds for currency, with running interest to the bank from the bonds, and capable of very profitable management, are yet, as the creations of public privilege, so subject to the political discussions and dissensions of the Republic, to constant change of conditions by Congress or by the Secretary of the Treasury alone, and to sweeping Federal control, that they cannot be said to be anywise popular among men of business. One of the first of the "national" banks instituted in Louisiana, having fallen under mismanagement, was seized by the Federal authority for some security of its own and forcibly wound up, with great loss to the creditors, under a state of the bank's affairs which is declared to have shown assets sufficient for all its liabilities. This event has tended to swell the deeper currents of objection to "national" banks, and it is more than doubtful whether any companies under this form of constitution can overtake the vacant ground in any great place like New Orleans.

The halcyon days of light taxation have gone from this country, possibly not soon to return. Taxation in the United States is now, after the great war, necessarily heavy, while unnecessarily excruciating. Here in New Orleans, where tariff legislation represses every mercantile faculty, and prevents capital, so deficient, from multiplying, one feels this deeply. Against the Federal revenue there is no use to protest, save in the one cardinal point of how most lightly and equally to raise it—a branch of study heretofore happily not needing in the United

States to be much studied—but behind Federal revenue there are State revenue and City revenue, Alp on Alp, with confidence in the taxing power of State and City sinking almost to zero. State and City taxes in the South have been mounting up, since the war, to an altitude only short of that of the Federal taxes, with little or no power on the part of the taxpayers to help themselves and with loud complaints of stealing and corruption that are in the main wholesome, since they show that the spirit of liberty and self-government are by no means dead in this country. The total infliction is without doubt very severe. Take a merchant or manufacturer in New Orleans, with a capital (say) of 10,000 dollars, a house worth 6,000, and furniture worth 2,000 dollars. In the first place he pays a licence duty to the State, for the mere liberty to pursue his avocation, of 100 dollars; and another licence duty to the City, varying somewhat, but still to him 100 dollars. If selling spirituous liquors be any part of his business, he must pay another 100 dollars of licence duty to the Federal Government, and if he be one who professes to be a "rectifier," very few can have any bowels left for him at this point of the screw. But he pays, besides, direct taxes on his capital in business, on the value of his house, and on his furniture and personal effects of every kind, *minus* 500 dollars—in all to the amount of 4⅝ per cent. At the same rate he is taxed on money outside his business, if he have any, at interest, or in ships or sailing craft, or railway and other stocks. When all his means and substance have thus been taxed, a demand is made upon him for 2½ per cent. to the United States on his income from all sources, and he must thus part with a portion of his stock and of its annual produce at the same time. There are also stamp duties on bills and promissory notes of 5 cents per 100 dollars, on cheques 2 cents each irrespective of amount, and on deeds and instruments of every kind. His consumption of dutiable goods also pours heavy sums every hour of the day into the various treasuries. Assuming his profits of trade to be 6,000 dollars, which is supposing him to be very prosperous, he will have paid during the year in direct taxes alone at least 1,500 dollars if he make an honest return. If he is not so prosperous, if his profits be little or nothing at all, his capital will have been shorn and cut down by the inexorable shears of taxation on means and substance. Any rapid increase of capital among the citizens of New Orleans is thus unpromising; for many of the most fortunate are glad to remove as soon as possible to some clime where they will run the risk of being taxed to death no more. There is a practice in the United States of assessing real estate on its capital value instead of its annual rental, which has some unfavourable consequences, discouraging extensions and improvements of house property, and keeping many of the streets where a large traffic is carried on in an inconvenient and semi-dilapidated condition. Owners of house property are more averse to enter into the improvements needed by the occupiers when their assessment on capital is sure to be increased *pro rata* by the whole cost of the improvement than they would be were taxation confined to the increased rental, and shared with them equally by the occupiers. The result is that the owners are apt to stipulate for an increase of rent so disproportioned to the capital outlay as to stagger the occupiers, and prevent the desired operations.

The facts I have stated are enough to show that Taxation, without dwelling on the Misgovernment which is declared by so many witnesses to be its only return, is indeed severe and exhausting, and that the whole fiscal polity of the United States will have to be carefully revised and adjusted if New Orleans is to rise to the level of her great commercial position, if her captivity is to pass away "like streams of water in the South," and, going forth with precious seed, she is to return with sheaves in harvest joy and gladness.

CHAPTER XXX.

Trip in the *Bradish Johnson* down River.—The Sugar Plantations.—River
Traffic.—Passengers.—The Scenery.

[NEW ORLEANS. — *Jan.* 25 to *Feb.* 14.]

THE *Bradish Johnson*, though only a plantation boat, and in
dimension much inferior to·the floating palaces on the up-river
navigation of the Mississippi, is yet a gem of its kind, and,
while swallowing barrels of sugar and molasses with wondrous
capacity on her flat lower deck two or three feet above water,
opens on her second story in such a creamy brightness and
gilded luxury of saloon, boudoir, and sleeping chambers as
might befit a king and queen of the East with their brilliant
train of courtiers. The barge of Cleopatra, save in a few mere
poetical embellishments of Shakespeare, was not more gay, more
soft and silken, or more burnished in its equipments, than the
middle region of the river steamers on the Mississippi. The upper
story, seldom visited, is not so agreeable ; but the genius of the
American shipbuilders has here devised a watch-tower for the
steersman, and an ornamental cupola with azure roof and golden
minarets, bright as the colours of the Southern sky, and giving
to a white exterior without line of beauty an aspect of stately
grandeur, as if there were a Nabob somewhere in the interior of
the curious three-decker. For a combination of rough, raw, ready
traffic, with pleasure and luxury of accommodation to passengers,
no structures have been put on the waters to compare with the
Mississippi steamers. But for an unhappy tendency to take fire
or to burst their boilers, which can only be the result of carelessness, they would be perfect.[1] The *Bradish Johnson* is an
instance here, simply because it was in that steamer, at the
courteous invitation of Mr. Bradish Johnson, her owner—a
gentleman known alike in New Orleans and New York as a
great sugar-planter and merchant in one—that I passed down
some fifty miles from the city among the sugar plantations; and

---

[1] Six or seven Mississippi steamers, within about as many weeks, have
come to a bad end this winter.

though the circumstance, I fear, will not give her any immortality yet in passing one must touch, however lightly, on what one sees.

The sun was shimmering warmly over the levees and waters of the Mississippi, with the buildings on either side, at noon. All in the distance was so low that the funnels of the steamers looked even taller than they were, and a sensation of being too near the furnaces stole over one in an atmosphere quivering with heat. It was only when the *Bradish Johnson* pulled in her ropes, and her paddle-wheels began to revolve, that one wakened up to the delights of sailing on the Mississippi in periods of the year when the sun must be much more fierce. The vast body of cool, deep water, and the great fan of air produced by a movement of ten miles an hour, cannot fail to render the famous second story of the steamers the most pleasant of retreats in midsummer. The scenery, indeed, is not very captivating, because it is so monotonous. But the *Bradish Johnson* has no sooner got under way, now in the current and now among the driftwood, than she begins to row, in fine commercial cadence, betwixt great ferry-boats as big as herself, from one side of the river to the other—taking in a drove of lean Texan cattle on this, and giving out barrels of flour and sundry parcels on that, and sweeping bravely on, though making little progress as one thinks, through the great bends of the river. Large ships were moored to both banks; a revenue-cutter or two were in the stream; and a couple of Monitors, their brown iron decks lying as squat on the water, and much the same in shape, as the backs of a couple of soles, with a round-house only above the wave, where the guns are, and the crew conceal themselves, with under-water passage to works below, giving, very likely, hidden powers of motion—most singular marine reptiles, which, since there is nothing to shoot at, must be run down and crushed with an iron foot if their sting is ever to be extracted. An American patriot points out a monument in commemoration of a great swamp where President Jackson, at the head of the Federal army, repulsed a British infantry expedition, and killed a considerable number of Highland soldiers marching bravely to death, at the word of command, without the ships that were an essential part of their line of battle, a whole month after peace had been happily concluded in London betwixt " father and son;" and, quite close to the monument there is a vast sugar-mill, with thousands of acres of plantation in a state of dilapidation and decay. But the river environs of New Orleans have more agreeable objects of contemplation. The signs of manufacture native and proper to the city are not very marked, cotton-oil works being the most prominent; but there are many fine residences, and a Federal barracks under trees, with groups of

happy children playing on the clover lawns among sweet-scented
shrubs, and long planked walks to the water edge, where maidens
in white robes and fascinating curls, blonde and dark, come
down to bid adieu to parting or welcome arriving friends.
There was on this occasion, as usual in these river boats, a large
number of passengers, ladies as well as gentlemen—fine old
French seigneurs with all the polite affability of the olden time,
with other civilized persons of probably as ancient lineage, but of
quite a modern monetary aspect, as if bent on looking narrowly
into the securities—and stout honest ditchers, going down among
the plantations to negotiate a contract. There were also many
negroes, or at least coloured people of various hues, the men in
tweed trousers and jackets, and the women in modestly draped
serge or printed calico, according to taste or age, with emblems of
mourning not infrequent; some of the younger and sprier fellows
wearing pegtop pants with high-heeled boots and cane, repro-
ducing the costume of Bond Street dandies many long years
ago with remarkable exactness; and, in the matter of heel, long
cultivated in the South, giving to the Darwinian theory a quite
disturbing confirmation. One old portly woman of colour, who
had bound her head in a kerchief with hanging loops over the
ears, and mutton-chop whiskers of natural or artificial wool
brought down over her broad brown cheeks, and who was always
running about, on saloon deck and lower deck, upstairs and
downstairs, everywhere one happened to be, with something
eatable in her hands, and munching something similar in her
mouth with a strong and apparently unappeasable appetite—was,
in the first place, amusing, and in the second, suspicious or even
hateful. The first impression was that this old lady must have
some supreme connection with the cooking department, and that
the dinners of the ship were disappearing rapidly; and this
impression grew in exact ratio as any one on board wished to
have anything to eat. But it was a delusion. A very choice
dinner was served in due time in the saloon, with a supply of
good claret to the white people, while the negroes had their meal
under an awning on the saloon deck, where they had been
sauntering freely all day; and the old negro woman, shade of
Barmecide, turned out to be a genial old soul who keeps a shop
somewhere on the levees of New Orleans, and spends most of
her time on the river, up and down, executing small commissions
with the most trustworthy accuracy, and speaking French and
English to the genteel families with a fluency equal to her fine
gastronomic qualities. An intimate and cordial acquaintance-
ship prevails all through this riverain territory; and the banks
of the Mississippi south of New Orleans—so numerous are the
plantations, and the people on them brought into so frequent
intercourse by the river traffic—are in reality a great rural town,

where all classes, high and low, know one another better, and live in a more social spirit than in the streets of large cities.

The Mississippi at this point is scarce half a mile broad, with a slow and placid flow, yet full of the latent power and majesty of waters that run deep, and, as the sun falls on its surface, revealing rolling volumes of the most various colours, from bright red to brown and milky, as if all the great rivers swallowed up in this common channel were being twisted, like the strands of a cable, into union, and yet remaining separate and intact. The banks are so low as to lip the edge of the stream, with a fringe here and there of long willow saplings; and the horizon on either side is bounded by a dark grey wood, bursting at this period into streaks of green, at a distance of a mile to three-quarters of a mile from the *batture;* the sugar-cane fields, sometimes lower than the river, filling up the middle space. The Mississippi, in its progress, describes a series of curves round one great tongue of land after another, and as one looks forward athwart these windings, all that is of bank and forest fades down in the bright sunshine till it seems but mere drift-wood floating on the surface of the waters. But as the steamer ploughs its way round the curves, there is no want of life and cultivation along the margins of this swelling channel. Every sugar plantation is a little village in itself. The planter's mansion—sometimes elegant, always comfortable, seated amidst bright orange groves and fields of white clover, more radiantly green in its new spring growth than can be described—is flanked by rows of negro frame-cottages, windowed and painted white, with verandahs extending along the whole front, while close at hand is the sugar factory, with its great square chimney-stalk, broad shingled roof, and numerous outworks. Back from the river, more than half way to the wood, there is on most of the plantations a small building with a chimney-stalk, where a steam-pump helps the drainage of the fields out into the swamp. The planters have brought down the leaves of the sugar-canes to the *batture* in front, and behind the bank thus garnished there is usually a large heap of coals, transported by boats from the Ohio, and drayed by the mules as needed to the sugar-house. As the steamer presses its heavy bulk against this dry and yielding beach, one notes how admirably the Mississippi vessels are constructed for the work they have to do. The open lower deck laps the water edge of the *batture,* and with the help of a heavy plank, and sometimes without, the most easy entrance and exit are made for goods and passengers. On approaching, the steamer wheels round, turning her prow to the stream; backing out makes another semicircle, carrying her into the middle of the river, and nearly half-way to the landing on the other side, where she goes through a similar movement; and thus, describing in many series the figure 8, she steams, with heavy but fluid grace, her waltz-like dance along the Mississippi. Down river from New Orleans there is not much freight to give out, but as there is always a message or demijohn to deliver on one side, and an old negro woman who has hoisted her cotton handkerchief as a signal to be taken up on the other, the calls one has to make are numerous, if not universal. On the up voyage it is different, and nearly every plantation on both banks has barrels of sugar and molasses at this season to be shipped—the planters who have the best lands generally being most behind-hand in their pre-arrangements for the steamer. One planter, having the finest oval of a farm ever seen, descending in high and dry furrows spaciously to the river, no steam-pump necessary, after keeping us more than two hours under a hot sun—his barrels of molasses all uncorked, and his sugar hogsheads to be waggoned two by two from the sugar-house, more than half a mile away—when the steamer at last moved off, took a furious gallop to himself on his brown gelding across the fields, by way of making up for the delay so unconscionably inflicted on his neighbours and fellow-creatures. The Rev. Mr. Peregrin, Episcopal Methodist minister of Cincinnati, observed to me the sad want of churches and schools along this great sugar-growing and sugar-making causeway, and was sure a small skeleton temple the *Bradish Johnson* was approaching must be one of those blessed fruits of Northern gospel spirit and philanthropic principle everywhere since the war spreading over and regenerating the Southern States. But the "skeleton" turned out to be a Roman Catholic place of worship. The white population along this Mississippian territory is largely of French origin, and Roman Catholic; the Church of Rome, more-over, from New Orleans southwards, is one of the *livest* of ecclesiastical communities. And thus the day wears on, the sun declines more and more towards the West, and all terrestrial out-look assumes a more strange and unaccustomed shape. Towards sunset, when the orb of day is sinking on one bank of the river, and the full moon rising on the other, pale, ghostlike—the faintest adumbration of a heavenly body—and sun, moon, and intervening sky are brought so very near that in fancy one could almost touch them, an idea of proximity to the line of the Equator—the outmost bulge of "the orange flattening towards the poles"—steals over the imagination, till, as the shades of night gather round, the land on all sides slopes down out of sight, and nothing is left above the narrow horizon but the Mississippi, with this great water-fowl of a steamboat skimming, as it were, with heavy white wing over some deep and reed-bound tarn in the bosom of eternal shadows, and in the birthday of time when light and dry land began to be. The sun sets in these parts with startling rapidity. One moment a round fiery disc

glows in the West, as if it were big, fierce, and profound enough
to set the universe in a blaze, and the next it has disappeared,
leaving only an effulgence of gold and purple along the western
sky, as soft, and inexpressibly beautiful to behold, though a
million times as grand, as any tropical flower. And the orb of
night, with almost equal suddenness, advances from its pale
outline to fiery red, from red to pure silvery brightness, and then
casts a sheen over the waters, palpitating with every ripple, and
broadening as it palpitates, till the great river gleams and shines
like a lake of liquid ore. The plantation houses flash out now
and again in the moonlight from the darkened banks, and great
fires, of whose existence there was no trace during the day save
in trails of smoke hanging like specks of vapoury cloud in the
sky, flare up in the night air, telling that far beyond the plantations and the woods there are savannahs and prairies trembling
amidst swamps and bayous, where vagrant negroes may be
snatching some pasture land from the wilderness by flames, or
keen and eager hunters by like means beating up their prey.

The *Bradish Johnson* left New Orleans at twelve noon, and
arrived at Woodlands Plantation—forty-five miles of river—at
eight p.m.   But one-half the time must have been consumed in
crossings and stoppages at the various landings.

CHAPTER XXXI.

Woodlands, Point Celeste, and Magnolia Plantations.—The Sugar Mills.—
Sugar-refining Apparatus.—Culture of the Sugar-Canes.—Fowler's Steam
Ploughs.—Thomson's Road and Field Steamer.—Large Fixed Capital of
Sugar Estates in Louisiana.—Chinese Labour.

[NEW ORLEANS.—*Jan.* 25 to *Feb.* 14.]

MR. JOHNSON has two large plantations—Woodlands and Point
Celeste; and marching with them along the river front, and
extending round one of the river curves, is Magnolia Plantation,
the property of his neighbour, Mr. Lawrence. These plantations
are among the finest sugar estates in Louisiana, and their mills
and refineries are on a scale of the most liberal amplitude. The
reader may please to step in for a minute or two to the sugar-
house at Woodlands—an immense fabric covering more ground
than most town factories—a mill and refinery in one. First is
the sugar-mill, where the canes, carted in from the fields, are
carried by an endless rail under two ponderous rollers, seven feet
long, probably more than half as much in diameter, and have the
saccharine juice expressed from them; and where the bruised
and fibry refuse, or "baggasse," as it is called, on issuing from
the rollers, is taken up again by the endless rail, and carried
direct into a furnace, in which it is burned, and makes part of
the steam-power necessary to drive the great iron wheel of the
mill. It is worthy of note, as part of the economy of the process,
that the "baggasse" makes steam enough to drive the mill
proper, and that the canes, as far as steam-power is concerned,
really express their own juice without other fuel. On going
down to the ashpit of the furnace, what remains of the cane
there is as like the coke of coal as two things can be. For the
steam required by the refining processes, in which it is largely
consumed, there is another furnace and set of boilers fed with
coal. The juice as expressed by the rollers is an impure and
turbid liquor, with much earthy and vegetable matter in it,
needing to be quickly looked after, else the liquor will sour and
spoil. When one cuts a sugar-cane through the middle and
looks at the juice welling out from the interior pores and arteries,
nothing could seem more pure, more like spirit of ether itself,

than this saccharine essence; and if it could be sucked out as perfectly as it is every hour of the day in the cane-fields by the masterly and exquisite lips of the negroes it would crystallize and be the finest sugar immediately. But though great ingenuity—English, French, and Spanish—has been exerted on this mechanical problem, and the sugar-growers are bewildered by new processes and new modifications of old ones, yet nothing equal to or resembling the mouth of a vigorous negro boy or girl has up to this time been invented. So, upon the juice and other matter crushed out by the rollers, the clarifying process, repeated and developed to the last stages of refinement, has to begin and be carried out with an elaboration and outlay of capital to be seen in all our large refineries, and marvellous to find here within a few paces of the fields where the sugar-cane itself is grown. The juice passes through a series of open trays, with steam-pipes, copper or iron, coiled along the bottom, where the scum sent to the surface by the heat is taken off; then through bag filters and "bone-black" filters (the latter being large round pans filled with burnt bone-dust, through which the liquor percolates with excellent clarifying result); then through "evaporators," differing little in appearance from the clarifying trays, but bringing the liquor to a lower degree of heat; through "bone-black" again, and next into the vacuum pans—large tower-like vessels, in which, from the lower temperature at which the syrup granulates *in vacuo*, the grain begins to be perfectly formed, and is completed either by being passed into long rectangular wooden troughs or "coolers," or into semi-cylindrical vessels of the same capacity as the vacuum pans, with slowly revolving paddles to keep the sugar in its half-liquid state until it gets to the centrifugal machines, the last touch of all— little round shallow vessels, cased with two or three layers of the finest copper wire-net that can be made, through which, by revolutions of 1,200 in a minute, and mere force of whirl, every drop of molasses or liquid still incorporated with the sugar is squirted out, leaving only the dry sugar of commerce, to be put into hogsheads, sent to market, and sold to the highest bidder. The sugar thus produced on Woodlands is the finest powder sugar of the market; but were it put through the "centrifugals" again, with some water added, it would come forth in the purest crystals, to be moulded into snow-white loaves if necessary. The molasses cast off are, by pipe and sub-floor arrangement, lapped up and re-boiled, and sent through the centrifugals again to make "seconds" and even "thirds," with molasses still over, which are not to be confounded by any means in the market with the prevailing molasses of New Orleans. Even the "bone-black," once used, is put through a kiln and re-burnt, and sent back to the filters, so that no economy appears to be overlooked.

The sugar-house on Magnolia differs little, save in mere detail, from the general process on Woodlands. The sugar-mill, instead of two great rollers, has three of somewhat smaller dimensions, giving a second squeeze to the canes, which is believed to be beneficial, and may as well be given as not. The whole arrangement of the factory is admirable; and from an office upstairs in the centre, one looks down through the mill on the one hand, and the refinery on the other, with the eyes of an Argus. The reader has only to consider the maze of various mechanism underlying every square yard of every floor of the sugar-house, and extending outward in cisterns, boilers, and furnaces, which all this process involves, in order to perceive what an elaborate combination or complication of chemistry, manufacture, and agriculture sugar-making on the great scale in Louisiana must be.

Going over the fields on Woodlands, there are large spaces of rich open land, ribbed with the furrows of last year, untilled, but ready, with little labour, to receive a new course of seed-canes. Labour is at present at a stand. The negroes, enjoying a long holiday since Christmas, are chaffering with the planters, sugar falling, for higher terms. They had sixteen dollars a month last year, and rations equal to five—twenty-one dollars a month, or rather more than a pound sterling per week. The planters, to make short dispute, have offered a round dollar a day without rations, or twenty-six dollars, or 5*l.* 4*s.* 6*d.* a month; but the negroes, thinking there is something in "rations," doubt whether last year's terms may not be better after all. The great law of demand and supply in the matter of labour operates here under curious difficulties, the supply neither knowing what it is worth nor what it wants, and the demand, having no other shift, forced to try all kinds of dodges, offering sometimes less or more indifferently, in order to get the supply to begin, which is the main thing for both. The perplexity of this state of affairs, especially to men accustomed to the system of slave labour, with its fixed quantity of rations and clothing, must be taken into account in all questions of Southern production, with a large consideration in favour of employers in the South, who, under the abolition of an old and bad system, have yet to grope in the dark for the elements of a new and better without exactly finding them. There is no sharing of crops with the negroes on the sugar as on the cotton plantations, the large outlay of capital in the sugar-mill and refinery, and the amount of white labour necessary in this branch of industry, forbidding that simple but questionable solution of immediate difficulties. The soil on Woodlands is cultivated much the same as, but with stronger mules and somewhat deeper ploughs than, in the cotton districts. The plantation, almost level, is intersected by waggon-roads and broad drains, more like canals than ditches. When the water flows down through these channels to the Mississippi it is well; but when it backs the other way there is a steam-boiler house, driving not so much a pump as a broad-feathered wheel or revolving fan set in the canal, which lifts the water five feet, and sends it out into the wood and swamp behind. Vast swarms of blackbirds—not of the singing species—cover the Indian corn patches, doing little harm on the sugar plantations, but very plaguy customers on the rice farms, to be rabbled off by a smaller swarm of negro boys, only a little less black and voracious than themselves; and, on this occasion, a dense wing of the countless army had settled down on a mound covered with straw on the cane-fields, not far from one of various wooden sheds, where the workers run for shelter in a heavy shower. In this and similar mounds the sugar seed-canes of the year are treasured—fine, carefully-selected, purply-coloured stalks, six to eight feet long, and about as thick as one's wrist, with ring-joints at every six or eight inches, from which heart-shaped buds, two or even three round the joint, are springing, and clinging while they spring. The sugar-cane, as thus seen, is quite a picture of beauty in colour, art-symmetry, and modestly-budding vitality. When the drills are opened, the tall seed-canes are laid in twos or threes laterally along the bed —the great object of the sugar-planter being to bring up as many canes as possible; and, on the whole, the cultivation of the sugar-cane is less elaborate, minute, and troublesome than that of the cotton-plant. Riding down one of the waggon-roads of Woodlands to the common way along the *batture*, there was a fine breeze under a cloud-tempered sun rippling the great river, which was six or eight inches higher than the day before, and as it laved the roots of the moss-draped trees on the one hand, and the soft air rustled the leaves of the orange-groves round the blacksmiths' shops and the villas and hostelries on the other— the said groves yielding to people in these parts, with little trouble beyond the original cost of planting, some thousands of dollars per annum—a sensation of health and pleasure vibrated through one's whole frame, and in its full glow I was met by the doctor of these plantations, who reported a fairly clean bill of health, but three loving wives, prominent ladies of the district, had died since last fall, and their decease had cast a gloom over the whole district. On the other side of the river a small town with notable buildings was visible, to which people have to go to worship on Sundays, and to sue and be sued on other days of the week, crossing the Mississippi in boats—the head town of the "parish"; for the Louisianians, following old tradition, call their counties "parishes," the minor divisions being mere wards and sub-divisions of parishes, and this trace of ancient nomen-clature makes one feel a little more at home. But if anything could recall the memory of Old England here, it ought to be

" Magnolia" plantation, spreading round a loop of the river in
a firm, dry, and well-braced semicircle, and yet in parts divided
into square lots as level as a bowling-green, where two sets of
Fowler's stationary-engine steam-ploughs, costing 15,000 dollars
each, were turning over the soil $2\frac{1}{2}$ feet deep, and laying
furrows so straight and handsome that mule and negro-ploughing
in comparison must be pronounced the most barbarous workman-
ship.   In the courtyard was an enormous grubber, or cultivator,
of the same manufacture, with prongs a yard long, and so
adjusted as to pass down on either side betwixt the sugar-canes,
and stir up the soil round them afresh.   There was also in one
of the ditches a machine for scooping out the gathering mud and
decaying vegetable matter without hand-labour, but from some
defect in the motive-power, it had come into passing desuetude.
One cannot but admire the splendid courage and enterprise of
bringing all these costly mechanical inventions to the hard and
necessary work of the soil.   Mr. Lawrence, in conversation, discovered a contempt for Thomson's road and field steamer,
ploughing only eight inches deep, and sticking fast at the end
of the furrows ; so unlike Fowler's, which works with perfect
balance and so much deeper.   Mr. Johnson, though not finan-
cially committed to steam-ploughing, yet observant, could as little
conceal his regret that the trial of Thomson's engine lately in
Jersey State was a failure, and that the ploughs, inextricable at
the ends of the field, had to work round in a circle.[1] And Dr.
Wilkinson, as old and vigilant a planter probably as either,
observed that Thomson's steamer, were there no ploughing in
the matter, would be worth its cost (some 5,000 dollars) on the
sugar-plantations for nothing more than hauling in the sugar-
canes to the mill, which is one half the battle.   These questions
of steam-power applied to agriculture—nowhere more important
than in the Southern States—must be left to experience.   But,
putting agriculture aside, too much complicated as it is on sugar-
estates with manufacture, what have we ?   Magnolia, from 600
acres of cane, has manufactured 850 hogsheads of sugar in two
months in its sugar-house, the cost of which latter cannot be
estimated at less than from 200,000 to 250,000 dollars ; the

---

[1] It must be observed that the trial of Thomson's engine in New Jersey
was not a trial of its adaptation to ploughing at all.   Only an engine had
been sent to New York.   There was no ploughing apparatus attached to it,
and the trial was made with a seven-gang plough, consisting of the ordinary
ploughs of the country.   For ploughing, Thomson's engine requires such a
special ploughing apparatus as Lord Dunmore has applied in Scotland.
Mr. Thomson's patent right in the United States has been transferred to
Mr. Williamson of New York, who is producing a seven-gang plough that
will lift quite easily at the end of the furrows, and cover a narrower surface
than was possible to the improvised ploughs in New Jersey—about eight feet
wide.

sugar-house on Woodlands must have cost about as much, and that on Point Celeste probably not much less; and Mr. Johnson, if he has got his canes into the mills with the usual expedition, will have made about 1,500 hogsheads of sugar. So that, within four or five miles of one another, three perfectly equipped sugar-mills and refineries, costing probably near a million of dollars, have made some 2,300 hogsheads of sugar for the year, which they have done in two months, standing idle, with the necessary staff of skilled labour, all the other ten months of the year, and wearing down in idleness probably near as much as if they were all the while in active operation. This is the system of development on which sugar culture in Louisiana has hitherto proceeded. No other system can yet be said to have emerged under the assumed necessity of having the best sugar-making apparatus close at hand on the cane-fields, so that the canes, when ripe, may be treated and sugar made before they are injured by the first touches of frost. But it is not a desirable system. It is a system which betrays a great defect somewhere, whether in mechanical invention or in division of labour, and is burdened with a weight and waste of capital that must be hazardous, I greatly fear, to the proprietors, as well as a formidable obstacle to any rapid recovery and extension of sugar-cane culture in Louisiana.

The scarcity of field labour appears to be a source of much anxiety to the sugar-planters, and hence the readiness to introduce steam-ploughs and other labour-saving machines, were their practical fitness assured and their cost within reasonable bounds. But the difficulty of engaging hands is not greater than I have found in many cotton districts, while the terms of remuneration are not so high. One planter on this Mississippi coast has entered into a contract with twenty-five Chinamen for three years, and squads of that race are found at work in various capacities in the neighbourhood of New Orleans. The Chinese element is just so extant as that a few pigtails may be seen any day in the streets of the city; and efforts are being made from time to time to induce a larger immigration from the "Flowery Land."

CHAPTER XXXII.

[NEW ORLEANS.—*Jan.* 25 to *Feb.* 14.]

THIS city of the South is large and lively enough to present the
most varied objects of interest to a traveller. If his object be
information, there are a hundred branches of inquiry in which
the knowledge to be obtained is alike new and valuable; if he
seek amusement, he can be well amused; and if any one would
write a history of New Orleans, social, political, and commercial,
he must make up his mind to stay a long time, and produce a
large volume. But almost the first question put to a stranger,
is, whether he has seen "the Negro Legislature?" and the
Legislative Assembly of the State, as at present constituted,
seems to be regarded much in the light of a joke by most of the
citizens.

I went to see the Legislature of Louisiana. There were a few
carriages, and some knots of people round the door of the
Mechanics' Hall, in which the Legislative Body sits. The
lobbies were crowded with negro men and lads "from the
country," with a sprinkling of more white and sharp-visaged
townsmen; and negro women were selling cakes, oranges, and
lollipops up to the door of the Chamber of Representatives.
Within the Chamber itself were seated in semicircle round the
Speaker's chair, with little fixed desks and drawers full of papers
before them, a body of men as sedate and civilized in appearance
as a convention of miners' delegates in Scotland or the North of
England. On close inspection, a few Africans were visible, but
yellow men seemed to predominate. The Senate differed little
in general aspect or composition, but was presided over by
Lieutenant-Governor Dunn, a really black man as far as could
be seen in the shadow, and was being addressed by an honourable white Senator of an intellectual cast of head and face, who
appears to have gained more notoriety than all the rest by
marrying a black woman. There is no supreme law of taste,

and negro suffrage and love together combine to produce occasional startling effects. But having seen a few coloured men
sitting among a great majority of whites in the House of Representatives, and two gentlemen of decided African blood in the
Senate of Virginia, with no want of cordiality and honest political
intent, I am not disposed to attach radical importance to the
" incompatibilities of .colour " in legislation, albeit the spectacle
of a majority of coloured and negro-worshipping and negro-
marrying legislators in Louisiana and South Carolina be matter
of passing amazement and regret. It is strange, abnormal, and
unfit that a Negro Legislature should deal, as the Legislature of
Louisiana has been dealing, with the gravest commercial and
financial interests, dispensing not only the State taxes and
patronage, but the levees of the Mississippi, and the sugar sheds,
warehousing, and cattle marketing of New Orleans to private
companies, with unlimited powers of compulsion and taxation
over the community of merchants, planters, and white people of
business and industry, who, though a numerical majority of the
population, have as little power in the government as if they
were inhabitants of another sphere, and are forced to speak
of it only as a grim jest, or as a playful though melancholy jibe.
This state of things is not any advancement of the negro. It is
only his exaltation, through the exigencies of Federal politics
since the war, into a delirium of folly and corruption, which,
under the action of parties at Washington, will assuredly, soon
or late, be reduced by two inevitable amendments, nowise incon-
sistent in principle with the "fifteenth," viz. the restoration of
proscribed people in the South to their equal rights under the
Declaration of Independence and the Constitution, and the
limitation of the suffrage to citizens, white and black, who have
a local habitation and pay their taxes. It is not so much
universal suffrage that misgoverns the United States as a loose
misconception and strong-handed abuse, wherever practicable,
of what universal suffrage, even on the broadest theory of representative democracy, really is. The poll-tax—the only tax
levied on the negro masses—seems still worse paid in Louisiana
than in other Southern States. " At present," says Mr. Graham,
the Auditor, in his report for the session of 1871, " it is paid by
a comparatively small number of those who are subject to no
other State tax. Except in comparatively rare cases, it is paid
only by property holders." And the expenses of collection, he
shows, exceed by a hundred and forty per cent. the net proceeds
of the poll-tax paid into the Treasury. The poll-tax is set apart
to the support of free schools, chiefly, though not wholly, for the
negro children. The tens of thousands of negroes who fail to
pay the poll-tax, vote not only once, but occasionally several
times over in the same election, and no one seems to think that

the exercise of political *right* over the life, liberty, and property of the whole community has anything to do with the discharge of political *duty* to the community, in the direct line even of absolute personal and parental responsibility. While this is the state of the poll-tax on negroes for schools, what is the action of the Education Department? The State Superintendent, said to be a Northern Baptist minister, is enforcing a rule, that has received some sanction from the Legislature, for what he calls "mixed education," and the sitting of white and black children on the same school benches, and being taught in the same classes. The rule is as little desired by the coloured people as by the white; it is open to the gravest technical difficulty and objection in respect of the mere art of school instruction; and even though it were sacred in principle and morality, yet it is not within a thousand miles of the legitimate sphere of compulsory legislation. The rule, of course, cannot be enforced practically save as a mere disturbing wedge; but the savour of it destroys confidence, and New Orleans, which before the war had a munificent free school system for its white children, and was going gladly on to give the same to the children of the negroes, is drifting back into private schools in connection with the various Churches—Presbyterian, Episcopalian, and Roman Catholic— maintained by the subscriptions and fees of those who have to pay the whole, their own and the negroes' shares included, of the free school taxation. This source of public discontent— paying for one's black neighbour and for oneself twice over, and spoiling a noble national work in the process—is kept full steam up by a reign of Federal misrule, which can only be of the most temporary character. The American people must be acute enough to perceive that, in this and various ways in the South, they are not only imperilling the unity and indivisibility of the Republic, but putting the fool's cap on Republican principle.

The Governor of Louisiana, Warmoth, is a young man of spirit and ability, who came down to New Orleans at the close of the war, and by dexterously "fugling" the negro vote, got himself advanced to this high position, in which he seems to be growing wiser if richer, and is tacking about, not without skill, in the present calm. The outcry against him has been loud and deep; but all that can be said is, that whereas he was once poor, he is now very rich, and that his wealth, if the wages of corruption, has been so deftly acquired that no one can lay his finger on the foul spot. It is not uncommon to hear in New Orleans that Dunn, the negro Lieutenant-Governor, is a more trustworthy man than his superior in office; and while there is no doubt that the fair Desdemona of the State has been foully wronged, it seems a puzzle whether Othello or Iago be the more to blame. The New Orleans Chamber of Commerce succeeded by an Act and "self-denying ordinance" of the Legislature, last session, to get decree that the State debt shall not exceed twenty-five millions of dollars. The coloured legislators in the Mechanics' Hall are "pottering" over bills three millions beyond the prescribed maximum; but lenders on State security in Louisiana are not without warning.

Have you been at the French market on a Sunday morning betwixt four and five o'clock? at the Opera House? at the Masked Ball? at the —— where "youth and pleasure" (and sometimes age and misery) meet? at the Cemeteries? are questions which follow in rapid succession, as one hears the miscellaneous voices of New Orleans. I have been chiefly pleased by the success with which, amidst abounding temptations, a quiet and happy social intercourse is cultivated by the people of New Orleans. But the great and serious interest here, amidst all distractions whether of politics or pleasure, reverts mainly, and by natural gravitation, to sugar; and to that subject I shall briefly revert.

Woodlands, Point Celeste, and Magnolia plantations, as I have described, are "model" plantations. They are plantations on which what is called "the steam train" is brought into operation in all its completeness. But almost every form and modification of process, from the old arrangement of wooden rollers and horse mills, adopted when the Jesuits first introduced the cultivation of the sugar-cane about the middle of the last century, to the higher and later improvements, are to be found in this and other sugar-growing regions of the American Union. Horse and mule power in the mills, indeed, has rapidly given place to steam, and now remains in only 153 plantations, while steam-power claims possession of 664. The old process, however, of boiling in "open kettles," to which the fire is directly applied with much waste of fuel, as well as darkening of the colour of the sugar and other economical disadvantages, prevails in no fewer than 683 of the Louisianian sugar plantations; on 81 there are "open pans," giving evaporation under lower temperature, and improving on the "kettles" pure and simple, but the saccharine matter from which has to be put into hogsheads with perforated bottoms to let the molasses drip out, so that in making up two hogsheads of merchantable sugar a third is required from which to fill up the other two, as the percolation proceeds; and in only 53 of the Louisianian plantations have "vacuum pans," equal to, or resembling the splendid sugar houses of Mr. Johnson or Mr. Lawrence, been introduced. The "open kettles" make excellent sugar, though in smaller quantity from the same weight of cane than "the steam train and vacuum pans;" and they yield molasse exceeding as much in quality as in quantity the final molasse of the "centrifugals" in the

more expensive refineries, and fetching from 40 to 60 cents per
gallon in the market, while the other goes at 15 to 25. Still,
molasse in sugar-making is only leakage more or less perfectly
recovered from total loss. There can be no doubt that the
" open kettle " process is a rude process, and does not give the
planter the full saccharine juice grown in his fields. Yet, such
is the burdening effect of large outlays of capital in machinery
for which there is only a few weeks' work in the year, that the
" open kettle " people seem to get on as well as, if not better and
safer than, their more advanced neighbours. There is a large
foundry at New Orleans which has survived all the changes of
forty-five years, employing from 300 to 400 hands at three to
four dollars a day, and is at the top in sugar-making apparatus
and other branches of ironwork. From Mr. Mitchell, the working chief of this establishment, I have received some valuable
information as to the cost of the various kinds of machinery in
use on the plantations. The old horse-mills, but with iron
rollers, cost, according to dimensions, from 450 to 900 dollars,
exclusive of wooden frame and erections. The cost of the boiling
apparatus used in connection with one of these mills, and consisting generally of four semi-spherical cast-iron kettles—capable
of boiling, say three or four hogsheads of sugar per twenty-four
hours—is about 300 dollars, exclusive of erection, costing about
as much. The mills, on the other hand, driven by a steam-
engine, with necessary pipes and appurtenances, are made for
prices ranging from 3,000 to 25,000 dollars, according to size,
making from four to forty hogsheads per twenty-four hours.
The cost of kettles suitable to the steam-mills, similar to the
foregoing but larger, and generally used in sets of six (when
more than twelve hogsheads a day are required two sets are
employed), is about 1,000 dollars per set, exclusive of erection.
The kettles, where steam-power has been introduced, are frequently modified by the use of a steam granulating pan or
" batterie," generally of copper, the cost of which, with coil of
pipes, valves, and tanks, is usually about 2,000 dollars. Then
comes the open steam-train process, by which the kettles are
dispensed with, and the price of which, with suitable boilers,
varies from 10,000 to 30,000 dollars. If a vacuum pan be
added, with pumps and centrifugals, a further expense is made,
according to capacity, of from 8,000 to 28,000 dollars. There is
another process effected in what is called " the Rillieu apparatus,"
costing from 20,000 to 50,000 dollars. It will be observed how
rapidly the absorption of fixed capital proceeds as the process of
refining sugar on the plantations is pursued from one improvement to another, and that if there are defects in the ruder
processes at the one end, there are drawbacks no less serious in
the higher processes at the other. This is the more worthy of

consideration, since the production of sugar in Louisiana does not thrive as could be wished, and makes little or no progress towards the development attained before the war, though the reason does not appear on the surface. Soil and climate are suitable. Improved sugar lands can be bought for 25 to 40 dollars an acre. The newer and cheaper the soil, it is often the more vigorously fertile, and the growth of the sugar-canes has to be retarded rather than stimulated. But on the old soils, a crop of field peas ploughed down gives them a new power for the growth of the canes. The average produce is 1½ hhds. (1,100 lbs. to the hhd.) of sugar with molasses per acre—say 1,500 lbs. of sugar at 8 cents per lb., equal to 120 dollars, and 80 gallons of molasses at 25 cents per gallon, equal to 20 dollars—in all 140 dollars of produce per acre, contrasting favourably with the 200 lbs. of cotton lint at 12 cents per lb., or 24 dollars per acre, of the cotton fields. Yet how different the progress of these two great branches of Southern production since the war! Were tranquillity to be restored to Cuba, or that island to be annexed to the United States, the sugar-planting interest in Louisiana, under its present conditions, would probably be placed in peril. The Cuban insurrection, by disturbing the system of slave labour, can only have been a help to the Louisianian planters, while the duty on Cuban and other foreign raw sugars is like so much money put into their pockets by the Federal Government, which Congress at any hour has the power to withdraw. There may be little time to lose in probing the difficulties of sugar-production in Louisiana to the foundation, and in removing the defects under which it labours, the chief of which appear to be an inefficient extraction of the juice of the cane alike where the fixed capital is small or moderate; greatly too costly machinery and apparatus where the process is more perfect; and the difficulty, not peculiar to sugar-culture here, of attempting to do on the plantations what had better be done, under other capital and responsibility, in the refineries of the large towns.[1]

[1] I am not sufficiently informed on the culture of sugar in Cuba or the British West Indies to compare it in any way with the sugar culture of Louisiana. The processes of sugar-making are very probably as varied and as little determined to any common basis of economy in the West Indies as in Louisiana. But the great activity of trade in sugar-making apparatus, more especially in Glasgow, for many years, and the great amount of skill and ingenuity exerted in the adaptation of apparatus to every size of estate, and to various degrees of sugar-refining, are sufficient proofs that outside the United States very close and eager attention is being paid by planters to this question. I have been courteously supplied by Messrs. Mirrlees and Tait, of Glasgow, with their "prices of machinery for sugar plantations," from which a comparison may be made between the outlay that a planter in Cuba or Demerara makes in machinery and the similar outlay of a planter in Louisiana. Discarding the cattle mills and old "open kettles," which are clearly behind the times, and avoiding, on the other hand, the "vacuum pans" and

An apparatus has been patented by a large refining firm in
Manchester, called "the Sugar Concretor," and not unknown
though not yet in use here, which, with much economy of fuel and
labour, concentrates the whole juice of the cane, after the ordinary
defecation, into a concrete mass, without making molasses, and
preserving, in fact, both sugar and molasses in one bulk for the
operations of the refiner.   Something of this kind, if moderate
in cost, economical, and labour-saving, would seem suitable for
the many sugar plantations of Louisiana that cannot be brought
into culture from the twofold difficulty of labour and want of
capital.   There are one or two refineries in New Orleans, but
they are of little account in the sugar-making of the State; and
it is surprising, while the town of Greenock, for example, on the
distant Clyde, has such a multitude of refining establishments,
adding largely to its wealth and population, that New Orleans,
with an almost boundless sugar-growing region of its own, and
within a few days' sail of the Sugar Islands, should make so
little figure in this growing and profitable branch of trade.

"centrifugals," which belong more to the sugar refiner than the sugar planter,
and taking, as the most suitable to Louisiana, with its numerous uncultivated
sugar estates, the machinery where steam is introduced both for driving and
boiling, the results are as follow :—In Louisiana a sugar mill driven by steam,
sufficient to make four hogsheads, or 4,400 lbs. of sugar in twenty-four hours,
or 183 *lbs. an hour*, costs 3,000 dols. ; set of kettles to suit 1,000 dols.—in
all 4,000 dols, equal, at an exchange of 4¾ dols. for the pound sterling, to 842*l.*
In Glasgow the price of a steam sugar mill, sufficient to make a ton, or
2,240 lbs. a day of ten hours, *or* 224 *lbs. an hour*, with set of pans (600 gals.)
and a steam clarifier (400 gals.) to suit, complete, and at the highest value
they are made, is 450*l.*   It will be observed that the Glasgow apparatus,
at a cost of 450*l.*, makes 224 lbs. of sugar an hour, while the Louisiana
apparatus, at a cost of 842*l.*, makes 183 lbs. of sugar an hour.   Yet the
Louisiana apparatus does not include a " steam clarifier," as the Glasgow
apparatus does, and it is usual in Louisiana to add to the "kettles" a " steam
granulating pan," which costs 2,000 dols. more.   These results, as near a
common point of comparison as can be approached, support more than a doubt
whether the Americans, by the tariff and its tendency to exclude all inter-
action of commerce and industry with other countries, are not starving their
foundries and stemming back the development of their sugar estates at the
same time.

CHAPTER XXXIII.

[NEW ORLEANS.—*Jan.* 25 to *Feb.* 14.]

THE resources of Louisiana lie so profuse on the surface in the remarkable vegetative power of her river lands that it seems an almost useless digression to speak of mineral deposits, which may here, indeed, be as inconsiderable in value as they are unnecessary to the attainment of the highest prosperity. Mr. Bigney, the enlightened editor of the *New Orleans Times,* has shown me specimens of *lignite* found on the Ouachita (Washita) River, and another specimen, more strongly carboniferous, black and glossy like coal, though very light, found by Mr. Todd, a Scotchman, on the Red River, in a seam three feet deep. Also, a small cake of quartzose-brecchia impregnated with metallic specks, and evidently bound together by the action of oxide of iron on pebbly or flinty beds. But the presence of such conglomerates is not always an indication of seams of ore, and any one who has examined the undoubted mineral regions of the South in Alabama and Tennessee and parts of North Georgia, and seen the hilly ranges, traversed by layers of coal and iron, yet cloven in two, and washed into valleys, can be at no loss to conceive how widely the mineral treasures, thus broken up, may have been dispersed, and falling slowly and irregularly from the waters in which they were suspended, may have left their traces on many a distant landmark. Yet there are two remarkable mineral developments in Louisiana, which seem capable of immediate and profitable utilisation. The first is a discovery of rock salt on an island within a few miles of Vermilion Bay, an arm of the Gulf. This rock salt is found by chemical analysis to be almost a pure chloride of sodium. It has been mined, and reduced to the grain of Liverpool coarse salt ; and has been brought in large quantity to market, where it has commanded general acceptance. The price of Liverpool salt in New Orleans was 1¾ dollars per sack of 210 lbs. The Louisiana was offered at 1·35 dollars, and the Liverpool was at once reduced to, and still remains at, the same figure, though the production of the Louisiana, from some hitch betwixt the interests concerned, appears to have suffered a temporary interruption. The Federal Congress, with its usual opaqueness on commercial matters, has imposed an enormous duty (18 to 24 cents per 100 lbs.) on foreign salt, the whole benefit of which goes to a single salt manufactory somewhere in the North, and all the loss to the American people; but the development of this mine of salt on the Bayou Petite Anse, for curing and packing purposes, would be a great advantage to Texas and Louisiana. The second mineral discovery is what from all accounts appears to be a rich deposit of crystalline sulphur on the Calcasieu River in the south-western part of the State. The strata are peculiar. There is first a bed of yellow clay 160 feet deep, then grey and yellow sand 173 feet, next a blue sandy limestone 48 feet, under which there is a deposit of pure crystalline sulphur 108 feet thick. This is followed by successive beds of gypsum containing sulphur and of pure crystalline sulphur, to a depth, so far as bored, of more than a thousand feet from the surface. The land was leased to bore for oil, sulphur was found instead, and a litigation, of course, ensued; but so valuable a discovery can hardly be long locked up " in Chancery."

Straying through Carondelet Street one finds the "new riches" of Louisiana displayed on every hand. There was a sale one day of *Ramie*—a plant whose fibre is incomparably superior to flax or cotton, and only inferior, if inferior, to silk, and though of Japanese origin is attracting some speculative attention here and in Alabama—and so I went into the sale-room, found it was a sale of a few boxes of roots, and understood at once that *Ramie* is for the present in the introductory and planting stage, and will have to pass through a long and severe ordeal. *Ramie* has hitherto been inquired after chiefly by the manufacturers of Bradford, a fact in itself conclusive of its fate, for the *Ramie* fabrics as soon as they appear will be discountenanced and depressed in the market by Federal duties, and the belles of New Orleans, whose Southern patriotism is only surpassed by their exquisite taste in matters of costume, will be compelled, much against their will, to array themselves in silk. I could not help remarking to *Paterfamilias*, " How richly, and yet how tastefully, your ladies dress! Considering the enormous price of every article of apparel in this country, I could hardly have deemed it possible." "Yes," he replied, "you probably think they dress only too well. As Republicans, we endeavour to repress this feminine frivolity as much as we can, and heap on duties in the hope or the pretence of compelling a general simplicity of attire. But I am afraid this is one of those wars against Nature which not only defeat their own object, but increase the very evil they profess to war against." I was tickled by the *naïveté*, as well as the wisdom, of this observation ; for the fair sex all in all are not insensible to economy, and if there be any remedy for the so-called weakness of women it must be in spreading before them as great a profusion of ribbons, laces, silks, and *ramies* as possible, every new beauty more cheaply beautiful than another. Taste and even tasteless desire become wonderfully bewildering amid great variety of choice, and are most sure to be driven back on the right course when economy is on the side of what is most pretty and becoming. *Ramie* is a new sensation in the market, while tea is quite an old one. Yet, the cultivation of tea is also commanding some attention in Louisiana, and thousands of seeds and plants are being distributed by the Department of Agriculture at Washington for the propagation of this new industry in the Southern States. But I confess I have been more engaged by the arrival in the Mississippi of a cargo of tea direct from China than by all these enterprising efforts of General Capron. The Southern people have been plied so long by the vilest corruptions of green tea, and the saying " it will do for the Southern market " is so common in the tea streets of New York when a particularly bad invoice turns up, that the consumption of the Chinese beverage has been rapidly going out as the " Heathen Chinée " themselves have been coming in, and a direct importation of sound tea into New Orleans would probably make more satisfactory progress than the importation of pigtails. For if coffee be good in the morning, tea is an agreeable change in the afternoon ; and in these hot climates cold tea lemonade, iced, is declared by the few who have tried it to be more fragrant and refreshing than the most liberal libations of soda-water or other effervescing liquids.

The city of New Orleans, amidst all its wants, has now got one thing which suits it exactly—an ice factory—the sweetest, cleanest, most scientific, artistic, and beautiful of all factories ever seen or imagined, where 72 tons of ice a day are manufactured from distilled Mississippi water by fire and steam-power, in a general atmosphere equable and temperate. This marvel has been accomplished by Carre's apparatus, founded on Faraday's discovery of the intense cold produced by the volatilisation of liquified ammoniacal gas ; and the commercial agent here has been a company, with half a million of dollars capital, who have reduced the price of ice from 40 and sometimes 60 dollars to 15 dollars per ton, and dividing 25 per cent. of profits, to the utter dismay and confusion of the Northern ice importers. The ice is brought out from the machines in the purest rectangular slabs, which, on being placed one on top of another, become a solid mass. It is somewhat more porous than the " Wenham Lake "

product, and is not so fit in the bar-rooms of being poured out
of one glass in which it has been once used into a clean one; but
this is a difference on which the bar-keepers maintain a discreet
reserve, for only to few of the frequenters of these establishments
is it known that they are served with ice that has been sucked
in a sherry-cobbler, or mouthed in a cocktail, by previous votaries
of Bacchus. The success of the ice factory in New Orleans is
spreading the same scientific adaptation into the Southern towns,
from Atlanta to Shreveport.

The Board of Health in New Orleans publishes an annual
report. Though statistics in this country have no very exact
basis, yet they are always interesting and instructive. I asked
the President of the St. Andrew's Society—where in the wide
world is there not a "thin red line" of Scots?—what good work
the St. Andrew's, having the night before jovially celebrated the
anniversary of Burns, has done, or was in the act or intention
of doing; and his reply was—" The St. Andrew's Society, Sir,
during my incumbency, has built a cemetery, which, let me tell
you, is one of the first necessities of life in New Orleans." But
this was said with a smile neither grim nor Sardonic, and with
a happy soul in his eyes shining through and overflowing his
spectacles from such a depth of genial and lustrous humour as
proved at once that he did not mean what he was saying, albeit
the St. Andrew's Cemetery is a fact. The unhealthiness of the
Southern cities, I still think, is generally exaggerated. The
total number of deaths in New Orleans last year, excluding still-
born children (449) was 6,942, which, on the basis of population
given by the census, is about one in 28 of the inhabitants. But
New Orleans is just as likely to have 250,000 souls as 191,512;
and there are included the " blacks and mulattoes," 50,499 by the
census, among whom the recorded deaths in 1870 are 2,560, or one
in 20, swelling in the total the apparent mortality of the whites,
among whom the number of deaths on the census basis is not
more than one in 30. The deaths from yellow fever in 1870
were 587; but the sacrifices of that occasional plague are
exceeded by the more permanent burnt-offering of consumption,
which had 757 victims; and small-pox, ravaging chiefly the
negroes, carried off 528, almost as many as yellow fever. Of
other deadly fevers there was scarcely any trace. Of natives of
Scotland 31 died, of natives of England 99, of natives of Ireland
551—the Irish being next to the negroes the most mortal.

During the hot sickly season in New Orleans, people go away
as most people try to do in other large cities of the world; while
in the pleasant and healthy periods, such as now, few care to
leave the gay and busy town, although there are retreats at
hand when they happen to have such a desire. There is, for
one, the suburb of Carrolton, up river on the levee, where Dan

Hikcok, a retired Mississippi captain, has "fixed up" an hotel and gardens with much taste, and whither the city cars go and come every hour of the day. On getting into the shell road towards Dan's hostelry, no one can fail to observe the comfort and elegance of the residences on either side, and the white clover covering all the banquettes with the brightest green carpet, and springing up even under the iron rails as if traffic itself were to be defied by sheer power of the most sweet and succulent verdure. The day of my visit was one of those mildest of April in England when great patches of white light are spread over a cloudy sky, and Nature, withdrawing herself behind veils and draperies, seems poising with easy wing betwixt the poles of an infinite variety. The deep winding river was smooth and bright as a mirror under broad and steady gleams of light from the heavens, while its flow was not more perceptible than the breath of a sleeping child. Yet let us not be deceived—there is a latent force in that mild current greater than the force of ten thousand giants. See the depth of the levee towards the land, and how far you have to descend to the stores and shanties on that side! If the Mississippi in its rise, or in the action of its many currents, were to overflow or pierce the bank, or (since the levees are now a public interest and "under government") through any jobbery, or corruption, or want of watchfulness on the part of the State, to make a "crevasse" in the mud wall, the enormous volume of water would rush through the breach with the roar and violence of a cataract, and submerge in total ruin the vineyards and vegetable gardens in which a multitude of plodding Germans are supplying by daily toil the demands of the New Orleans market. How sad if, in the very place where Government should be as reliable as a second Providence, it should prove utterly at fault! But there was nothing on the levee to suggest such disquieting reflections. Big geese were gabbling and flapping their wings along the bank, and slim negroes were talking French with the grimace, vivacity, and repartee of Parisians. A broken statue of pure marble lay on the side walk, a human male figure obviously, with back uppermost—truncated—head, arms, and limbs nowhere. On turning it round, not without serious damage to a pair of dog-skin gloves that cost me exactly 11½d. in the old country, and that I had begun from long and faithful service to look upon as no mean work of art in themselves, behold! a breast of Hercules modelled with almost divine art of sculpture. What could this be, where did it come from? Searching about, fragments of the same marble statuary were found—the draped limbs of a Venus, the head and neck of a greyhound with a finely chiselled collar—serving the "base use" of curbstones in one of the deep square gutters common here. All the information I could gather about these

fine-art relics was that they were dug out of the levee some
twenty years ago, and that the tradition *then* was that they were
part of the luxury of some grand French seigneur whose mansion
and parterres were swept down in the fury of a crevasse!
Strolling away from the unprofitable sentimentality of such a
revelation into Mr. Hickok's conservatory, a splendid *Bychnonia
Venosta*, or "Mexican Trumpet Vine," flowering from Christmas
to March, and stretching like a curtain with bright yellow
fringes of flower along the whole glass-house, consoled me a
good deal. Peaches, grapes, figs (a slip of which put into the
ground grows in a year or two into a goodly tree) were all vital,
and plum-trees already in blossom. Roses, in great variety, come
out towards the end of February, and when they are in their
first full blow the "Knights of Comus" and other "mystic ties"
of New Orleans will, on the annual festival of Mardi-Gras, be
covering the stage of the Opera House, and descending into the
streets, with gorgeous processions and *tableaux vivants* in all the
gay and demonstrative spirit of their race.

CHAPTER XXXIV.

Incidents at Summit.—Want of Towns in the Interior of Mississippi.—Mr. Solomon's Account of his Commercial Relations with the Planters and Negroes.—The Law of Lien.—Usury.—The Free-trade Question.—Some Characteristics of the Dram and Drug Shops.

[SUMMIT, MISS.—*Feb.* 15–16.]

IT were idle for a traveller to attempt to find in the names of places some index of their general qualities, and such an attempt would be especially inappropriate in the United States, where country towns are for the most part named after individual founders, the ubiquitous Jones carrying off a large share of such landmarks. But Summit, near the southern border of the State of Mississippi, really indicates an ascent from the low level lacustrine region about New Orleans to the gently elevated table-land that distinguishes more than two-thirds of the State from its famously fertile but sickly mortal bottom-land along the course of the great river. In another sense Summit may be so called, because it may be taken as presenting a fair sample of the summit of all that is wrong, adverse, difficult, and uncomfortable in the reconstructed Southern States. Strangers from afar seldom find their way to such a part of the American Union as this, or, passing through it in the night train, remain unconscious alike of its existence and its circumstances. On entering my name and country in the hotel book, I became an object of affectionate solicitude to the clerk, a grave, elderly man of the race known in America as " Scots-Irish," who wondered what had brought me here, still more what could possibly induce me to stay, and who seriously advised me to think better of it than to remain ! There was not the slightest trace of inhospitality in these remarks. The old man seemed to speak from the depths of a brotherly heart. Life and property, he assured me, were not particularly secure in Southern Mississippi ; there was no industry of any kind but growing cotton and hogs ; the planters were very poor, and had many grievances against which they exclaimed night and day ; and the white man had become as like the negro as two peas, only a little more so. Yet, to show what different estimates of the relative advantages of distant countries may circulate side by side, a youthful cavalier, with leather riding gloves of the pattern of the reign of Charles I., was ready to bet me a hundred-dollar bill that I would never see Scotland again, for "Scotland was the poorest country on the face of the whole earth." It would have been a pity to strip this young man of his hundred-dollar greenback, of which denomination of currency it did not seem likely that he had many to spare. Besides, it was so easy for him, with the help of his revolver, to win! In all the circumstances, I declined the bet, and shamefully allowed the honour of "Auld Scotland" to go to the hogs.

In a State of such territorial magnitude as Mississippi, never one-tenth part peopled and occupied, the attraction of settlers is naturally towards the best and most fertile districts—towards the "bottom," where the fertility is great, or the "prairie land," where, with scarcely inferior powers of production, there are superior sanitary conditions; while inferior territory—such as the land from this point along the lines of the New Orleans and Jackson and Mississippi Central Railways to Memphis—receives, with few exceptions, only subordinate attention, and presents society in a more rough and straggling condition than in many other parts of the same State. Thus, it often happens along the whole westward wave of population, North no doubt as well as South, that rude and almost inchoate elements of society are found in comparatively near propinquity to considerable developments of wealth and civilization. Looking out from Summit, there is visible only an expanse of not very majestic forest land, with few traces of culture or population on any side. The farms and plantations, of which there are many, seem to have been picked out, far apart from one another, in the recesses of the woods, without making any great impression on the natural wildness of the country. Summit is 105 miles from New Orleans and 120 from Vicksburg, which latter city, after sustaining a long siege during the war from its formidable bluff on the Mississippi, is now growing into a commercial emporium of more and more importance. The greater towns are the lights of industry in such regions as this, giving to the cultivators of the soil, markets, sympathy, encouragement, and help in the prosecution of their labours. The great distance betwixt such towns and the agricultural settlements is like a break in the chain of communication with the outer world, throwing the country-people back so far into barbarism, with all its passions of greed, rapine, and imposture. The planters of Mississippi, a large proportion of whom must feel the weight of this isolation, held a convention recently, in which they passed resolutions setting forth their grievances, chief among which is the enormous usury to which they are subjected in the purchase of their supplies and the sale of their produce, and sighing for closer and directer relations with the spinners of cotton, and for some participation in the ordinary rules and usages of mercantile civilization. The change that has passed over the Slave States has in the meantime dislocated the conditions of credit. When the planter was an owner of slaves, and had along with that ownership and fund of property, now swept away, an unlimited control over the labour necessary to bring his crop into market, he enjoyed great credit in the river towns and seaports. That is now gone, and the opening thus made is occupied by Jewish storekeepers, mostly young men pushed forward by an unseen force in the large cities, and operating with great power over the plantations, though themselves poor enough, and kept tight by the head at the farther end. It is doubtless owing to the greater distance of many Mississippi cotton-fields from towns and village centres of wealth and credit, where old local merchants of repute have survived the war, that this peculiar development is more conspicuous here than elsewhere; and that the system of paying the negro field-hands in part by rations is more prevalent in Mississippi than in any of the more eastern cotton States, where the liberal concession to the negroes of one-half the crop without rations, instead of one-third the crop with rations, has become the prevailing rule. The system of business here has been so well explained by Mr. Solomon—a wide-awake but ingenuous Jewish trader, who makes no secret of his transactions, and is animated by a humane spirit quite engaging—that I cannot do better than produce our conversation.

The monthly ration of a negro field-hand, Mr. Solomon assures me, is one bushel of corn meal, the first price of which is 75 cents, the second 1.50 dol.; 16 lbs. of bacon, the first price of which is 13 cents, the second 25 cents, per lb.; and one gallon of molasses, the first price of which is 50 cents, the second one dollar.

"But, Mr. Solomon, is not 100 per cent. of retail profit too much?"

"It ish large profit, but it ish profit in de books, not profit in de pocket."

"How so?"

"Why, de white planter is very poor, and de negro, who sometimes raises crop for himself, is very idle, and knows no accounts. He comes to me and says he will raise crop if he is fed and gets clothes, and we say, ' Well, raise crop and we shall see.'"

"And how do you do?"

"Do? We do great deal. I have three horses riding on saddle —my own one of de best pacers in de country; and when Sunday comes I say to my clerks, ' Go you dis way and dat,' and I go de other, and we see how de work is going on; and if negro is doing nothing we put them all," with a wave of his hand, "outside."

R

" Beg your pardon, Mr. Solomon, but what do you mean by
putting them all outside ? "

"Outside, ish it ?—outside de store, of course. De store ish de
inside of de plantation. If de negro wants bacon or molasses; we
give him half de quantity or none, and planter de same.   His
wife wants silk gown ; we give her cotton one or none."

" Do you mean to say, Mr. Solomon, that there are white
Christian people, possessors of large landed estates, in this
bondage to you?"

" Christians did you say ?   Many of dem, too many for de
books.   Christians ! Dey eat swine's flesh three times a day, and
call it goot living.   Ah ! you are joking about Christians !   But
many white men in de war are sold—father, mother, child, the
very clothes on their backs, all sold.   What is lien on de land?
It brings no monish.   White planter is la cavalier, but black
man must eat, and if he not work we put him outside with lien
on his crop."

Mr. Solomon, for the rations and goods which he supplies, and
on which he has 100 per cent. of profit, takes under his lien the
cotton, hides, and other produce of the farms at prices which enable him to turn them over with another profit in New Orleans
or Memphis, where very probably he himself is under stringent
obligations.   But in two or three years he ought to be very rich.
Yet these local Jew traders often run away, leaving their city
friends in the lurch.   For, as Mr. Solomon truly says in extenu-
ation of this offence, as well as of the hard and usurious conditions
on which the business is conducted, the large profits are often only
in the books, and the few industrious and successful planters
and negroes, who are squeezed to the last cent, do not always
compensate the trader for the many unable at the end of the season
to square their accounts.   It is difficult to get the negro, who is
now on the front either as a cultivator or a partnership-cultivator
of the soil, to comprehend the ordinary principles of commercial
obligation.   When he enters into treaty with a local merchant for
supplies, giving *per contra* abundant lien on the produce of his
labour, he goes on rejoicingly for the year; but the treaty, in his
opinion, ends with the year, and if the merchant has then a
balance on the wrong side, the negro thinks that it is fairly "quits"
between them—that the contra side of his account is obliterated
by the natural roll of the seasons, and that the new year begins
with new and clean paper.   Yet Mr. Solomon shows me many
debit balances carried over in his ledger, shaking his head, and
adding his usual ejaculation of " profit in de books," which, as
distinguished from " profit in de pocket," seems to him like
the dividing line betwixt light and darkness, order and chaos.
The law of lien in the Southern States has assumed a somewhat complex character.   At New Orleans and other ocean

ports there is a vendor's right to seize produce even when shipped in the harbour, if the original purchase-money has not been paid, which is evidently conceived in the interest of the planters, and which the banks, in becoming interested by discounting on bills of lading, can only surmount by seeing that the vendor's right has been legally discharged. In the present state of affairs, the law of lien is more frequently brought against the planter than in his favour. At the same time, as regards the land itself, the law assumes a lien in favour of the seller till the purchase-money has been paid ; and land rights are as carefully guarded, and titles as consecutively registered, as in any other part of the civilized world, although an inattention to precise conditions of the law leads to complications, feuds, and sometimes acts of violence of the like of which we read in the history of the old country two or three hundred years ago. As regards a lien on the agricultural crop, even where the negroes *sole* are the cultivators, under such arrangements as those of Mr. Solomon, with three saddled ponies in weekly service, it is all plain sailing, and the holder of the lien will get the whole crop, save in so far as Sambo may surreptitiously sell parts of it to somebody else! But in the more common case, where the negro, though a labourer, is a partnership-cultivator with the planter, it does not seem to matter much whether the planter undertakes to supply his negroes with rations, or, by surrendering to them a larger share of the crops, leaves them to provide their own commissariat, for in the latter case he gives his lines to the storekeeper for what the negroes want, and thereby becomes responsible for the final discharge. The storekeepers like the planter's " line," because it gives them another eye over the plantation, and an additional element of security. But where the planter gives his " line," there is now lien upon lien—the whole crop is his till he has settled up his " lines " with the negroes ; and curious scenes arise when an outside storekeeper, not observing strictly the rule of the plantation, sends his waggon to lift the share of the crop of a negro on whom he says he has a " lien," and the planter interposes, and, giving the preference to his own " lines " and the foregoing lien on which they are founded, endeavours to carry out a division on a basis of common honesty throughout. How the books on the plantations are kept I do not know ; but the share-crop system, though much favoured by many in the South as the only means of obtaining reasonable service from the negro freedman, seems liable to grave objection, and inferior in various points of view, as regards the true freedom and independence of labour, to the system of definite wages for work done.

There is no banking accommodation in this and many other districts of the State of Mississippi worthy of the name. Yet planters of means and substance can sometimes obtain loans on their personal notes at an interest of 20 to 30 per cent. per

annum; and, deplorable as this may seem, until country gentlemen in the South show more attention to their notes when due
by personal appearance, even at the expense of a ten or fifteen
miles' ride on horseback, it must be vain for them to think of
coming under the reign of ordinary monetary usance. Complaints
of bank and note collectors as to the cavalier indifference of the
onerous parties are very common, even where no doubt is entertained of ultimate payment.

Mr. Solomon, in his contract of supplying "rations" to keep
the plantations going, confines his obligation to meal, bacon,
and molasses—the primal necessaries of life, which, as direct
products of the soil, are abundant and cheap in the United
States, and which he sells at nearly double their cost—but it is
not to be supposed that the wants of the cultivators of the soil
are confined to these simple elements of existence. The "Dry
Goods and Notions Store," in which line Mr. Solomon himself
has a department, flourishes here as elsewhere in the United
States, and dispenses its heavily protected or heavily tariffed
wares at prices 200 to 300 per cent. above their real value.
A pair of coarse negro boots, one of the cheapest articles
in the stores, is charged five dollars. The Northern manufacturers themselves are sometimes astonished at the retail prices
of their goods in the South, and a boot and shoe manufacturer of New York informs me that it has been in consideration
by his trade in the North to open depôts in the South, with a
retail department to "force the running," to use a phrase of the
Turf, in retail prices. Very good; but I could not help asking
him whether it would not be well to begin by abolishing Customs
duties both on leather and on boots and shoes, and thus promote
at the foundation the descent from an inflation and exorbitance
of prices which, in relation to other great commercial countries,
must prove fatal to American prosperity. He remarked that
large quantities of the best English and French leather are
imported into New York; and this is quite true. The commercial aristocracy of New York are able and willing to pay
any sum asked for the best articles of clothing the world can
produce, and New York, being the great port of entry, where
foreign goods pass into manufacture and consumption with the
utmost facility, they have little beyond a mere 50 or 100 per
cent. extra—to them a small matter—to complain of. But
this does not meet the case of the great American Republic of
citizen farmers and negro freedmen, living or attempting to live
in the remotest parts of a vast territory, where the effect of
monopolies and artificial restrictions is to bring the article wanted
to the poorer consumer at a price to him much more severe.
The *Boot and Shoe Reporter*, a manufacturers' organ, meets the
complaints of dear boots and shoes by referring to the high price

of hides, in which, indeed, trade has been active for six or eight months past at a rise of two to three cents per lb.　But this trifle, while giving to Mr. Solomon or his constituents a better return for part of their raw produce, is obviously insufficient to account for the excessive dearness of manufactures of leather. The retailers, it is true, do lay on their figures very heavy, and will only resile from high profits under some strong necessity ; for they do not seem to see that they gain nothing; that what they exact from others, others exact from them; and that they are simply engaged in limiting business and making it unsound throughout.　The baneful effect of high monopoly prices of articles of consumption on what is the main interest of the United States—the successful occupancy and cultivation of the land—and how difficult they must render the growing of cotton with profit at the price that cotton is now likely to command, are applications of this question that must be plain to every understanding.

"Let us liquor," says an American friend on whom I have been pressing these observations; and "liquor" we attempt to do.

"Is this brandy French brandy, or brandy from the juice of the grape?"

"No, sare," quoth the honest barman.　"It is applejack from Massachusetts, and quite as good as brandy."

"Humph!　A little of your best whisky, and be sure it is whisky without compound of turpentine, or benzoin, or fusil oil, or any more noxious ingredient."

"This whisky, sirree," rejoins the barman, "comes from the rectifiers."

"Hang your rectifiers!　Good malt spirit, man, requires no rectification except plenty of cold spring water."

And the jolly barman, now put to his mettle, shakes up his black bottle with its gold legend of "Bourbon" or "Robeson County," and shakes it again to make the liquor sparkle ; but it is the sparkle, the glitter, of a snake.　"It biteth like a serpent and stingeth like an adder."　In no part of the world probably is liquor-drinking held in greater social disesteem than in the Southern States ; the ladies regard it with horror ; and strong drink seems all but banished from private houses.　But there is much drinking, nevertheless, about the bar-rooms and liquor saloons, and the effect of the whisky of the country on the wild youths and loafing negroes of Mississippi is a caution for any one to see.　It makes them rage and bellow like bulls of Bashan, and in the reaction and prostration of excess the consequences must be terrific.　A bar-room in America, with its long rows of labelled bottles, its piles of drinking vessels, its odours of pharmacy, and its varied paraphernalia, as if for operating medically

on the human system, has always looked to me like a drug shop.
On the other hand, the drug stores in the smallest towns are the
neatest, most attractive, sweetly perfumed, and restaurant-like
places of that kind to be seen in any country; and in hot
weather they really do dispense spiced and cooling drinks of a
refreshing quality. I do not know whether the frauds and
vices of the drinking system have anything to do with the prosperity of the drug trade, but the sale of quack medicines has
attained a magnitude to be found nowhere else. It is more than
probable that people who begin by taking drugs in the bar-rooms,
and refreshments in the drug shops, proceed to doctor themselves
in the light of the quack advertisements, and thus by one false
step at the outset, inverting the ordinary rule of life, are carried
on for the cure of the more inveterate disorders to such firms as
" Circumventible & Co., India Herb Doctors "—a style-and-title,
by the way, that is no invention of mine, but is copied from an
actual signboard in Chattanooga.

CHAPTER XXXV.

[JACKSON, MISS.—*Feb.* 17-20.]

ONE is struck, in passing through the central region of the State of Mississippi, by the roughness of the country. Lazy yellow creeks flow through a sandy clay soil of much the same kind as that of the Atlantic States; greenish pools rot the roots of the trees in the woods; the ditches on the cultivated parts are overgrown with weeds and bushes, and the fields after rain are saturated with water. To this general character there are some exceptions, and the country improves as one advances northward towards Memphis; but want of settlers and of the hand of fertilising and civilizing industry is conspicuous throughout. Yet as a field of white labour this wilderness is probably more congenial than the fat bottom lands, where, with marvellous productiveness, there is more than equal natural wildness, and a malaria fatal to European constitutions. It is observed of the German Freehold Associations in the North and West, which are just beginning to turn their attention southward, that they do not look at rich lands, but rather at those depreciated by the natives, on which, through good and careful husbandry, a comfortable and independent result may be attained. The negroes, under free labour, are drawn off from such regions to places where cotton grows more abundantly with less toil, and where in the matter of health they have no competitors, and consequently have easy masters. The cry of want of labour is thus universal; but supposing that white labourers could be brought here to work under planters and farmers, which is somewhat chimerical, there is an insuperable obstacle in the want of such housing as white men could be expected to occupy, as well as in the high rate of negro remuneration. If negroes cannot be retained with all the reward and privilege offered them, which are just about as much as they like to ask, what terms are to be made with white labourers? Nevertheless, there is a continuous line of railway communication through all this central part of the State, and the lands in this respect are within the available limits of occupation. The New Orleans and Jackson and the Mississippi Central, uniting at Canton, are managed under trust, and in "maintenance of way" are by no means perfect; but they keep the country and means of transit with due regularity open.

Jackson, the capital of the State, is a town of 5,000 inhabitants. There is a spacious State House, like nearly all State Houses in the South, under repair, a commodious mansion house for the Governor, a city hall, several churches,· and many private residences denoting a large proportion of people of taste and culture. The business part of the town, including a large hotel, was burned down in the war, but has since been rebuilt, and goodly streets of stores and offices have risen up, with fewer foreign, that is German or Jewish, names than I have observed in some other inland Southern towns. I sought an interview with the Governor, Mr. Alcorn, who is a man not only of much social consequence in the State, but of great mark in the politics of the Federal Union, and was politely received by him in his rooms at the Capitol. Mr. Alcorn, in the times before the war, was what is called an "Old-line Whig," and was thus opposed in the political contests of Mississippi to Mr. Jefferson Davis, who was a Democrat. Like many more in the South, while disapproving or but faintly and doubtfully approving the "secession ordinances," Mr. Alcorn felt the force of his allegiance to the State, and, I believe, took up arms with his compatriots. But the old difference betwixt him and Mr. Davis would seem to have been too much for harmonious action in the new state of affairs, and an apparent slight on the part of the President of the Confederation in the distribution of military commands, caused Mr. Alcorn to retire at an early period of the war. When the struggle closed, Mr. Alcorn naturally came to the front, and, applying himself to the reconstruction question with all his practical ability, was elected Governor of Mississippi, to the satisfaction of the Radical party and the negroes, while at the same time his position in the State as an eminent lawyer and an extensive planter rendered him more acceptable to the conquered Southerners than many of the State Governors who rose into power on the tremendous reactionary wave that followed "the surrender." Mr. Alcorn is past middle age, but in the full vigour of his faculties. I found his Excellency busy in the discharge of the duties of his office; and in the casual business of the hour, such as the appointment of county treasurers under proper sureties, the displacement of sheriffs who had allowed riotous assemblies to insult law and order in their districts, and the adoption of measures for organizing and calling out the militia in support of the civil power where it was too weak, had some insight into the details that devolve on the Governor of a Southern State. Mr. Alcorn was ill enough pleased at the prevalence of murder and homicide in Mississippi, but maintained that the powers of Government within the State were amply sufficient to enforce an impartial execution of the law, and complained chiefly of the difficulty on the border lines of the State, where violent and lawless persons had an opportunity of organizing and perpetrating crimes, and escaping from justice with provoking facility. I had just read in the papers an account of a fire which a few days before had broken out in the large gin-house on Mr. Alcorn's plantation at Friars' Point on the Mississippi, by which 500 bales of cotton were consumed in a few minutes, and two gins and saw and grist mills, furnished with the best steam-power machinery, were reduced to a heap of ruins—the people, who were all busily at work, having barely time to escape. The fire was purely accidental. The destruction of property had been roughly estimated at 100,000 to 150,000 dollars. Mr. Alcorn admitted that his loss would probably not be less than 70,000 dollars. The policy of insurance had expired only a day or two before, and the Governor, busy in the capital, had allowed this essential matter of private business a few hours' grace. He was in the act, indeed, of directing a renewal of the policy when the news of the calamity reached him. The negroes on Mr. Alcorn's plantation are paid by one-third the crop with rations, and he has a store, of course, with salesmen and clerks, and a large establishment in which there must be overseers, mechanics, and other white persons paid by salaries. I asked him whether the negroes, having a common property in the crop, would not bear with him the loss from the fire to the extent at least of one-third of the 500 bales of cotton. His reply was that, in point of legal right, that question would depend on whether a discharge for the year had taken place betwixt the planter and the negroes anterior to the accident. The rule was for the planters to sell the whole crop, and to credit one-third of the proceeds as "wages" to the negroes in the books; but this might be done as soon as the crop was gathered, or at a later period. I understood from Mr. Alcorn that, having settled with his negro labourers for the year, the loss would fall wholly upon him, which is a strong corroboration of what I have more than once indicated, namely, that while the existing pact of capital and labour on the Southern cotton plantations partakes of the largest communism probably ever attempted in any part of the civilized world, it is not an adjusted system, in which the labourer shares with the planter the losses as well as the profits of the common enterprise. The negro is in one sense more, and in another sense less, than a partner. Desirous to have the opinion of a gentleman of practical knowledge and experience on a point on which glowing statements are usually made, I asked Mr. Alcorn what the average production of cotton on the Mississippi "bottom" might be. His answer was that planters were disposed to talk of the large crop on their acres, but what they did grow was not so discoverable, nor when discovered was it always equal to their own assumed standard. Take an acre, or ten acres, of the best bottom land, and try by experiment what it would yield, the result, attending to nothing else, would be great—a whole bale, or even more, per acre. But this was little else than theory, and two-thirds of a bale (of from 400 to 450 lbs.) was a very favourable crop over the best plantations in "the bottom." Some conversation followed on political affairs, in which I alluded to what I had heard outside, that Mr. Alcorn might probably be the next Vice-President of the. Republic. The Governor did not express himself as a man enamoured of political life even in its most attractive guises. He had done his duty to the State of Mississippi; the office of Governor had nothing to confer upon him for the personal sacrifices which an efficient discharge of its duties involved; and as for the Vice-Presidentship, he did not think the Northern people would consent to elect any Southern man to so high a post in the Republic. Mr. Alcorn was probably somewhat depressed by his recent loss, as he might well be from its suddenness and magnitude, and was thinking more of the permanent interests of his family than of any personal ambition. But events must prove. Mr. Alcorn impressed me as a gentleman of sincere politeness, extensive culture, and much administrative ability.

I did not leave the Governor without congratulating him on the great pains he had taken in his Message, recently delivered, to illustrate by statistics the moral, social, and vital condition of the population, and more especially of the negroes, which is a department of the public interest worthy of the closest attention in the Southern States, as elsewhere, or even more than anywhere else. Some of the facts educed in this Message deserve notice.[1] Mr. Alcorn, while confessing his misgivings and apprehensions as to some results, moral and social, of negro emancipation, is, nevertheless, from his full acceptance of the new order of things and his political responsibility, favourably disposed to the negro in his present state, not of personal freedom only, but of electoral power and privilege—more inclined, indeed, to discover a virtue than to insinuate a fault, and to prophesy well than ill—a state of mind that, if somewhat unique in the Southern States, only

---

[1] Annual Message of Governor James L. Alcorn to the Mississippi Legislature, Session of 1871.

augments the value of his testimony.   From thirty-one counties
of Mississippi that have returned full answers to his interroga-
tories, Governor Alcorn is enabled to state that the number of
marriage licences issued to coloured people, which in 1865—the
first year of emancipation—was only 564, rose in the following
year to 3,679, and, with the exception of 1868, when it fell to
2,802, has kept very near that mark ever since.   The number of
marriage licences to negroes in 1870 was 3,427.   The Governor
considers this manifestation of adherence by the negroes to the
legal formulas of marriage the more surprising, since, up to the
close of the war, they were incapable of making a marriage
contract, by which incapability, of course, he no doubt means an
incapability without the consent of their owners, who mated
them, and kept them to their marital duty; and, in an inversion
of moral obligation, did for them in this respect what they
were supposed, like children, to be unable to do or to care to
do for themselves.   It is not the less gratifying that the
negroes, when freed from all control, should have entered into the
marriage state of their own accord at this ample rate, more
especially as the cost of a marriage licence had been increased
from *one* dollar under the old system to *three* dollars under the
new—a tax on virtue at the critical moment, which the Governor
unhesitatingly and indignantly condemns—and social history
will probably be searched in vain for any more striking proof
that marriage and other laws, when based on nature, duty, and
religion, command an unfailing homage from the humblest
understandings.   The whites in these thirty-one counties of
Mississippi do not appear to marry in nearly equal proportion to
the blacks; but while the superior number of marriages may
fairly be taken as a proof of virtue in the one case, an inferior
number must not be pronounced a proof of less virtue or greater
vice in the other; for, as the Governor himself hints, the negroes
had many old and bygone marriages to ratify, and the circumstances since the end of the war may not have been so productive
of that exuberance of spirit so favourable to the married relationship in the case of the white people as of the negroes.   Taking
1870, though not a fair annual mean, the number of marriage
licences issued to a white population of 189,645 was 2,204; the
number issued to a coloured population of 239,930 was 3,427.
In the whole six years since the war, 1865 and 1870 included,
the number of marriage licences issued to the white people in
thirty-one counties of Mississippi was in the proportion of 1·61
per hundred, and to the coloured people in the same counties in
the proportion of 1·22 per hundred per annum.   Though this
result does not convey the same impression as the Governor's
Message, which is that of a larger number of marriage licences
among the blacks than the whites, yet it is the same statistic, and

the only difference arises from the various ways in which figures may, with all integrity, be presented. I find that in the United Kingdom in 1869 the number of registered marriages was only in the proportion of 0·73 per hundred of the population, and so it would appear that both whites and blacks in Mississippi are going on, in the matter of marriage, much more favourably than even the " most favoured nations." Yet marriage is one thing, and the observance of virtue before and after marriage is another; and so the Governor, in his Message, advances from marriages to births, and from conjugal love to its offspring in population. But the inquiry at this stage drops down from thirty-one counties to six, from which only statistics are available. In the six counties thus selected, the number of children born to white parents was in the proportion of 6·02 per hundred of a white population of 33,092 ; while the number of children born to coloured parents was as high as 7·30 per hundred of a coloured population of 43,748. There is no division in Mississippi statistics betwixt " legitimate " and " illegitimate " births, which with so much particularity gives so much pain in the old countries, and in this matter of births we are no doubt travelling more or less out of the marriage record. The number of registered births in the United Kingdom in 1869 was in the proportion of 3·37 of the population,[1] which is so much less than the proportion of births to population in the six counties of Mississippi as to sink the question betwixt whites and negroes into comparative insignificance, and to show that as both races are far ahead of the old country in the proportion of marriages to population, they are still farther ahead in the matter of births. Though these results in their first impression almost tempt a doubt of the accuracy of the Mississippi statistics, yet they are probably, with defaults of statistics on both sides to be taken into account, not more different than might be reasonably expected from an old country on the one hand, and a virgin country on the other ; and coming back to Governor Alcorn's point of view, which is that of Mississippi *per se*, there is no contest of the principle that the number of births per cent. of the population is a fair general test of virtue, and even on the lower ground of material interests is not without a strong recommendation, seeing that there is no want in the Southern States more apparent than the want of population. It must be remarked of the South, as of other parts of America, that anxiety as to how to maintain children is not so notable as in the Old World, and that parental solicitude more usually takes the form of caring how the children, when grown up, will choose to dispose of

---

[1] It may be well to state that the data here of marriages and births in the United Kingdom are taken from the " Statistical Abstract for the United Kingdom," Parliamentary Return, 1870.

themselves—a problem to which the very abundance of openings and resources for young people in this country seems to give an unfavourable solution. American youth do not evince quite as much disposition to avail themselves of their opportunities of a happy and successful life as the youth of countries where there is greater competition for places in the world and a more anxious training. It is hardly to be imagined, however, that the negroes are, meanwhile, much controlled in their marriages and births by refined considerations of prudence, and therefore Governor Alcorn, after " a tribute of justice " to the tender *nursing* faculty of slavery, proceeds to the question of saving infant life, and shows, as conclusively as arithmetic can make it, from the census returns of the six counties, that 6·02 per cent. of white births giving 10·52 of white children of one to five years of age, 7·31 of negro births ought in like proportion to give 12·89 per cent. of negro children of one to five years of age ; whereas the number of negro children of that period of life is only 11·16 per cent. ; the negro population thus losing in greater infant mortality more than it gains in greater proportion of births. There can be no doubt that this is the great defect in the vital condition of the negro under freedom. However he may propagate, he cannot preserve life as well as the white man. Yet the statistics adduced by Governor Alcorn in regard to negro marriages and births are encouraging, and show how idle may be the predictions of a speedy extinction of the black race in the South. Other results in this Message are no less gratifying. The number of churches for a coloured population of 179,677 has been increased from 105 in 1865 to 283 in 1870; the number of preachers employed by a coloured population of 163,733 has increased in the same period from 73 to 263. The number of schools open to a coloured population of 180,527 has increased from 19 in 1865 to 148 in 1870; the number of teachers employed by a coloured population of 167,421 has increased in the same period from 18 to 170. There is thus proof of a wholesome activity among the negroes, since the abolition of slavery, in founding churches and schools and providing the means of moral and intellectual improvement. The statistics of the material condition of the State are by no means so satisfactory, and, notwithstanding an annual progress from the desolation of 1865, only go to prove how much poorer and wilder Mississippi must be now than it was before the war. Governor Alcorn takes six counties from which returns are available as a basis ; but as these extend across the middle belt of the State, embracing bottomland, upland, ridge, and prairie— all varieties of soil, as well as all proportions of white and negro population—they may be regarded as a fair representation of the whole State. The value of farms in these six counties has fallen from 20,946,075 dollars in 1860 to 6,415,161 dollars in 1870, being a decrease of 69 per cent.; the production of cotton from 115,865 to 42,880 bales of 450 lbs.—a decrease of 63 per cent.; of Indian corn, from 3,367,140 to 1,159,458 bushels —a decrease of 65 per cent.; while of swine there is also a difference betwixt the two periods of 65 per cent. Of minor products, such as wheat, peas and beans, potatoes, cheese, honey, and orchard fruits, the decline is still more enormous; and probably cotton, the quantity of which this season is much larger than in 1869–70, has made more progress to the ante-war level than any other product of the soil of Mississippi. Governor Alcorn finds some consolation for these melancholy figures in the great increase since before the war of general stores and of shoe-makers' and smiths' shops; and his explanation, no doubt correct, is, that the breaking-up of the close system of business under slavery has enabled a much larger number of tradesmen, by serving the public instead of an individual, to establish a business for themselves. But the freedom which enables the negroes to do well in so many respects, enables them also to do ill in some others, and the number of dram-shops has increased greatly more since 1860 than the smiths' or the shoemakers'. At the same time there are significant indications that some of the better class of negroes are rising in wealth and independence. In twenty-three counties 40,561 bales of cotton were produced in 1869, and 50,978 bales in 1870, by coloured tenant-farmers. In twenty counties 6,141 bales of cotton were produced in 1870 by coloured *owners* of the soil.

There is a proposal afoot just now likely to attract much attention beyond as well as within the State—viz. to redeem the old repudiated debt of Mississippi, amounting to 20,000,000 dollars. Many, afraid of the jobbery with which the operation may be attended, and still more perhaps of the formidable addi-tion it would make to the taxes, shrug their shoulders at the mention of this scheme; but Repudiation is happily everywhere felt to be so complete a bar to the credit and prosperity of a community, that it may not be surprising if Mississippi, following the example of some other defaulting States, should one day make a serious effort in this direction. The revenue of the State shows some signs of elasticity. The receipts at the Treasury in 1870 were 1,066,092 dollars, while the disbursements were 1,061,249 dollars, showing an almost even balance; but the Auditor, in his estimate for 1871, anticipates a revenue of 1,536,500 dollars, and an expenditure of 1,319,626 dollars, which would give a surplus of 216,874 dollars.

CHAPTER XXXVI.

The " Mississippi Bottom."—Plantation at Austin.—Obstacles to Cultivation.

[AUSTIN, MISS.—*Feb.* 24.]

AUSTIN is a small town with a jail and court-house, on the Mississippi River, and in the "bottom land." It was much knocked about during the war, the jail having been burned ; but the place still retains the form and semblance of a village, where the steamers, on being signalled, call and take up passengers from the plantations in the neighbourhood. The river at this point describes an almost circular bend, and within memory has greatly changed its course, leaving dry much of what was formerly its channel. A little farther down on the opposite bank it receives the waters of the St. Francis flowing from Lake St. Francis, in the north-eastern corner of Arkansas.

The "bottom land" of Mississippi extends from Memphis to Vicksburg, a length of near three hundred miles, and is about thirty miles deep from the river bank. Much of " the bottom " is traversed by an interior river system, the chief member of which, the Yazoo, or "River of Death," as it was called by the Indians in their usual picturesque way, flows over a great part of its course much farther in the interior of the State than the thirty-mile verge of the "Mississippi Bottom," and has many large tracts of rich bottom land of its own partially occupied and cultivated. But three-fifths of the bottom land along the Mississippi River are not in cultivation, and cannot be cultivated on account of their liability to floods, both ordinary and extraordinary. The ordinary annual flood covers large spaces of the soil with deep water, and when it subsides and the hot sun begins to act on the slime, insects spring up in a pestiferous abundance that is fatal to the cotton crop. The insect life of this region is amazing. Horses and oxen are often worried to death in a few hours by swarms of venomous flies ; and the greatest care has to be taken at certain periods of the year for the preservation of stock. A plantation near by was bought by an experienced planter attracted from his so-called "worn-out " land elsewhere to the fat virgin soil of "the bottom," in 1860, when war was scarcely yet credible, and when he could transport his negro slaves along with him as a guarantee of labour. The price was 30 dollars an acre, with 300 acres cleared, a loghouse, and a few cabins. All the rest of the plantation was forest and cane-brake. The cotton-tree, oaks, hackberries, sassafras, and persimmon-trees prevail most in the woods. A few red deer are found in the forest. The cane-brake seems to grow over all parts of the ground not cultivated, very dense, often to a great height, and is the haunt of small black bears, and even panthers. There is a half-moon lake behind the cleared land called "Beaver Dam Lake," in which there may at one time have been beavers, but the chief inhabitants of which at present are swans, pelicans, and other wild birds, with probably some trout, and certainly a few alligators, that are occasionally seen plunging among the reeds in the lake or basking in the sand and mud of the shore. Fruit-trees flourish well when planted, but there is very little indigenous fruit; and flowers and aromatic plants must be introduced and tended round the farmhouse. There was a great stand of cotton on this plantation in 1861, eight to ten feet high, but not a great crop of lint. The next year there was a very large crop, but the hurly-burly of armed men had by this time approached even Austin, and the plantation was rendered useless during the rest of the war. After 1865, the planter and his family having been driven away by chills and fevers, the plantation was let out at an annual rent, and has since been sold to an active and unencumbered man who is prepared, for sake of the extra fertility in cotton, to encounter all the difficulties of the situation. This is the general course of plantation-property in "the bottom." There are a few great proprietors, like Governor Alcorn, who, without residing on their farms, carry on the work of cultivation with vigour and direct responsibility; and there are others who, being not so rich or independent, live on the spot, and make the best they can of the soil and climate; but many more have abandoned their plantations to negro and other tenants, and one not unfrequently finds that a planter ruined by the war and sold out of his homestead in some more healthy part of the South, while still in the prime of life, has settled in "the bottom" with the hope of working up a new freehold estate at any risk or sacrifice to himself and his family. A plantation in the "Mississippi bottom" is regarded by others in the light of a speculation; and energetic men, with command of more or less money, throw themselves into the breach, and, without wholly giving up their domicile elsewhere, superintend their crops and operations with a home-retreat to run to as often as may be necessary. Too often, even in such cases, a glowing account of the crop is accompanied with complaints of some sacrifice of health. The negroes, after two or three years of acclimatisation, agree better with " the bottom" than white people; but their contracts end with the year, and such of them as have a surplus earning take sanitary excursions over hundreds of miles, like their employers, and there is a scramble to engage the necessary number of good hands for the next season. With all these disadvantages, the wonderful agricultural productiveness of · " the bottom" is beyond all dispute. Heavy crops of wheat come, by a little scratching of the soil, under trees the sap of which has been turned off by a scarification of the bark round the trunk in the gradual process of clearing. As for cotton, on the cleared ground, it is difficult to say when the picking season begins or ends. There is the tendency of all rank soil to give more stalk and fibre than proportionable fruit, but there is not so much fear here that bolls may not mature as in many other parts of the " Cotton Belt," and it may be said generally that in the "Mississippi bottom" cotton wool comes earlier and ripens to a later period than elsewhere. The picking season extends far into the new year, and at this date planters, weary or hopeless of gathering all their cotton, are turning cattle or sending negroes with bill-hooks into fields still partially white in order that they may prepare the next crop.

The reclamation of the " bottom land " in Mississippi is a work of time, and the efforts made, in the spirit of American adventure, will render it by successive stages much more habitable than it is at present. Yet one must look at existing conditions, and, in the light of these, it must be owned that the superior productiveness per acre of such regions as this is attended with some formidable disadvantages. One often hears of the " sharp intelligent countenances " of the American people, and the mass of Americans have that superior kind of aspect. But a large proportion of the faces one sees in these parts, with all the " sharp intelligence " desirable, seem intellectualized not a little by heat and sickness, and sharpened by hardship and suffering.

CHAPTER XXXVII.

Progress of Memphis.—Receipts of Cotton.—Buying on Spinners' Orders.—
Through Bills of Lading.—Import of Foreign Goods at Memphis.—Politics
and Railways of Arkansas.—Extensive River Communications.—Definition
of "the Cotton Belt."—Banking and Insurance Capital.—Jefferson Davis.
—The Southern Presbyterians and the Free Church of Scotland.

[MEMPHIS, TENN.—*Feb.* 25-30.]

ANYONE whose impression of Memphis has been formed from
the accounts of its condition at the close of the war, would be
agreeably surprised by its present well-built, well-paved, and
comfortable condition. The city, from its high bluff on the
Mississippi, overlooks the surrounding country, embracing great
parts of Tennessee, Mississippi, and Arkansas. Its local lines
of river steamers, carrying upwards of 10,000 tons, not only
conduct a regular traffic with the plantations on the Mississippi,
but, ascending the branch rivers, penetrate into the interior westward over distances as great as many sea voyages. Its railway
connections are also very advantageous, placing it on all the
great routes north and eastward; but, not satisfied with present
attainments in this respect, Memphis is as strongly moved by
the enterprise of opening new lines of railway as other Southern
towns. It is pushing to get down direct by rail on the mineral
region of Alabama; to shorten its communications with Savannah, Charleston, and Norfolk; and the question as to the future
Atlantic seaport *par excellence* has been as keenly canvassed here
as in other great cotton centres of the Southern interior. The
Chamber of Commerce has come to the conclusion that Port
Royal, an embryo port in South Carolina betwixt Charleston
and Savannah, may be the destined "gateway of Memphis to
the sea," because the distance is only 728 miles, as against 959
from Memphis to Norfolk in Virginia, and may be reduced by a
projected short-cut betwixt Atlanta and Decatur to 658 miles in
all; and so the Chamber looks with favour on the line working
along from Port Royal in the lowlands of Carolina to Augusta
in Georgia. While thus glancing eagerly and far into the future
eastward, Memphis is not unmindful of the great country behind
it to the West, from which it draws immediate support, and

which is bound from year to year to swell its prosperity and raise it ultimately into one of the great cities of the American continent. A line is now open from Memphis to Little Rock, the capital of Arkansas, and others are projected through that State to Fulton on the borders of Texas, and to Fort Smith in the Indian territory. That there is a rich harvest to be gathered by Memphis from the gradual development of the great agricultural resources of Arkansas is already seen in the rapid progress of the city. Its population, which was 22,623 in 1860, is now given at 40,230 by the census taken last summer, when a large number of the inhabitants were absent. The probability is that the population of Memphis has fully doubled in ten years —five of these being years of war and devastation—and has thus made good an increase of inhabitants which has nowhere been surpassed, if equalled.

The total receipts of cotton at Memphis in the season 1869-70 were 290,737 bales. The receipts already this season have been 386,149 bales. The receipts at same date last year were 212,818 bales, showing an increase this year of no less than 81 per cent., which is greatly more in proportion than the total increase of receipts at the United States ports this year as compared with last—the figures being, total receipts this year, to Feb. 25th, 2,786,149 bales, and last year to same date 2,113,533 bales, an increase of 32 per cent. The total increase of cotton at United States ports at this date being 672,616 bales, and the total increase at Memphis 173,331 bales, the consequence is that Memphis has above 25 per cent. at this time of the whole increase on last year at all the great outlets of cotton.[1] This result speaks favourably, in the first place, of the increased production of cotton on the Mississippi River, in the State of Arkansas, and the Tennesseean and other districts round Memphis; and, in the second place, of the energy and advantage for sellers and buyers with which the market here is conducted. The classification of cotton in Memphis is the same as in New Orleans—the two markets being supplied from almost precisely the same varieties of soil and climate—but the Liverpool standard is the prevailing basis of transactions. The cotton of Memphis, till within the last two or three years, was almost wholly sent to the Atlantic seaports to be there resold; but the establishment

---

[1] It is hardly necessary to exhibit statistical results, which will appear more properly at the end of the season through all the ordinary channels of intelligence. But it may be worth while to state the percentages of increased receipts of cotton, so far as developed, at all the ports, as a passing landmark. They are as follow:—Texan, 2 per cent.; New Orleans, 16; Mobile, 24; North Carolina, 41; Virginia, 43½; Charleston, 48; Savannah, 52; Memphis, 81; other ports, 9 per cent. At New York the increase is 76 per cent., but as the New York receipts pass through, and are mostly recorded in, the Southern ports, they do not enter essentially into this comparison.

of *through* bills of lading by the various railroad companies in connection with the ocean steamship lines from New York has introduced a new mode of business, which promises to have important results. The present freight rate of through bills of lading is seven-eighths of a penny per lb. of cotton from Memphis to Liverpool. Insurance for the whole route is also effected in one transaction with the English companies at three-fourths per cent.; so that a spinner or merchant in England can buy in Memphis at first hand from the producer, with all the selection of grades the market affords, and have the cotton delivered to him in Liverpool by rail and steamship within three or four weeks of the purchase, not only with advantages of freight, but without the cotton being handled, tared, or stolen at any intermediate point, and with no more than one series of necessary commission charges—viz., at the place of purchase. The advantage of this mode of business has been found considerable enough to be now giving it some play; and having heard the cry of the planters in Mississippi for more direct relations with the spinners, I can scarcely conceive how, in present circumstances, this object can, with equal benefit to producer and consumer, be better realized. Memphis, as the greatest inland mart of cotton, has been the first to feel the force of this movement, but there is no reason why at any point amidst the plantations, with means of transit, the same class of operations may not be carried out. One or two of the cotton brokers in Memphis began, after the war, to turn their attention to the execution of direct orders from Liverpool; and so contagious is a good example, that already, I am told, one-third of all the cotton business in Memphis is done on this principle. The telegraph gives the buyer in England the power of controlling his orders, reducing or extending his margin, or closing it up, and regulating his shipment of cotton per week or month, in the nicest adaptation to his views of the course of the market or to his manufacturing wants. It is gratifying to find such proofs of closer commercial relationship betwixt parties working to each other at such vast distances; and yet, beneficial as this directness of trade betwixt the planter and spinner must be in the matter of cotton, there is not less ground of rejoicing in the smaller fact at present as estimated by dollars, that Memphis, availing itself of an Act of Congress by which it has been made a port of entry, and under rather hard conditions of inland transit, may pay its own import duties on the spot, instead of in New York or Boston, has in the year ending 30th June last paid 41,140 dollars in duties on European goods imported direct to the order of its own merchants. The cotton growers may rely that, substantial as the advantage may be of a more direct disposal of their product to the manufacturers of Europe, it is not a hundredth fraction of the advantage which would accrue if the laws of the United States allowed to Europe anything like equal liberty of paying them its products in return, which products, as measured in the exchanges of the two continents, are in reality, whatever the laws of the United States may enact or prescribe, the price of cotton to them. The fact that Memphis, notwithstanding the severity of the tariff and the restrictions with which the removal of goods in bond to inland ports of entry is accompanied,[1] should have paid so much as 41,140 dollars of Customs duties in the past year, is no insignificant proof of the mercantile spirit and enterprise of the city; and if so much has been done under existing difficulties at Memphis, it becomes the more obvious how greatly a free exchange would increase the volume of trade with the Old World, how much larger and better value the United States would receive for its exported produce, and what a healthy and invigorating influence would be exerted on American industry and manufactures to the farthest limits of the Union.

The politics of Arkansas would appear, from an extraordinary struggle going on at Little Rock for possession of the governorship, to be in one of those tumults which are too frequent under universal negro suffrage. Governor Clayton, who has been elected one of the Senators of the State in Congress, and is willing to go to Washington, should lay down the one office before entering upon the other, but refuses to do so because his lawful successor in the governorship, while one of his own party, has of late been somewhat too independent, and is not likely to continue with due succession the Clayton dynasty and rule. The partisans on both sides are greatly excited, threatening armed force against each other; and, reading the Little Rock newspapers, one would conclude that the capital of Arkansas must inevitably be drowned in blood. But these political frays seldom fulfil either their threats or their promises, and the crisis will probably end in some trick or intrigue that will raise a hearty laugh on one side or the other. Memphis looks with deep interest on the wide and fertile State over against it on the west bank of the Mississippi, of which it is the gate to the East; and, notwithstanding the unsatisfactory condition of government in Arkansas, the increasing production of the State is annually conferring on Memphis increasing advantages. A stream of white emigrants, though chiefly from other cotton States, is slowly occupying its richer lands; the cotton of Arkansas comes in larger quantity and of superior quality to market; and whatever

---

[1] The new warehousing regulations require, among other provisions, that goods in bond conveyed to inland towns named be conveyed in cars of iron, that the cars be doubly locked, that they be locked by a particular patent lock, and that they be under the constant inspection of officers appointed for the purpose.

present difficulties may be, there is that confidence in the future, buoying the American community more than any other in the world, which, however slow and elusory in its particular realization, has in the aggregate lines of history and experience all the assurance and stability of destiny. There is a general testimony as to the fertility of the lands along the rivers in Arkansas. Until the projected lines of railway are completed, the State will labour under no common difficulties of transit. In the meanwhile, the rivers are the chief means of communication, and the extent to which steam-vessels thread the narrow and sinuous channels of this inland navigation is wonderful enough, in some of its most general facts, to be worthy of record. Steamboats regularly leave Memphis to the mouth of White River, down the Mississippi, and thence ascend to Jacksonport, which is 700 miles by this waterway from Memphis, while the distance overland, by " air-line," from Memphis to Jacksonport is only 75 miles. Some of the boats on the White River go to Pocahontas, 150 miles farther than Jacksonport, and within 15 miles of the Missouri line, or only 85 miles overland from Memphis. But the navigation of the Upper White River above Jacksonport is only practicable at irregular seasons. Though the railway from Memphis to Little Rock is now open, steamboats continue to make trips from Memphis to Little Rock by the Arkansas River in six days, and this line of navigation is pursued from Little Rock by the Arkansas River as far as Fort Gibson in the Indian territory. But this is not all. Fifty miles south from Little Rock, and 200 miles from Memphis, is Archidelphia on the Washita (Ouachita) River, which joins with the Red River away down in Louisiana before the confluence of the latter with the Mississippi, and is thus more within the navigable sphere of New Orleans than of Memphis. Steamboats, carrying 2,000 to 3,000 bales of cotton, penetrate from New Orleans by the Red River to Camden on the Washita in Arkansas, 700 miles ; and at Camden other boats of lighter draft, carrying 400 to 500 bales of cotton, go up and down the Washita to Archidelphia, which is but 55 miles from Little Rock, where there is an " air-line " railroad to Memphis. This is only an Arkansas branch of the New Orleans river steam navigation. Pursuing the main Red River channel, the New Orleans boats traverse a distance of 1,100 miles. Fulton in Arkansas is the general head of navigation on Red River, but the steamers, by getting round through the bayous a raft formed by drift timber in the upper waters, occasionally reach still more distant points. All the principal branches of Red River, such as Bartholomew, Saline, and Mason bayous, are also regularly visited by boats from New Orleans. Cotton bears a freight over this vast river route of sometimes eleven dollars a bale. The steamers, indeed, passing as they do along the rivers where the farms and plantations mostly are, perform a minute service of traffic and convenience which railways themselves, however important, are not so able to discharge. The masters of river steamers one meets with at Memphis and New Orleans are generally men of fine disposition and of great intelligence, social and agreeable to strangers, and liking nothing better than to see and be useful to families of European settlers.

At this point one may take a glance, by way of definition, at the "Cotton Belt" of the Southern States. Memphis is a little north of the line of 35 deg.; it is nearly a whole degree north of Wilmington in North Carolina, and it is in North Carolina, with the exception of some border counties of Virginia, where one travelling South first comes on flourishing fields of cotton. Memphis, therefore, albeit from its situation on the rich bottom lands of Mississippi and Arkansas one might fancy differently without looking at the map, is very near the northern limit of the cotton region, which is usually held to be 35½ deg., while its southern limit is now recognized to be 31 deg., or, to take a local point, say the mouth of the Red River. Though the cultivation of cotton may not be strictly confined to precise lines of latitude, yet there are natural causes which tend to hold it within these limits. Beyond the northern limit of 35½ deg. short seasons and early frosts are apt to rob the crop of the means of full maturity; while below the southern limit of 31 deg. its liability to be devoured by worm and rot is no less adverse to its successful culture. The slow result of experience, indeed, has been to reduce the southern limit of the cotton belt greatly more than the northern limit. There was a time when, under the prevailing impression that longer seasons, more and more sun, and absence of frost, were the all-essential conditions of the cotton plant, Natchez, or about the line of 32 deg., was deemed the centre of the American cotton belt, but few would probably now venture to place the centre line farther south than the mouth of the Arkansas River, or 34 deg. On the southern limit cotton comes into rivalry with the sugar-cane, whereas on the northern limit it has only the production of northern climes to contend with; and it seems true of cotton as of wheat and other products of the soil, that they yield as well with necessary care on their northern verge as on any other part of their congenial space. Hence cotton clings much more closely and steadfastly to its technical northern limit, and beyond it, than to its southern limit, which is so far a diminishing quantity; till passing the equator line, in South America, a new and reverse series of natural conditions come into operation. The product of cotton in the southern latitudes of Texas does not present in these days any result approaching to the expansion in North Carolina, or even Virginia.

The total capital of the "National" and other banks in

Memphis is 1,700,781 dollars, which is a small amount in proportion to the commercial interests of the city, but does not compare so badly as in other Southern cities with the banking capital before the war. The bank capital of Memphis in 1860 was given in round numbers at 2,000,000. The bank deposits are 2,226,919 dollars, being considerably less than the proportion of deposits to banking capital in New Orleans. The native fire and life insurance companies, which in Memphis have a total capital of three millions of dollars, employ their funds in various modes which practically relieve the pressure upon the banks, and help out a deficiency of banking means which would otherwise be severely felt. The fire and life insurance companies established since the war are usually prosperous. The stock of the Planters' Company, a fire office established eighteen months ago, is at 15 per cent. premium, and the dividends have been 50 per cent. on the money paid up. This company lends on various classes of security at one per cent. a month. Though dividends of this amount are only too good, yet a large portion of the savings of the community is likely to be invested in insurance companies in the South, where the operations of foreign companies are extensive. The capital of foreign life companies represented at Memphis is 73 millions, and of foreign fire companies 41 millions of dollars.

Mr. Jefferson Davis, who is at the head of one of the large American insurance companies, lives very quietly here in the Peabody Hotel, and, save when the negroes get a hold of him in the street or on the landing-stage at the river, and make him the object of an ovation, is seldom heard of in public. The popularity of Mr. Davis among the negroes is a fact which cannot be easily explained, and in Abolition circles would probably not be readily understood if it could. There is much peace and good feeling in Memphis among all classes of the population. No fewer than five daily newspapers are published in the city, and, judging from the well-organized staff of the *Avalanche*, must be well qualified to inform and enlighten the community. Among the novelties of manufacture, one of the two gas companies of the town supplies *gasoline* made by vaporisation from the mineral oil of Pennsylvania, and giving as pure and bright a light as the best cannel coal gas. The fame of this experiment has spread so far as to bring a deputation all the way from Milwaukee on Lake Michigan, who are much pleased with the result. But the second gas company of Memphis, who look askance on gasoline, say that with coals at 75 cents a barrel, and the high price got for the cinders and tar, there is little margin of economy. Either way, I daresay, gas supply is a profitable business in the Southern towns. The price of gas to the consumer is four to five dollars per thousand cubic feet.

I attended divine service in the Second Presbyterian Church of Memphis on the Sunday, as it happened to be, before Communion. The minister, Mr. Boggs, at the close of the services, having occasion to urge the claims of the Sustentation Fund of the Southern Presbyterian Church, remarked that it was founded on the model of the Sustentation Fund of the Free Church of Scotland, which, with much eulogy of Dr. Chalmers and the Free Church, he finally declared to have been contributed by "*the poorest classes of that poorest of all countries, Scotland.*" I do not know how, though flattering to them in one sense, the thrifty and wealthy people north the Tweed may be disposed to receive such a compliment. There was a time, in the days of Dr. Samuel Johnson perhaps, or probably earlier, when Scotland, in working out the redemption of Protestant Europe, and laying on the common altar a great deal more than her reasonable share, might have been pronounced a comparatively poor country among the countries of Europe. But all this has passed away, and it sounds strange in European ears to hear the richest people, head by head, in the world—America not excluded—proclaimed from the pulpit the poorest of all peoples, and the Free Church, the "Hero Church" of the Scotch, the poorest of this poor. The truth is, I believe that there is little or no communion betwixt the Presbyterians of Scotland and the Presbyterians of the Southern States. The Southern Presbyterians complain that, under some unaccountable monopoly of disposition in favour of the Northern Presbyterian Church, they are deliberately excluded from correspondence and representation in the General Assemblies of the parent Churches in Scotland, which, if true (as I have no doubt it is), appears, without any further explanation, to balance the account, and to reveal that the Free Church of Scotland is probably about as imperfect in knowledge of Presbyterianism in America as any Southern Presbyterian ministers may be of the material condition of the Scotch people.

CHAPTER XXXVIII.

West and Middle Tennessee.—Backwardness of Rural Labour.—Proportion of
Corn and Cotton Crops.—Spring like "Glorious Summer."—Necessity of
an approved Rotation of Crops in the Cotton States.—Similarity of
Cotton and Turnip Husbandry.—City of Nashville.—Disorder of the State
Finances.—Farming in Tennessee.—Fallacy in the question of Free v.
Slave Labour.—Conclusions as to the Prospects of Cotton Culture.

[NASHVILLE, TENN.—*March* 1-15.]

THE citizens of Memphis who love to have a country house, going
to and from town by rail for business, have built residences along
both sides of the Memphis and Charleston road, several miles
out from the city, on fine dry sites, with well-kept gardens and
lawns, and amidst much pretty sylvan scenery. On leaving
these environs the train passes into the ordinary American landscape, with wild forest roughness as its principal characteristic.
But in West and Middle Tennessee there is a large amount of
agricultural industry, and the nearer one approaches Nashville
the country becomes more fine and cultivated. Maury County, in
the middle region of the State, is probably unsurpassed in the
beauty of its scenery and the variety of its agricultural products.
Grass, more natural than farther south, is more cared for; stock
is more abundant; and broad fields of clover and winter wheat,
the latter sown in the fall on the Indian corn-fields of the previous
year, clothe the soil with brilliant verdure. But at this point
north, one is passing rapidly out of the "Cotton Belt;" and along
the southern Tennessee border line, where cotton and Indian corn
are the sole agricultural staples, there is more natural roughness
and absence of busy rural life at this period of the year than in
more northern parts of the State.

Over a hundred miles of such country only one plough, a single-
horse, was seen at work, and the corn and cotton fields lay as
they had been at the close of last year. There is a hesitation on
the part of planters as to what to do this season, how many hands
to engage, and what proportions of the two great crops to plant.
There will be less cotton and more corn, if the resolutions passed
from mouth to mouth can be trusted. A very common proportion
of the two crops last year on the larger plantations was two-thirds

cotton and one-third corn—a proportion that, when the price of cotton is higher relatively than corn, is profitable owing to the abundance and cheapness with which corn is usually supplied from the North-Western farms, but, when the price of cotton is low, and the needful " staff of life " from other States has to be paid for in cash which the cotton proceeds do not yield, is uneconomical and insupportable. There will be a change this year to at least one-half corn and one-half cotton, save on small farms, where the proportion of corn was probably at no time lower than one-half. But the slowness in preparing the land for either one crop or other is remarkable. The cotton plant may not be advanced by early sowing, since heavy falls of rain or sudden blasts of cold wind may be injurious to a too early growth; but the preparation of the soil is another matter, and if the fields had been well ploughed even before the keen frost of last winter, it were contrary to all experience not to find them greatly improved by the process in the destruction of insects, and in their refinement and invigoration by the atmosphere. The weather along the northern limit of the cotton region in early March is what one may call "magnificent spring ; " and yet this euphuism may fail to convey an adequate conception of its favourableness for agriculture to many whose experience of spring has been confined to more northern climes. Spring in the South is " glorious summer," with occasional brief but heavy falls of rain that flood the creeks and swell the great rivers, and tornado-like winds that sweep along a narrow space in breadth, but over great distance in length. Helena in Arkansas and Pocahontas on the northern border of Mississippi appear to have been blown down in one night by a wind which at Memphis was scarcely perceptible. Yet these are but incidental phenomena, and Nature is now bursting forth with copious energy. The peach-trees, rushing into fruit before they have put forth their leaves, are in full bloom, and the wild plums along the country roads and in clumps in the fields are covered with cream-coloured blossoms as thick as English hawthorn in May. The vines are warping themselves with new life round the fences and up the stems of the sassafras and thorn trees, while the winter-reft and winter-soiled edges of the forest, splashed in colour as with the clayey mud of the ditches, become more bright every day, the brilliant light green of the willows in particular touching the landscape with hues of Eden. The transparency of the atmosphere probably moves one more than all—an effluence of ether in which the wing of a gnat is visible to the eye, and the gay blue or scarlet plumage of the shyish birds, as they fly into the recesses of the woods, or flutter in the air, is more flashing and more exquisite than the silken coquetry of a drawing-room. This, as one walks or rides along amidst the deep silence of these parts, without heat or glare of sun anywise oppressive, and with an exhilaration of lung and spirit, imbibing only what Nature shows and gives, is a source of felicitous sensation which one would rather not attempt to analyse or describe.

To do for farming in the Cotton States of the South, under negro emancipation, what rotation and green-cropping have done for farming in England and Scotland under free trade—to give it some regular plan or order of cultivation fitted to develop all the best qualities of the soil, and to attain the great ends of permanent profit and improvement—is an object now of the first importance, alike to the good of the Southern country and to the future of cotton supply. The old system of corn and cotton for ever on the same fields in uncertain proportions can no longer suffice to give a stable interest to the land; and if a large area and low price of cotton one year are to be followed by a small area and high price the next, and gambling in the cotton-market is to be complicated by gambling in the growth of the staple, a most unfavourable blow will be given to cotton manufactures throughout the world. It was the property in slaves that gave to the Southern plantations permanence of value and regularity of crop before the war: the substance that a British farmer possesses in his sheep and cattle, and that remains behind whatever reverses of yield or price may befall the crops of a year, the Southern planter had in his negroes; but this property in human beings having now been swept away, the cotton farmers of the South must seek to fill up the gap by live stock of another kind, and stock-raising and stock-feeding imply much variety of culture, and may be said, indeed, to open an entirely new agricultural problem in the Southern States. One sees, though rarely, a small flock of whitefaced sheep or merinoes on the cotton plantations, but usually lean, and with few lambs in proportion to the flock. The heat of summer spreads a desolation over grass which it does not speedily recover, and the want of moisture is unfavourable to turnip culture. But the fertility of clover, and the small modicum of care and labour by which the tender blades of rye or barley are brought away in abundance all winter and spring, seem to cover much other defect, and to afford means of nutritious feeding to sheep and cows. On asking a gentleman, who has made Southern agriculture a life-long practical study,[1] what crop there is or may be to occupy the same place in a system of rotation in the South as turnip culture in England, I was agreeably surprised by his reply, that cotton is the counterpart of green crops in England, seeing that it requires the same careful preparation of the soil, the same weeding and hoeing, subserves the same purpose of cleaning the land, and is the point in rotation where manure may be profitably applied. The idea was so sug-

---

[1] Colonel Saunders, North Alabama. See note p. 127.

gestive, and so obviously apposite, that I asked further what his rotation would be, and to this question his answer was—" Two years of clover, one of Indian corn, one of wheat or other small grain, and one of cotton." It would follow from this arrangement that one-fourth of the ploughed land on a plantation would be in cotton, instead of two-thirds or one-half; that the yield of cotton per acre would be so much greater as to render the smaller area nearly equal in productive power to the larger; and that the market price of cotton, seeing that the planter had various sources of return, would be less trying and fateful than it is, and the supply more regular and assured than it can be, under the present system of flighty and fluctuating adventure. Changes of this magnitude, amounting to revolution, in agriculture, and mixed up in the Southern States with difficulties of labour greater than in most other parts, are only slowly accomplished. But that men of intelligence, with interests in the soil, should approve and conclude on some line of action having the promise of lasting prosperity and improvement, is fraught, in the present circumstances of the South, with unusual importance.

A commanding view is obtained from the State House here of the surrounding country, with the Cumberland River sweeping round the city. People are still living who came to Nashville when it was only an advanced post in the wilderness, with a change house and a store or two. It is now a large and prosperous town. The inhabitants tell of the rejoicing that took place when the boat made the trip to New Orleans in ninety days; but the captain, in returning thanks for the compliment paid him on that occasion, said the time would come when the trip would be done in as many hours; and the prophecy has been about fulfilled.

The dictatorship of Parson Brownlow, who was Governor of Tennessee during, and for some time after, the war, has passed away like a nightmare. Mr. Senter, the present Governor—a Republican, but a prudent and temperate man—will be succeeded this year by Mr. Brown, a Democrat. Until within the last six months not more than one white man in five had a vote in Tennessee. The result of the restoration of the respectable inhabitants to their political rights is a complete change in the State administration. The Secretary of State was an officer in the Confederate army; the Comptroller of the Treasury was also a Confederate; and—as an old citizen of Nashville, of the same side of politics, said to me, when ascending the steps of the Capitol, with all the corrupt and terrorising rule of past years in his memory—" We are now getting up-stairs pretty well at last " seems to be the general feeling of the white people of Tennessee. Among other forms of misrule, the Brownlowites threw the finances of the State into utter disorder. State bonds and State endorsations of bonds were issued with a lavish hand, and voted away in some cases to persons and corporations unworthy of confidence. In one instance bonds to the amount of two millions of dollars were issued for a railway in the eastern section of the State, not a mile of which has been made, and the money, so far as realized from the bonds, has been embezzled and squandered. Some idea of the corruption that prevailed, and of the dishonest persons who got into public office and trust, may be formed from the statement of the Comptroller of the Treasury in his report dated December 1870, that the collected taxes in the hands of defaulting and delinquent tax-collectors amount to 1,283,115 dollars, and that the trouble of getting them out of the hands of collectors is not less than that of getting them fairly assessed and levied from the tax-payers. Much of the public revenue thus intercepted "is held for private speculation by collectors and their sureties." Nor are the assessors any better than the collectors. The Comptroller declares three-fourths of them to be utterly incompetent. The tax rolls exhibit the most scandalous exemptions and under-valuations. The real estate of Davidson County, while set down in the United States Marshal's books at over 22,000,000 dollars, appears in the State books for only 8,000,000. The Comptroller insists on a cure of all these evils, and on an assessment of 75 cents per hundred dollars of real estate, which even on the valuation of 1870—252,882,874 dollars—would bring in near two millions to the Treasury. Though the disorder left by the Radicals is great, and to cleanse their Augean stable would seem to require the might of a Hercules, yet the process of reform has begun—the State Government is reducing the State debt, and would ere now have been resuming the payment of interest but for the necessity of first redeeming the circulation of the Bank of Tennessee. The total debt of the State—chiefly railroad and turnpike debt—is 38,539,802 dollars ; but from this amount has to be deducted the resources of the railroads, many being substantial and prosperous concerns, and some already in process of retiring their bonds—the estimate of which resources available to the reduction of the debt is 21,982,844 dollars. Though the new Legislature is a great improvement on its recent predecessors, yet the railway interest is largely represented in it, and there may be some little danger that this influence may be exerted to impede the measures necessary to restore the credit of the State. But it is gratifying to see the spirit of honour by which the new Governments rising in the South are actuated, and the determination evinced, alike by the Executives and the Legislatures, to maintain the strictest economy and good faith in the finances.

Nashville enjoys, what is rare in many parts of the United States, an abundance of hard stone. Stratified limestone, of a bluish-grey colour, is plentiful under the site of the town, and in elevated bluffs around it. The State Capitol—an imposing edifice of the Ionic order—is built of stone quarried on the spot, and with paved streets in the city there are good *macadamized* roads in the environs. Round the base of the Capitol numerous squads of convicts from the penitentiary, mostly negroes, clothed in a common dress of striped stuff, are employed in breaking stones, making new roads, and other hard labour, with men armed with loaded guns on guard at the various points of exit from the place of work. The chance of escape is small, and the convicts, nearly all stout young fellows, apply themselves to their task with a commendable spirit of diligence and resignation.

The farmers of Tennessee have gone more extensively into the culture of cotton under the stimulus of high prices than was probably prudent, and Nashville of late years has been a brisk cotton market. The reduction of price this season will send many of the growers back to grain and stock, for which the soil and climate are well qualified. Yet the cultivators of the soil in Tennessee, as in other parts of America not supremely adapted by nature to the growth of any peculiar product for which there is a great demand in foreign markets, have difficulty in apportioning their crops, and are always ready to introduce or extend whatever promises a better return. The Tennesseean farmers began some time ago to grow broom-corn—a wild grass of great length and tenacity of fibre, requiring a strong soil, of which house brooms, very neatly got up, are made—and found it profitable a year or two, while there were comparatively few growers. But this season there has been an over-supply of broom-corn, and the price has fallen below the remunerative point. The circumstances cannot be much different in the great agricultural regions of the West, where wheat grows luxuriantly, but grows luxuriantly in so many other vast spaces of the globe that in meeting the changes of the foreign market and the expenses of transportation it often yields to the Western farmer only a petty return. The superabundance of land in America, and the ease with which, under its now advanced stage of occupation, any ordinary product may be supplied beyond the limits of profit, form the great difficulty of agriculture in the United States; and the British farmer, with a rent to pay, but with a demand round his steading for everything he produces always in excess of his supply, labours under but a milder form of the evil which besets the American farmer, with the soil his own or given to him for nothing, yet forced to look to distant countries for a market for his staple produce, and uncertain whether he will find one that will repay him anywhere. The cultivation of the soil in the United States has thus a much more speculative character than in Europe; and as the American farmer is not content by hard manual labour to earn a rough livelihood only, but seeks to grow richer as he works on, there is more changing from one system of crops and from one tract of land to another than, and probably quite as much dissatisfaction in the result as, in most other countries.

In the cotton region, with the exception of a certain steadfastness imparted by the staple produce, there is a full share of the uncertainty and indeterminateness that mark the general condition of American agriculture, together with some unsolved perplexities of its own. There is a competition betwixt "exhausted" land and new land, and betwixt the poorer soils of the Atlantic slope and the richer bottom soils of the West, inviting change and migration, and discouraging improvement in many fine parts of the country where cotton has long been produced. The system of labour presents some singular anomalies—partaking, on the one hand, of a communism extended to the negro freedman in the despair that followed the war, and a pauper dependence, on the other, that belonged to the freedman when he was a slave—and cannot be said to be yet established on any settled basis. And more remarkable than all, because exhibited in juxtaposition on the same tracts of country as well as fraught with much weight of practical result in the future, is the competition that has arisen betwixt the larger plantations, on which the negroes are chiefly employed, and the smaller farms cultivated by white people under their own hands, with as little negro labour as possible. This feature of cotton planting in the South is at present conspicuous; for I hold it, from observation as well as testimony, to be certain that the larger proportion of the annual expansions of the cotton crop since the war is due to the energy, on small farms, in gardens, and in crops taken on waste and unoccupied plantations, of white labour. Some few of the negroes no doubt contribute independently to this small-farm movement; but the *ad captandum* mode of arguing the superior efficiency of free negro labour—viz. that so many negroes perished in the war, that negro women do not now work in the field, that negro children are put to school, and that nevertheless the crop being all but equal to what it was under slavery, it follows that the negroes free must produce greatly better than when slaves—is superficial, and does not touch the substantial merits of the question. It does not embrace the fact that scarcely any of the plantations on which cotton was grown under slavery are nearly up to the mark of production before the war; and it leaves out of view the great number of small white farmers who, under the disability of the former growers, have begun for the first time to raise cotton, the numerous bands of white labourers who have availed themselves of the abundant opportunities of renting

and cropping from year to year, the white villagers who have
thrown their sickles into the common harvest—though small
their patches individually, yet considerable in the aggregate—
and the cloud of white planters and their families, reduced to
poverty, who have been the foremost to go down into the
Western bottoms, and there and elsewhere have bent with noble
fortitude and ardour to labour in the fields. It would be a mis-
apprehension to take the cotton crop now as the product of negro
labour in the same sense as it was before the war. The inter-
mixture of white labour in the cotton culture of the South is
already large, and though the forms under which the lands are
cultivated are various yet the general distinction betwixt large
plantations wrought by negroes under white employers, and
small farms wrought chiefly by white people, remains a prominent feature of the new state of things, the practical force of
which is felt more year by year. The economical conditions of
the two forms of culture may be briefly stated thus :—The large
planter looks almost wholly to cotton as his paying crop, whereas
the small farmer, making sure of meat and bread, milk and
butter, fruit and vegetables as his chief means of livelihood,
raises a small crop of cotton as an extra rather than a main
element of profit or subsistence. The large planter depends
almost entirely on negro labour, and must take it with all its
qualifications, and pay for it, as the arrangement now is, by advances equal to one-half the value of his crops ; whereas the
small farmer is less dependent on this negro-communism,
may even save his cotton crop by the labour of his family
and white people about him, and, when needful, have as
good an opportunity as the large planter of engaging negro
labour at wages for work done. So that while the one must
recoup all his expenses, including his payments in dollars
for special work done on the plantation, from his 500 acres of
cotton, the other, without anything like a similar ratio of charges,
looks only to the produce of his 10 or 20 acres, whatever price it
may bring, as the means of obtaining a little ready money to pay
for coffee, sugar, and other extras in the village stores. The value
of cotton in the market is thus a much more crucial point to the
large planter than to the small farmer, and in any severe depreciation one might expect to find the latter keeping afield longer
than the former. The discouragement from the reduction of the
price of cotton this season, as a point of fact, is more marked
among the large planters than the small farmers. It would be
unreasonable, indeed—and pitiable if it were reasonable—to
despair of the large cotton farms of the South, which continue to
be the main root of cotton production, as well as the main centres
of free negro labour ; but they cannot meanwhile be pronounced
in a satisfactory condition. The larger planters may always, in

any great fall of cotton, improve their affairs by adopting greater
variety of culture, and rendering themselves less dependent on
external supplies, while economising more fully the resources of
their lands, although even in this direction the extraordinary
compromise made with negro labour operates as a serious obstacle.
The most powerful instrument of improvement on large plantations would be a steam plough, neither too costly nor mechanically
elaborate, to break up the waste lands and prepare the soil for
crops so much better than the negro-and-mule can do, or rather
what they cannot do at all, and to give the planter some power
over the direction of labour on his property. In such mechanical
means, and in the development of stock and varied produce, the
Southern planters have hitherto unopened sources of recuperation
and sustainment. With these improvements, more especially
backed by a just and genial Federal policy, advantages great
and signal would arise to all classes in the Southern country:
without them, one may doubt the result.

CHAPTER XXXIX.

Concluding Remarks.

[WASHINGTON.—*March* 20.]

AT Nashville, travelling north, one loses sight of the " Cotton Belt," and the task I had set myself is now about accomplished. North Tennessee and Kentucky is a country of grains, grasses, and stock—of an undulating surface with good natural drainage, and elevated ridges often fantastical in shape—much more thinly wooded than the cotton region, an undergrowth of verdure gleaming brightly under the trees. There are considerable breadths of winter wheat, which, though said to be somewhat backward this season, is thriving in appearance, and gives a grateful aspect of cultivation and plenty to the land. A degree or two north of Nashville the difference of temperature is quite perceptible, and while the weather in the middle of March is genial and pleasant, the morning air is rawer, the sky more grey, and there is a colder nip in the winds than farther south The farm-housing is mostly all of a more substantial character than on the cotton plantations, but, save on some tobacco farms of Kentucky, inferior to the steadings on the farms of England or Scotland; and it is obvious that, owing to the difference of climate, the protection of stock from the weather is a matter of much less concern to the American than to the British farmer. Pens are sometimes built with a flat wattled roof covered with loose straw, and where such contrivances are wanting the cattle eat their way through the middle of large stacks of fodder, leaving an arch of straw or hay overhead that forms a shelter in the storm. On many of the fields of winter-sown wheat the Indian corn-stalks of the last summer are still standing, and probably serve some useful purpose to the growing crop; but their protracted occupation is scarcely consistent with the careful preparation of the soil for crops of wheat that prevails in the most advanced parts of Europe. Agriculture in the United States is altogether less elaborate, and more easy, not to say careless, in its modes than in the thickly peopled countries of the Old World. Yet I have not found that the yield of wheat per acre in these parts, while more easily produced, is nearly equal to the yield per acre in the more highly cultivated wheat lands of the United Kingdom.

Lebanon in Kentucky, inclosed on two sides by an amphitheatre of conical hills, covered with cedars, is one of the many charming spots in that rich and lusty State. The Mammoth Cave, within thirty or forty miles, is a constant attraction, as it must always be, to streams of visitors both of the holiday and scientific orders; but any description of its wondrous natural curiosities would be out of place here. There is in Lebanon one of the largest and most completely equipped steam flour-mills ever seen in any small country place, producing 300 barrels of wheat flour per day of ten hours. With wheat-growing all round, the supply of grain is purchased with every advantage; but what is chiefly notable in a work of the most recent origin is the facility with which a profitable market has been found for the product, the flour of the Lebanon mill being entirely absorbed by a single town in Georgia.

Approaching Louisville, the largest city in Kentucky, and one of the most flourishing seats of trade in the West, a traveller cannot but mark one proof more of the vast extent of American territory in the rough and all but waste condition of fat and level soil up to the environs of the town. It is only on entering the suburbs that one becomes apprised of a large and thriving population by numerous clearances, staked off in building lots, indicating a rapid increase of handsome suburban residences. The population of Louisville is now 120,000. The city has prospered much since the war. The merchants of Louisville held out a helping hand to the planters and storekeepers of the South, and established a character of friendliness and enterprise that will long give them a favourable position in the Southern trade. The sale of heavy bagging for cotton bales has here attained considerable magnitude; and the favour of the planters, under the high prices of cotton wool, for the heaviest bagging that can be made has led to a great extension of domestic manufacture of this material, with which the heavy cloth of Calcutta alone seems to compete. There are 390 power-looms in the United States making 250 yards each of flax-and-jute bagging, $2\frac{1}{8}$ to $2\frac{1}{4}$ lbs. per yard a day, or, at 250 working days say in the year, 24,375,000 yards per annum. There are besides 95 hand-looms making cloth of Kentucky hemp, 2 lbs. per yard, at the rate of 128 yards a day, or 2,968,750 yards per annum. Of both kinds there is thus a total domestic supply of 27,343,750 yards, which in the proportion of six yards to each bale of cotton is adequate to cover 4,557,291 bales, or more than the whole crop of this season. Of the Calcutta cloth similarly used the impor-

tation this year is said to be 25,000 bales, or enough .to cover a
million and a half bales of cotton.　There is thus an over supply:
prices have been drooping during the season, and the domestic
manufacturers are probably not too well satisfied with the prospect.　But, as long as the demand of the planters is for the
strongest heavy material, the looms of the United States will
supply the main part of this special branch of the trade in bagging.　For the lighter descriptions of cloth for grain, cotton-seed,
manure and other bags, the use of which is annually extending,
the jute factories of Dundee and Glasgow have an advantage
which they may long retain.　The tobacco market of Louisville
presents the commerce of the city perhaps in its grandest aspect.
There are six or seven tobacco "houses" or salerooms, placed in
the same street, where the hogsheads are presented daily, and
the dealers pass with the auctioneer from one "house" to the other.
The tobacco undergoes a strict official inspection, the samples
bearing the official seal; but before sale the hogsheads are
thrown open, spikes driven into the mass at various points, and
the tobacco seen from the top to the bottom as the auctioneer is
crying his bids.　The rapidity with which all this is done, the
presence of buyers from all parts of America and Europe, and
the large amount of business transacted in a few hours of the
day, convey a very animated and favourable impression of the
tobacco trade of Louisville.　The sales of tobacco last year in
Louisville amounted to about four million dollars.

The falls of the Ohio at Louisville spread the waters of the
river over an imposing breadth, and among the various interesting sights of the city the first and grandest is the iron railway
and foot-bridge, connecting the two States of Ohio and Indiana,
and the Louisville and Indianapolis with the Louisville and
Nashville and the Memphis and Louisville railroads—the *chef-
d' œuvre* of Mr. Albert Fink, whose railway bridges at Florence,
Decatur, and other points of the South cannot fail to attract the
attention of every passenger.　The bridges built by Mr. Fink
are of two kinds—the triangular and suspension truss—and have
largely contributed towards removing the prejudice against iron
as a material for bridges, and advancing the introduction of iron
bridges on the American railroads.　Of the suspension truss the
bridge at Louisville is the most recent and the most important
illustration.　The total length of the bridge superstructure is
one mile and 14 feet; the number of piers and abutments
twenty-eight; and the length of the spans from 30 to 400
feet.　The height of the track above high water is about 50
feet.　The quantity of iron in the structure amounts to 8,723,000
lbs.　The work, from the laying of the first stone to its completion for the passage of trains, was done in two years and a half
at a cost of a million and a half of dollars.　The great compass

of the bridge, the lightness of its structure resting over the stone piers like threads of gossamer in the wide landscape, and the facility of adaptation with which the channels of navigation have been kept open, are very striking, and well entitle Mr. Fink to the highest estimate as an engineer.

From Louisville to Cincinnati one has choice of going by rail or river, and the latter, though longer in point of time, will not disappoint any one whose object is to introduce as much variety into American travel as possible. The approach to Cincinnati at early dawn with chaos brooding over the morning, many tall chimneys belching out columns of smoke more dense than the clouds of night in gradual process of dispersion, and the Ohio not so much flowing as smoothly agitated, like a river of oil, under the paddle wheels, is quite as moving to the spirit as sunset from Louisville the previous day. On nearing the mooring-place of the steamboats a long line of lights, like stars in the sky, arrests attention; and on coming to anchor these are found to be simply the lamps of the suspension bridge, probably one of the most remarkable works of the kind in existence. As these lights in the dawn had perplexed me a little, and put all my astronomy out of reckoning, I did not fail to make some inquiry after them during the day. The Cincinnati Suspension Bridge is the work of Mr. J. A. Roebling, the celebrated engineer to whom the world is indebted for the Niagara Bridge, the Alleghany, and various other notable works of the same kind on the American continent. But in the bridge over the Ohio, connecting Cincinnati with Covington on the Kentucky bank, Mr. Roebling may be said to have brought his principles of wire-cable for suspension bridges to the highest perfection. To conciliate objection on the part of the river steamboat interest, a finely turned arch has been thrown over the whole breadth of the Ohio at low water, fully 1,000 feet from tower to tower, with flanking spans over high-water space, giving an easy ascent from the streets on either side. The bridge floor, consisting of a strong wrought-iron frame, overlaid with heavy planking, is hung by suspenders at every five feet to two wire cables, composed each of 5,180 wires laid parallel to each other, forming a cylinder $12\frac{1}{2}$ inches in diameter, with stays of the same material marvellously increasing the general support and strength of the structure. The bridge is used for teams and foot passengers, but it is believed that very little more strengthening would adapt it to the passage of railway trains. The great bridge at Cincinnati seems a model for suspension bridges elsewhere under much more easy natural conditions, and there can be no doubt that few objects will be found more interesting in a city that is very solidly and scientifically built throughout, full of life and trade, and presenting many substantial attractions to any curious passer-by.

I left Cincinnati on Saturday night a little before ten o'clock on my way to Washington by the Ohio and Baltimore road, and arrived at Parkersburg at day-break, where a great bridge laid on solid stone piers has just been opened over the Ohio; thence passed into Western Virginia, and having entered the Southern States on the eastern side, was glad to hail the limits of the "Old Commonwealth" again. The country is marked by mound-like hills with narrow ravines, where humble farmers extract such scanty livelihood as the peasants of Wales or the Highlands of Scotland from the milk of a few cows and from Indian corn-stalks scarcely bigger than an ordinary walking stick. But in this poorish land, mineral traces begin to appear, and the oil-field, outcropping from Pennsylvania, has received considerable development in Western Virginia—one place being so marked in its supply of oil as to have received the name of "Petroleum." The railway, while pursuing a devious route in the ravines, gradually ascends by steep gradients a hilly region watered by saffron-coloured streams. The hills, of no greater height at first than 500 to 1,000 feet, increase in bulk till on the Shoot, a dark and rapid river, they become stupendous; and the road being cut along their sides, the ravines below seem as deep as the rounded crags are high above. The people are mining coal and iron among these sandstone rocks, and tracks of rail, passing sometimes sheer down the steep and sometimes parallel to the railway, are often seen. The line of road strikes the head waters of the Potomac, and a canal to Baltimore, the Potomac, and the Railroad, pass over a large tract of country through the same defiles. Piedmont, the centre of a great mining industry, with railway machine-shops, long lines of coal trucks, and many young and spirited mechanics from the "old country"—Cumberland, a much larger town of similar fibre, on leaving which one catches on the western horizon the Northern lineament of the great mountain range of the same name, the farthest Southern spurs of which were seen in Georgia—Martinsburg, where on a lower geological level sandstone hill and mountain disappear, and the buildings of the town seem as if carved out of the limestone rock—and Harper's Ferry, where there is a singular concentration alike of striking geographical features and equally striking historical reminiscences—are all points on this Ohio and Baltimore route that are highly interesting, but must here be touched in the most cursory fashion. The train arrived in Washington at 11.15 p.m. on Sunday night, March 19—a distance from Cincinnati of 610 miles accomplished in twenty-five hours some odd minutes.

It was about the same day of October last I began in the American capital these remarks, now to be brought to a close in a few sentences.

The last year's crop of cotton in the Southern States has abundantly demonstrated their great power of increasing supply under the stimulus of a high range of value. Yet this power may suddenly contract when the expectation of price has not been realized; and the last year's experience has brought the extent of cotton culture in the South to a passing ordeal. The Southern planters can always modify their agriculture, under the vicissitudes of the market, by growing smaller or larger proportions of corn and cotton. Yet this goes but a small way towards a satisfactory condition of agrarian industry; the farms require to be more efficiently cultivated, more abundantly stocked, and to be made the arena of a more varied husbandry, in order to supply the loss of former profit arising from the abolition of slave property, in order even to give desirable permanence and success to the culture of cotton; and hence the revolution in the South, though the vast changes it has made are in full and so far hopeful progress, cannot be said to have spent its force or to have reached a complete or durable settlement.

The system of free labour has been attended with a degree of success to which the planters themselves are the most forward of all in the Southern community to bear testimony. Complaints are rife enough of negro legislators, negro lieutenant-governors and office-bearers, and of the undue political elevation given to the coloured people by the transitional state of government through which the country has been passing since the war; and even on this effervescing subject I have found it necessary to distinguish, on the one hand, betwixt the outcries of the bar-rooms and the street-corners—the echoes too often, it may be feared, of undone slave-traders and overseers—and, on the other, the true public opinion of the white population; but apart from this vexed question of politics, on which there are substantial grounds of grievance, I can scarcely recall an instance in which any planter or other employer of negro labour has not said that the result of emancipation, in its industrial bearings, has been much more favourable than could have been anticipated, or who has not added an expression of satisfaction that slavery, however roughly, has been finally effaced. Yet now proceeding on my own observation, the introduction of free labour in the Southern States has been bound up with such novel relations betwixt employer and employed, in particular the payment of the field-labourers by one-half the produce of the land, that I confess I have had the greatest difficulty in attempting to reconcile them with any sound principle. One may understand how an agricultural communism among a group of people on a farm might be carried out; but the project would require an economy and mutuality of arrangement betwixt the members of the group to which there is no resemblance in the existing conditions of a Southern cotton plan-

tation.[1] While payment by share of the crops affords the careful
and hard-working labourer an opportunity of doing well, in which
his employer participates, it tends to introduce a confusion of sense
as regards right and duty, and an uncertainty and fluctuation of
reward for labour, that are more likely to be adverse than favourable to the formation of steady industrious habits among a race so
lately freed from the most absolute dependence. The few negroes
who are wise enough to thrive under this system take advantage
of the abundance of land to rent and crop for themselves, while the
planter is left to struggle with the mass who abuse the opportunities and privileges they possess ; so that the worst results of
the system are apt to be reproduced, if not aggravated, from year
to year on the great majority of the farms. The share system is
so stoutly defended by many persons of practical experience that
it requires some hardihood of conviction to avow an opposite
opinion ; but the judgment I have formed must be given, however deferentially. I cannot think that the payment of field-
hands by shares of the crop, however liberal, is consistent either
with the well-being of the negroes or with the agricultural development of the South. It is more like a half-way slavery than
any relation of capital and labour of an advanced type ; and its
incompatibility with progress will be seen more and more clearly
as the Southern farmers proceed to keep live stock, to introduce
deep or steam ploughing, to diversify their crops, or to carry out
any improvement on their lands.

Though the weight of taxation in the Southern States is an
obstacle to their prosperity that forces itself on attention, yet as
in some respects inevitable, and as lying within the political
action of the people and the governments, it is one on which I
have wished to touch as lightly as possible. The Federal revenue,
swelled beyond all American experience or anticipation by the
gigantic war, must be borne by the South in common with other
sections of the Union. But the State and other local revenues
of the South, owing, on the one hand, to the immense collapse of
assessable property resulting from the furious struggle, and, on
the other, to the new demands of expenditure arising, such as the
building and endowment of free schools for the whole population,
railways, and other public works, have become much more
onerous in proportion to the assessable basis than in any other
part of the United States, and require all careful and prudent

---

[1] *Metayage,* a mode of letting farms prevailing over a great part of the
South of Europe, under which the proprietor furnishes part of the means of
cultivation and shares the produce with the cultivator or *metayer,* is somewhat
similar to the share system of the cotton plantations. But *metayage,* so far
from being beneficial, has an inferior reputation, both as regards the culture
of the soil and the well-being of the cultivators. Yet the share-arrangement
of the cotton planters in the Southern States is not even so well planned as
metayage, and differs from it in some essential points for the worse.

consideration.   Heavy as these burdens would have been under
any circumstances, the State and other local taxation of the
South has been grossly abused by a corrupt and reckless administration since the war, which, under the reviving control of the
taxpayers, is now receiving a check likely to be permanent and
effective.   The Federal taxation, I will observe, is rendered unnecessarily oppressive and injurious by the American weakness
of "protection to native industry," and the American ambition
of "paying off the National Debt," both purposes involving some
of the highest principles of political economy and finance, in regard to which there is a wide field of controversy.   Remarks on
the tariff of the United States can only be made by a British writer
under a certain amount of restraint, as indeed all criticism from
without on the internal affairs of any country can in any case be.
The American Protectionists have a short and easy way of closing
every demonstration of the international advantages of free trade
by declaring, especially to a British advocate, that the laws of
the United States are to be made not for the interests of England or any other foreign country, but for the interests of the
United States themselves.   This argument, however captivating
to a narrow patriotism, too often circumscribed within the still
more limited circle of personal interest, has little intrinsic weight:
since, taking it at its strongest point, the fact is that England
having thirty years ago—a long period in the history even of
nations—solved this question for herself, with some of her greatest
interests more threatened by the action of free trade than the
greatest interests of any other country in the world can well be, it
comes with ill grace from American citizens to exclude on a
fallaciously selfish or doubtful plea any wisdom which the example
or attainments of England in commercial polity may afford.   And,
indeed, the question of free trade betwixt America and Europe
engages incomparably greater interest among the people of the
United States than among even the manufacturers and merchants
of England, who appear to entertain extremely little concern on
the subject, save as one among many other principles affecting
the general progress and civilization of the world.   If free trade
cannot commend itself on American soil in the interests of
America alone, there is an end, of course, to the question there.
The United States' policy of "paying off the National Debt" of
two to three thousand millions of dollars, by monthly instalments of a million dollars or less, brought into association with
the question of the tariff through the common *nexus* of taxation,
if it err at all, most surely errs "on virtue's side," and it becomes
foreign criticism to be more abstinent on this point than even on
the other.   The Secretary of the Treasury deems or finds it
necessary, in carrying out this policy, to have 100 millions of a
surplus always on hand; and as the only way of conveying to

people in Great Britain a faint conception of the importance
given to this question by the American people, I am forced to ask
what they would think if Mr. Gladstone or Mr. Lowe were
to insist, after providing for all the expenses and obligations
of the year, on levying twenty-odd millions sterling under
the profession of paying off the National Debt, with the
national taxation increasing in amount and weight during the
process, instead of annually diminishing, which is the common
object to be desired and attained? There are three ways of
reducing the burden of a National Debt. First, paying off the
principal; secondly, converting portions of the principal, as
favourable occasions arise, into a lower rate of interest; and,
thirdly, giving such play and freedom to the development of
national wealth as, even without touching the National Debt or
its rate of interest, must infallibly reduce its burden by a simple
rule of proportion. The American Government has pursued the
two first of these courses with inflexible integrity and with more
or less success since the war; but the third it has not only not
pursued, but has pressed the first two so closely as to run directly
counter to it, and to have all but produced the dilemma that the
more determined the nation seems to pay off the Debt, the less able
it becomes. These questions, opening a wealth of observation, are
canvassed with such spirit and ability by the leading American
newspapers, and in some instances with such admirable independence of party, that very few who, like myself, have lived in the
country for some months, but must own that they have derived
greatly more from, than they can hope to contribute to, the
discussion.

I trust that in these pages I have given no partial view of the
many topics that have passed under review, and that as respects
the general condition of the Southern States I have not failed to
afford to many the means of a fuller and exacter understanding —
at least a nearer and more intimate view—than they had before.
If I have given strong expression to convictions on such contro-
versial ground as that of legislation or politics, there seems an
ample vindication of this freedom in the chief desire and aim of
the American people, of all political parties, themselves. The
polity of the United States that may be said to surmount all
others, and to be national in the highest sense, is that of attracting
in copious volume the surplus labour and capital of Europe; and
the wisdom of this polity is indisputable, since, while directly
building up their own greatness, it is the course in which the
United States may render the greatest service to the world.
But it were unwise to rest this movement on the basis of mere
political or social discontent in other countries, while neglecting
sources manifold of discontent at home; the conditions of free
and equal government, as well as of social prosperity, have made

much progress in the Old World ; and the more thoroughly emigrants, especially of the United Kingdom, feel at home in the New World, under just and wise laws and all the blessings of a well-ordered society, the greater their number, the better their character, and the more lasting their usefulness as citizens of the United States may be expected to be. Betwixt the Tariff, in particular, and the main polity and interest of the United States, there appears to be a palpable contradiction, since it directly shuts out the capital of other countries, and renders the land of America less attractive to and less tenable by foreign immigrants. It is this consideration that has chiefly inspired any little political criticism in this book. I have been writing of States which, though not sharing hitherto in any equal degree with other sections of the Union the stream of labour and capital from Europe to America, present under fair legislation and good government a peculiarly rich and interesting field for immigration, agriculture, commerce, and the development of many branches of industry ; and were the balance in this respect now to be redressed in favour of the South, there would be in such good fortune a result no less gratifying to all American citizens than responsive to the deep interest which an heroic, not too wise, and unavailing struggle for independence excited throughout the world.